FULL CIRCLE

A JOURNEY IN SEARCH OF ROOTS

David A. Hecker, Ph.D.

To Sharon,
a family friends and
fellow educator

David A. Hecker

CRAB WALK PRESS

Bainbridge Island, Washington

CRAB WALK PRESS

Acknowledgment is made to individuals and publications for permission to reproduce photographs and to quote from documents in their possession.

Adam and Ruth Hecker of Salem, Oregon; Magdalena (Hecker) Reiswich and Maria (Reiswich) Kreiser of Neu Wulmstorf, Germany; and Selma (Hecker) Schmidt of Dickinson, North Dakota.

The prologue of this book will appear in different form in the winter issue 2011 of the *Heritage Review*, a quarterly journal of the Germans from Russia Heritage Society, headquartered in Bismarck, North Dakota.

----

www.SLAPress.com

ISBN: 1466423978
ISBN-13: 9781466423978
Library of Congress Control Number 2011913352
CreateSpace, North Charleston, SC

Printed in the United States of America
First Edition

To

The Next Generation

Coleman

Katelin

Aiden

THE
MARTIN & CHRISTINE HECKER FAMILY

MARTIN HECKER	CHRISTINE (SCHMIDT) HECKER
b. 1853, Munchen, Russia	b. 1859, Munchen, Russia
d. 1930, Dickinson, North Dakota	d. 1891, Plantersville, Texas
	in childbirth with stillborn son

MATHIAS 1873	FRANK 1874	GEORGE 1875	JOHN 1881
+ (Elizabeth Heiser) *Rosie*	+ (Veronica Brucker) *Catherine*	+ (Bertha Brucker) *Elizabeth*	+ (Anna Mary Herzog) *Magdeline* *Emanuel*
George	+ (Stewart Farmer) *Anna*	+ (Clarence Borden) *Joseph* *John* *Henry* *Agnes* *Jack*	+ (Mary Spies) *Martin*
+ (Pauline Ehrmantrant) *Mike* *Nick* *Frank*	+ (Ernest Singletary) *Margaret* *Frances*		+ (Frances Ziegler) *Msgr. Adolph* *Remigius* + (Catherine Ziegler) *Libertaus*
+ (Anna McKenzie) *Jacob "Jack"*	+ (Leslie Witt) *Frank, Jr.* *Stanley*		+ (Renilda Malsam) *Loraine*
+ (Eleanor Kubischta) *Frances*	+ (Eva Rothchilder) *Angeline*		+ (Ted Plucinski)
+ (George Keller)			+ (Russ Gorman) *Sally*
	+ (George P. Schmidt) *Benjamin* *Rose*		+ (Olin Colig) + (Mike Rogers) *Lucas*

MATHIAS (1873)	FRANK (1874)	GEORGE (1875)	JOHN (1881)
			+ (Elizabeth Walsh)
	Marion		*Gregory Julius*
	+ (John Wachtler) *Adam*		+ (Jeanette Peterson)
	+ (Lily Peterson) *Eve*		
	+ (Adrian Erickson)		

ELIZABETH 1883	ANGELINE 1884	MICHAEL *DIED AGE 11*	ROSE 1885	MAGDELINE 1888
+ (Conrad Hilsendager) *Jospeh* *John*	+ (Frank Brucker) *Frank*		+ (Harry Brown)	+ (Michael J. Frank) *Nickolas* *Margaret* *Frances*
+ (Johanna Meyer) *Magdeline* *Adam* *Martin*	+ (Alice) *Joseph* *Christ* *George*			+ (Robert Schneider) *Helen*
	+ (Vivian) *Katherine*			+ (John Schiller) + (James Ruby) *Rose*
+ (Jane Besser)	+ (Alfred Henke) *Anna*			+ (Leo Davis) *Katherine*
+ (Elise Werner)				
+ (Leona Kerkaby)	+ (Koch) *Pauline*			+ (Gerit Verheigan) *Henry* *Agnes*
	+ (Ted Boehne) *William* *Agnes*			

ELIZABETH	ANGELINE	MICHAEL	ROSE	MAGDELINE
1883	1884	*DIED AGE 11*	1885	1888

+ (Norbert Geiger)
Alice

+ (James Dove)
Bertha

+ (Henry Toch)
George
Maria

+ (Caroll Horten)
Theodore
William
Charles

The
Martin & Christine Hecker Family

Martin Hecker	Christine (Dillman) Hecker
b. 1853, Munchen, Russia d. 1930, Dickinson, North Dakota	b. 1870, Russia Married, 1892, at Plantersville, Texas d. 1927, Belfield, N. Dakota

Margaret 1894	Barbara 1895 *Died age 10*	Joseph 1896 *Died 11 mths.*	Roy 1897 *died 9 mths*	Martin 1898
+ (John Schocker)				+ (Barbara Stricker) Widow of Jacob

Jacob 1901	Casper 1903	Frances 1905	Monica 1907	Ottilia 1909 *died 1930*
+ (Barbara Stricker)	+ (Theresa Kubischta)	+ (Peter Loran)	+ (Anton Koch)	

Christine 1911	Eva 1913	Adam 1915	Magdaline 1917	Infant Boy 1918 *Died at birth*
+ (William Mahoney)	+ (Philip Cox)	+ (Ruth Maddox)		

Contents

PROLOGUE

BERESAN DISTRICT

May 2010

Our Mercedes Benz van shuttered as it moved ahead on the cobble-stone two-lane road. The vehicle's suspension system was taking a beating. We were not on the side streets of a Spanish hill town where you would expect this type of ancient road construction. I looked forward and saw that the stony road became dirt and gravel. On it semi-trucks turned side-to-side to avoid deep potholes. We were driving in the Ukraine, an independent nation after the Soviet Union collapsed in 1991, about seventy-five miles north of Odessa. We were on our way to visit Munchen, our ancestral village, founded by German colonists in 1809 in what was then South Russia. It had taken three hours to get this far, and our guide and driver were the only ones who knew where we were at, for the sketchy map they had shown us listed the names of highways and towns in the Ukrainian language. Being a map fanatic and a collector of charts and atlases of every type, I'm always sure of where I'm at when driving or traveling; consequently, I was uneasy. Serge, the guide I had hired, a Professor at the Polytechnic University of Odessa who did tour directing as a sideline, noticed my restlessness and said, "David, we're only fifteen miles from Munchen."

I guess my age was beginning to show. I was seventy years old and had been studying my family roots since I was forty-eight, the year I discovered that I was ethnically a German from Russia. Finally I was returning to this village that my Great-Grandparents Martin and Christine Hecker and children, including Frank, my future grandfather, had left in 1891 for America, one hundred and nineteen years ago. My emotions ran high, rotating between excitement and wonder. At the same time I was anxious about this visit because I knew the history of Munchen, South Russia. I was eager to walk on the streets where many Heckers had lived for over six generations, see the Catholic church they had attended, and touch the soil they had farmed. I wanted to look at what remained of a once prosperous German colony before the Russian Revolution of 1917 and the collectivization of the Stalinist regime.

Suddenly our driver turned the vehicle down a dirt two-wheel pathway that ran parallel to the highway and a grain field. The van picked up speed until we passed the semis above us. After about a half mile the driver turned back up onto the road. We swerved along, making better time, but we passengers were bouncing and swaying from side to side. Magdalena (Hecker) Reiswick, aged eighty-one and the only one of us who had actually lived in Munchen, sat between her two daughters, Irma and Maria. Both daughters were middle aged and had been born four years apart in the Ural Mountains of the former USSR many years earlier. After the Reiswicks immigrated to Germany, Irma set up a midwifery practice, married a German national, and gave birth to a son and daughter. Maria graduated from gymnasium, took a B.A. degree from the University of Hamburg, worked as a translator for a major auto manufacturer and then married and had two daughters. Irma and Maria were both trim and petite like their mother, and each wore slacks and jackets of fashionable design. Magdalena looked furtively out the front and side windows, looking for signs of her former homeland that she had left at age 16 in 1944. Magdalena, a widow and retired nurse, wore checked light blue and white slacks and a red hip length jacket that set off her white wedge cut hair. Magdalena lived close to her daughters and their families in suburbs of Hamburg, Germany. My wife Helen and I sat in seats behind our relatives, so we'd each have front and side windows for viewing. We were closest to Maria who served as translator for us. We lived on an island near Seattle, Washington, and were both retired educators.

Once again we encountered a cobblestone section of the highway. I recalled Magdalena telling Helen and me, on a visit we had made to her home in Germany in 1990, that her father Johannes Hecker had gone away from Munchen and his family for weeks and even months at a time to work for wages on road construction similar to the one we drove on. The family needed cash to buy flour, sugar, and salt as well as cloth and sewing materials for patching and making clothes and bedcovers. If they needed medical attention, they had to pay in currency for railway tickets to Odessa. When Stalin's collectivization program went into effect, the German colonists no longer had cash crops or farm animals to sell at markets in neighboring towns. They had to work a shift each day in a nearby commune for a noon-day meal. When Johannes worked on road crews, his wife Margarete Hecker had to work his shift. Magdalena, her older brother, Anton, and Olga, a younger sister, all youngsters in the early 1930's, walked to the field where their mother worked to eat their mother's noon meal, usually a few dumplings in milk gruel and bread. The Soviet foreman complained about this, for he wanted his laborers fit to work vigorously. Margarete retorted by asking him, "Should I eat and let my children starve?"

I gazed out a side window at the passing landscape. The land was flat, and the rich black soil was sprouting green foliage of what would undoubtedly become stands of wheat. Beyond the broad fields were wind belts, two or three rows of trees running the length of the field. These trees were planted to block wind from blowing topsoil into the next district. In the winter the trees kept the snow from blowing away, so it would melt in place in the spring, providing moisture for newly planted seeds. The scenery looked surprisingly familiar, like the fields of central North Dakota. Helen squeezed my hand to get my attention and then said, "It looks like our old home state." "Yes, I was just thinking that myself." I continued looking out the windows, but didn't see any farmhouses, barns, granaries or other out-buildings that were normal in the Upper Plains of the United States where Helen and I were teenagers in the nineteen-fifties. This area was established in the German fashion with houses and outbuildings in centrally located villages. Grain fields, orchards, and pastures lay just beyond on all sides. I thought how this drive on horrible roads to Munchen, not only ended a twenty plus years odyssey to find my family roots, but it also served as a metaphor for the many bumps, detours, and dead ends I had encountered along the way.

— RASTADT —

I continued to peer out the window, noting the gray May skies and low dark clouds. A few sprinkles of rain ran down the windows. All five of us had hoped for warm weather and clear skies for our visit. Heavy rain would have left us mired down on roads and pathways like these. Fortunately the drizzle stopped as quickly as it had started. I noticed for the first time that the fields were not cut crisply, and the windbreaks looked irregular and ragged. As we passed a Ukrainian cemetery near the village of Rastadt, Serge reacted to simultaneous expressions by Irma and Maria, "*Blick, mutter, ein friedhof.*" (Look, Mother, a cemetery.) Our guide leaned towards me and whispered, "David," and I looked at him. He winked and said, "Not yet, please!" He then explained that he has a tendency to dark humor. I nod and thought, *yes, Magdalena is eighty-one.*

The van driver turned onto the main street of Rastadt. All eyes were on Magdalena. This village was close to Munchen, and she had walked to it during her youth to visit an aunt and her family. Her eyes were sad and fearful, and when the van stopped in front of the school, she refused to get out. She held onto the railing in front of her seat and grimaced. Tears were forming in her eyes. Magdalena didn't believe that this was Rastadt, the village she knew sixty-six years ago. Our guide left the van and walked over to the next building, the city hall. Maria and Irma commiserated with their mother, urging her to step out of the van and look around. Magdalena cried out, "This isn't the school I knew!" Serge returned to the bus with a slim, well dressed, middle-aged women. He introduced her to us as the secretary to the Mayor of Rastadt. She spoke in Russian and German to Magdalena and then took her arm and led her out of the bus to the school. Magdalena submitted because of the familiar languages she learned here as a youth. The secretary then explained to all of us in Russian that the old school stood unused for many years and finally collapsed after serving as a storage building. Maria stood beside us and spoke softly in English, providing translation for Helen and me.

Magdalena's eyes softened, and she walked to the school that had been built by the Soviets after her departure. We all entered the two-story utilitarian structure that had high ceilings, long, wide hallways with windows on one side and classrooms on the other. We congregated at one end of the hall that served as office and supply center. Magdalena, Maria and Irma all spoke to the Russian teacher. They seemed comfortable in the language they had all used in the Ural Mountains before they were allowed to immigrate to Germany in 1974. As they talked, school children were released from classrooms for recess, and we all followed them outside. There wasn't a playground, but the pupils scattered in groups around the building. Magdalena talked to some of them in Russian. She then asked the secretary about a stream that she remembered was close to where we stood. The secretary then led us over to the other side of the road and pointed to where the stream had been. The bed of the stream was still there, but it was dry and filled with sandy soil and weeds. We all looked around and saw that many old houses and outbuildings on both sides of the street had been partially restored since the destruction the Russian Army left in 1944. Other buildings were empty and crumbling, and many lots had nothing but battered foundations.

— MUNCHEN —

The Rastadt secretary agreed to go with us to Munchen. On the way there we stopped at the former Rastadt Catholic Cemetery. We walked down a hillside with some open grassland and large sections of shoulder high shrubs. We pushed into the brush and found some headstones, bearing names of German colonists. Magdalena became excited as she pushed into clumps of shrubs to see if she could recognize any names. Then she saw a large granite headstone that announced *Hier ruhet in Gott* (Here rests in God) Raphael Seelinger b. in 1887 and d. in 1910. Magdalena started weeping. Helen hugged her as Irma and Maria came running to comfort her as well. Maria told us later that Magdalena cried not from misery but from joy. Because she knew the Seelinger family and the familiar caption on the headstone, *she finally was convinced that she was in her former homeland.* Magdalena believed her faith had saved her life and preserved her soul many times during her travails in Russia and the Soviet Union's work camps in the Ural Mountains.

We continued on to Munchen and arrived there in just a few minutes. If I had thought that Rastadt was in shambles, Munchen was much worse. There was no school, no store and fewer houses and outbuildings. Workers had abandoned many houses when the collectives had dissolved in 1992. Since they had no ownership of the places, they had let them fall apart and then left them when their work source vanished. Our van stopped in front of the Catholic Church that Magdalena was baptized in and had attended until she left at age 16. We climbed out of the bus while Maria and Irma supported Magdalena. She cried as she looked at the ruins that stood in front of her. The church had no steeple. The Soviet Army had pulled it off, and the steeple lay now on its side in weeds down the street. The secretary explained that the church had been used for storage and animal shelter. When the roof caved in later, the church was abandoned. We entered the church and saw that the back wall where the altar had been was gone. A side room where robes, bibles, and chalices had been stored now held debris and a dead dog.

— *Photo of Munchen Catholic Church* —

An old man wearing a ragged, mud-stained military uniform walked towards us from behind the church. He was Ukrainian and spoke to our guide. Serge asked him where the old German cemetery was located. He pointed to a hillside covered with scrubs in the distance. He led us to it where he pointed at some shattered concrete blocks with metal plates still attached, but the iron crosses and lead nameplates were gone. Serge noted that they had been taken and melted down to make implements of one kind or another. He said also that any headstones that had been erected by Germans in earlier times had been removed and were used to build foundations for buildings or bridges. With a gleam in his eyes, Serge added that in one case a bridge that had been built out of headstones collapsed the first time a horse and wagon crossed it. *Good I thought*. Magdalena looked about with tears running down her face. Her daughters hugged and kissed her.

Our Rastadt secretary took us to visit an ethnic Romanian family who had two buildings. One was a small house of German origin. Attached to the back of it were chicken coops and lean-tos for sheltering pigs and goats. The one story house had four rooms and two-foot thick mud and straw walls. Interior and exterior plaster held it together. Our guide identified the entry door as German colonist designed and made. I recognized the thick walls as being identical to the sod houses of the prairies of North Dakota that Germans from Russia had built in the 1890's after their immigration from South Russia. The entry hall led to a low-ceilinged front room with dining table and a few wooden chairs. A small kitchen was opposite the middle of the room through a narrow doorway. It held a small cabinet and a kerosene stove. At the other end of the entry hall were two small bedrooms. This house was too small for the ethnic Romanians who had moved into it in 1947, three years after the German Army and German colonists had retreated to Poland. In time they converted an old German built barn across the driveway into another house.

— *PHOTO OF GERMAN HOUSE* —

The reconstructed barn had high ceilings and larger rooms, including living room, kitchen and dining rooms as well as several bedrooms. The walls of the old barn had been thickened to provide protection against the cold of winter and heat of summer. The Romanian residents invited us to visit their root cellar, also of German origin, that was next to the main house. It had an igloo-like top and entrance to a subterranean room below. Stone steps led down about twenty feet to a dirt floor. Helen nudged me as we stepped down the stairway and said, " We had a root cellar like this on our homestead in North Dakota." I answered, "This is my first time in one, and I can see its value for storing and preserving food." Along the stairway were horizontal shelves that held canned food in glass jars. As it was the month of May, many of the shelves held empty jars with lids. The few full jars held tomatoes, carrots, beans, and onions. On the floor below small potatoes, beets, and radishes lay scattered about in small piles. The process of refilling this cellar was already beginning in the gardens, trees, and vines above. Since there were no stores in either Rastadt or Munchen, it was clear that these people lived a hand-to-mouth subsistence. They had horses and wagons but no auto or tractor. No gas-powered vehicles were visible at the other houses along the street.

— *PHOTO OF ROOT CELLAR* —

Back out onto the street we looked up and down at a village that once had four streets according to an old plat map from 1941. I saw nothing but other shabby structures and a line of small poles down the one lonely street, carrying electricity. The only other signs of modern conveniences were small tanks of what I supposed was propane, standing outside a few of the houses. Nobody was about except one villager who came in his bedraggled garments and offered to sell us his place and several acres of land for a couple hundred dollars. Serge winked at me and asked, "David, should we invest together and buy his land?" I smiled and shook my head side-to-side. A few of the houses had chickens and pigs running about their yards, and goats were staked out to graze on the areas of tall grass that bordered the street. We walked farther and located on our plat map an intersection where Ludwig Hecker's house and outbuildings had stood. He had been my great-grandfather's brother and the richest man in the village. We found four crumbled foundations filled with broken stones, debris and weeds. Two other Hecker lots couldn't be found.

In spite of the ruins I witnessed, I was pleased to be at Munchen and to see the church and cemetery that had been used by generations of my family. I was also glad I had visited a home that was built by neighbors of my distant relatives. I walked on the same ground that they had trod. I looked at the same horizon they had viewed. I saw the fields they had worked. But I also now gave my great-grandfather thanks and my gratitude for leaving here when he did. The ironies were many as I thought about how the Romanians had found shelter here. At the beginning of the cruise that brought us to Odessa, we were docked in Kiev on May 9, Independence Day for Ukrainians. They were celebrating the ouster of the German Army in 1944. There was much history here that could not be learned in the standard graduate history program offered in our universities. Over the past years I had learned other things about culture and history as I searched for my roots that could only be grasped by this sort of witnessing.

— ELSASS AND JOSEPHSTAL —

We boarded our van and drove back to Rastadt where we dropped off the secretary, thanked her for her hospitality and assistance, and started our trip back to Odessa. We had two more former German villages to visit, Elsass and Josephstal, the villages of Helen's ancestors. When my wife and I married, we had no idea how close our roots were. Just shortly before we left on this trip, we found the names of her ancestral villages where her grandparents, Wendelin and Richarda (Ziegler) Black, and family had lived. We couldn't drive directly across country to these villages even though they were located to the west of Odessa. That route was impossible from Munchen because of the severe winter damages to the dirt roads. We had to return to the beltway around Odessa and then drive directly west on the paved roads in that area. We were up to the trip because the weather had turned sunny, and it was only twelve-thirty in the afternoon. We had time on the drive to eat the lunches that had been provided by our cruise ship's kitchen, and we all needed the time to absorb what we had experienced. Along the way we did see a flock of geese. We made one stop at a Ukrainian village about ten miles along the way where we saw the contrast between the old and new in transportation in this region, horse and wagon and autos.

— *Photo of Horse and Wagons and Autos* —

After we continued the journey, Serge said to me, "David, what do you think about Obama?" I answered, "He's doing a remarkable job considering the economic circumstances and wars he inherited from the previous administration. Serge responded that he had hoped for a McCain victory. I asked him why? He told me about McCain's wife's foundation and how he and his ill daughter had been flown to Phoenix, Arizona for an operation that couldn't be done in the Ukraine. I replied, "I think McCain is a fine Senator, and I can understand why you support him." Serge went on to say that he favored an alignment with Russia for Ukraine rather than with the European Union. In fact he thought that the Ukraine should be divided down the middle, giving each side in the current political debate their own countries. I replied that some Americans had attempted to get that arrangement, and it ended in a brutal Civil War. Although I liked Serge's openness and the candid give and take that we had about Ukrainian politics, I was pleased that he fell silent because I knew that Magdalena, Maria and Irma had little sympathy for Russia and given their spirited natures, it wouldn't have been long before a debate started.

— *Photo of Irma, Maria, Magdalena, and Helen* —

We arrived in Elsass in about three and a half hours, having made one stop to get fuel, coffee and the use of the gas station's facilities. The fields around Elsass were large, well cultivated, and displayed sprouts of new grain. Tractors and other implements were in view. Helen was clearly enthusiastic to get to her ancestral village. She told everyone that she was the first member of her extended family to return to the village that her grandparents and father-to-be, Wendelin Black, Jr., had left in 1898. Given its closeness to Odessa, Elsass and its streets were in far better shape than those of Munchen. The old German built houses were in far better condition as well. Some residents still had farm animals, and I saw one woman milking a goat in the yard next to her house. The old German built Catholic Church still stood, but without a steeple. It was now used as an exercise facility for the community. Next to this building was a monument celebrating the two hundredth year of the founding of Elsass by German colonists. We stood to have our photographs taken with this monument, and much to our surprise and delight, school children from the neighborhood rushed to get into the picture with us. We couldn't talk to them, but they were so well mannered and enthusiastic that we welcomed them to join us as pictures were taken. Nothing like this monument stood in Munchen, but it demonstrated the changes that were taking place in Ukraine since they gained their independence in 1991.

— Photo of Memorial and Old Catholic Church in Elsass —

*— Photo of Helen, Ukrainian Children and Me
at German Colonists' Memorial in Elsass —*

Later when we stopped on a street to examine some old German built homes, a resident came out of his house and introduced himself. His house showed signs of updating with painted stucco exterior and TV disc attached to the roof. He told us that Anton Schell, a German colonist, had originally built his house. When he found out that Helen's ancestors had once lived in Elsass, he returned to his house to get her a gift. While he was inside, Serge said to me, "The improvements on this house shows that this man is well off." He came back with 8x10 photographs of German houses and streets from days when Germans still lived in them. He also gave Helen an aerial photo of the current village. Our next search was for the old German cemetery. Like in Munchen the old burial ground was covered with lilac bushes, that were typical of German cemeteries, but there were no graves or headstones, just a few concrete blocks. Unlike at Munchen the Ukrainians here gave recognition to this former cemetery by erecting a commemorative monument, a sculptural figure of Christ on a Cross in metal with decoration and a granite block base. In an adjacent plot of land next to the monument was a Ukrainian cemetery with many headstones, some with elaborate decorations and encased photographs of the dead. Flowers covered the area and showed the current reverence given by the Ukrainians for the departed.

Next we drove a few miles to Josephstal, the earlier residence of Helen's ancestors. We were all tiring from the long day that started at 7 a.m. and now it was nearing 6 p.m. As we approached the village a sign greeted us, acknowledging the founding of this village by German colonists in the early 19th century. We drove through some neighborhoods. One section had four and five story apartment buildings for commuters who worked in Odessa. The houses and streets of the old German neighborhoods were also in good condition. We wanted to look for cemetery and church, but Serge said they were gone.

— Odessa and Beyond —

As we drove back to Odessa and to our departure home, I again thought about the values of this trip to our ancestral land. It meant going full circle for me. It was the end of a two-decade plus journey where I had encountered many surprises, a few agonizing disappointments, and some detours that took me to places I didn't know existed.

These locations were not just geographical but emotional and mental as well. I became aware that my extended family had participated in historical events over the last three centuries that shook the very foundations of the western world. I was no longer a by-stander reading history from a comfortable vantage point. I was a participant, and I had obligations to those in the present and future who might also be caught in these vagaries of history.

I recalled the names and images of the many people who had helped me along the way. They had made my life broader, richer, and more relevant. I now knew of many relatives in other countries: Germany, Russia, Canada, and Argentina. How many books had I read about the history, cultures, and immigrants of these countries? They filled two shelves in our bookcases. How much census data and reference material had I accumulated? I have a filing cabinet full of it. I reflected on the depth of my understanding now of Central Europe, World War II, and our American participation in them. How much time, donations, and moral support had I given to help exploited people in the United States since this ancestral research began? I marveled at how my writing had shifted from academic papers and essays to poems, short stories, travel pieces and a historical novel.

How this transition came to be over this long time passage was still a matter of fascination to me. What drove me? What turns of fate made it possible? How many bumps, dead ends, detours, and roadblocks had I encountered on the journey? I had many questions, and the answers would take a good deal of sorting, thinking and careful writing. Fortunately I had kept all of the letters I had received, I had kept extensive journals, I had Helen's photo albums, and finally I had my memory, faulty though it is. Could I possibly put it all together in a coherent fashion? Would this be another way that I might influence the thinking and actions of people about ethnic differences, national backgrounds, and the welfare of all humans? Could I write a memoir and bring my quest to a broader full circle than it is now? Maybe.

PART I

GETTING STARTED WITH THE JOURNEY

August 1987

———————————

— Chapter I —

Exploring family roots can begin innocently enough. Adam Hecker of Salem, Oregon, answered my letter about our shared heritage by inviting Helen and me to his home for a weekend in August. Since we lived in Bremerton, Washington, where Helen taught primary school and I lectured at Olympic College, Adam's residence was only about a four-hour drive south on I-5, so we accepted the invitation although we had never met him or his wife. In fact I didn't know I had any Hecker relative in Oregon or any other western state except for an uncle and aunt living in Southern California and another relative, possibly a second cousin, in California with whom I had exchanged letters. That underestimate of family living in the western half of the United States would change dramatically before very long.

This trip wasn't entirely a leap into the dark. I had contacted the North Dakota Heritage Center at Bismarck about my paternal ancestry, and they responded with titles of several reference books as well as with the name of a person who was doing research on the Hecker family name. I mailed a letter to Emma Frank of California (the possible second cousin), and she answered, writing that she was in fact a North Dakota Hecker from Dickinson and had been working on a family tree for nearly twenty years. She also gave me the names and addresses of two other Heckers who were also seriously and dependably collecting facts about the Hecker clan. One of them was Adam

Hecker of Salem, Oregon, and the other was Selma (Hecker) Schmidt of Dickinson.

I thought it astounding that anyone would spend decades on a genealogy project, but I wasn't aware at the time of the many dead-ends and other problems in this type of research, nor was I aware of how compulsive the lure of connecting the dots of family lineage can become in one's middle years. Who are we? and Where did we come from? become mysteries to be solved. How I happened to have relatives from Dickenson was one clue that left me puzzled. I was born in Mandan, North Dakota, and had lived in the same neighborhood as Frank and Veronica Hecker, my grandparents, and I had aunts in Bismarck and another in Flasher, but that was the extent of my information about North Dakota Heckers.

The traffic flow on I-5 was heavy as usual for this time of year. Helen was reading a book, and I was listening to some Dave Brubeck on a CD. I thought about what Adam might look like. My dad, also an Adam Hecker but from Minot, North Dakota, was tall, barrel-chested with long, thin legs. He had a high forehead with deep-set brown eyes and a full face. His skin was slightly olive in color, and he tanned easily into a light brown with the slightest exposure to the sun. I had surmised that we Heckers were immigrants from Bavaria where skin color is somewhat darker than northern Germans. Helen and I had traveled to Southern Germany in 1986 and had visited a Catholic Cathedral in Speyer. The church had been built over a Roman altar that was preserved in its basement. Speyer and Rulzheim, where I supposed my family had immigrated from to the United States, were on the Rhine River that Roman legions had sailed on during the Holy Roman Empire era. I had let my imagination run at the time, assuming that my dad's coloring and those of other Bavarians I had seen had their source in intermarriage with the Romans or just plain couplings by these legionnaires with German women. My dad's physique could also have come from them as well. Might the Romans have bred long thin legs, tall frames, and barrel chests into their troops to cover easier the vast distances of Europe in the expansion of their empire? My dad also gestured with his hands when he talked, and he spoke incessantly, traits often associated with Italians.

After stopping for lunch near Portland, we continued down I-5 and arrived at Adam's home in Salem. It was a beige bungalow with brown trim in a quiet neighborhood in the north end of the city. Adam greeted us in German, saying *"Guten tag, wie gehts?"* (Good day, how are you?). When I responded that we knew very little German, he smiled as if to acknowledge what he expected. He explained that his wife Ruth was shopping with their daughter but would be home later to cook us dinner. Adam's appearance was not what I expected. He was compactly built, of average height, and had a receding hairline with thinning light brown and gray hair. He also looked a bit pale. He led us into the living room where a large coffee table rested between two sofas. The coffee table was covered with materials; sheets of paper, some filled with handwriting and others with typescript, shoeboxes full of photographs and envelopes, plus a couple of photo albums. We sat down, and Adam said that the "piles of stuff" on the table were the results of his investigation into the Hecker family tree. He told us that the search started when he retired from the railroad as an engineer and purchased this home and an RV. He and Ruth then traveled about six months out of each year around the American and Canadian western states and provinces, visiting Hecker descendants of the original immigrants to the United States and Canada. The search went on for many years.

Adam then handed me a photograph of an older man with large head, square jaw, and broad forehead, characteristics of my own father and the few male members of the extended family that I had met or had seen in photographs. "This is Martin Hecker, your great-grandfather." As I looked at the photograph, Adam asked if we minded if he smoked. Helen and I both assented even though neither of us smoked, and he reached for an ashtray and lit a cigarette. I handed the photograph to Helen. I then asked, "I suppose this picture was taken in the old country?"

— *Photo of Martin & Christine (Dillman) Hecker* —

"No," Adam responded, "my dad lived his last years near Belfield, North Dakota."

"But isn't Belfield a small town just west of Dickinson? What was he doing there?"

"He homesteaded on some farmland just a few miles north of Belfield."

I was confused to say the least, so I asked another question, "Did you say that Martin Hecker was your dad? If so, then you are my grandfather's brother."

"I'm your grandfather's half-brother."

"Is this possible? I was born in Mandan and lived in the same neighborhood with my grandparents. I was young, but I didn't hear any reference to Martin or you then or later when I visited them. Why is that?"

Adam explained that there had been a riff in the family. Martin's first wife Christine (Schmidt) Hecker had died in childbirth at Plantersville, Texas, leaving Martin with nine children. About a year later Martin married Christine Dillman, a widow of twenty-six who had a young son, and who would become Adam's mother some years later. Since the house where Martin and family lived was small and since Mathias and Frank, the oldest sons, were nineteen and eighteen years old, Martin told them to look for other places to live.

Adam lit another cigarette as he waited for my response. Again I was flabbergasted! It was enough to hear that I had a great-grandfather who had lived within a hundred miles of where I was born, but who was unknown to me until now, and then to add that Martin Hecker had a son who is my grandfather's half-brother. Then I'm told that I have a great-grandmother who's buried in Texas!

Helen and I looked at each other and shook our heads. Adam quickly said it was time for a break and offered coffee or beer. Helen said she'd like a cup of coffee, and I welcomed a beer. Adam walked into the kitchen and brought back a cup of coffee and some cookies that Ruth had made for the occasion. He then brought beers for the two of us. I held up my bottle and said, "Cheers." Helen lifted her cup of coffee and responded with "Cheers" also, but Adam said, "*Prost.*" Helen and I had heard this German word for toasting before, so we both added "*Prost*". I then told Adam that the things he had been telling us about my family overwhelmed us, but we were thankful that he had made the effort to help us get the record straight. I assured him that I had a number of questions for him about that information but that for now I would like it if he would tell us something about Martin's Belfield farm and maybe some comments about Martin himself.

Adam replied by saying his father was a strict man who had a sense of his own authority. Adam admitted that he, as a teenager, once challenged his father by telling him to "go to hell." Martin had chased Adam into a coal shed were he gave him a severe tanning. Because North Dakota winters were frigid, Adam recalled some clothing habits that his father had adopted. Martin always bought his overshoes two sizes too big so that he could stuff newspapers around his feet, wool stockings and shoes.

I could appreciate that gesture to stop frostbite and recounted for Adam our last winter in North Dakota when in the month of February 1963, the warmest it got was 10 degrees below zero at mid-afternoon. Under this frigid weather I had to start our car and let it run for fifteen minutes before departure in the mornings to get oil circulating enough to stop the engine from clanking. I added that I wouldn't have gotten the car started at all without the head bolt heater on all night. Even with the car's engine running smoothly, I had to rock the car back and forth from reverse to a forward gear to break the tires free from ice. In the late afternoons when we arrived home, the warm tires would once again melt into the ice and snow and refreeze within an hour.

Adam laughed when he heard this story about the Siberian conditions in North Dakota and then told us about his father's other protections against those brutal winters. Martin had worn a buffalo coat that came down to his ankles. This coat complemented his fur hat that came down to his neck and fastened under his chin. He built a sod house for the family that had two-foot thick walls and roof. With a coal burning stove and chimney in the center of the house, the family was warm in the winter and cool in the hot summers. The smallness of the sod house also contributed to the warmth, as did sleeping five and six people per room. Adam admitted, however, that the house was dark and musty inside with little ventilation. He lost the grim look on his face when he said that he was his dad's companion on evening walks on the prairie land. Adam's job was to retrieve prairie chicken, grouse, or rabbits that Martin shot. Adam smiled when he told about how he was allowed to take the reins when they rode to town in their wagon to get supplies. By now Adam was lighting one cigarette with the burnt remains of another one.

Just off the Dakota Badlands
on one-time Sioux treaty land,
Martin walked through sweet grass
on his hilly farm with
shotgun cradled in his arms.
He searched intently for stone figures
in the brush line of a coulee.
Adam, his youngest son, followed behind,
carrying two grouse by their necks,
victims of his papa's deadly aim.

The father's face wore disappointment
like a sculpture, not just because two grouse
were not enough for his large table,
but because the forces of history carved a life
that weeping could not touch anymore.

Uprooted twice, leaving three brothers and one sister
behind in South Russia—one brother shot
in the face by Bolsheviks trying to extort tribute. The others
died during Stalin's rule and World War II.
Losing his first wife in childbirth with their tenth child to a Texas grave,
he now homesteaded in North Dakota on barren land.

Chapter 2

After Helen and I took a break to refresh ourselves, Adam got each of us a fresh bottle of beer, and I pondered my next question. When we all where seated again, I launched into it. "How did Martin Hecker and family get into Texas?

"Their ship docked at Galveston in 1891."

"But why did they enter there when most immigrants from Europe entered at New York?"

"I asked the same question when I dug into this family business. My dad took his family to Argentina first. I don't know why they decided not to stay there. I think that some of your great-grandmother's Schmidt family lived there. Maybe they had trouble at the Argentinean customs. A family with nine children and a pregnant mother might have caused concern for their officials. Or it could be that conditions were bad and work scarce after they settled in, so they left for America. They likely would have booked passage on a ship that was headed to the nearest port in the United States and that would have been in one of the southern states. Also it's possible that there were other Germans who had already immigrated to Texas."

What next, I thought to myself. Helen was just as mystified as I was about my family's past. She looked through some of the albums that Adam had offered her earlier, and Adam and I continued our conversation.

"How long did Martin and Frank, my grandfather, stay in Texas, and why did they move to North Dakota?

"My dad's two older sons, Mathias and your grandfather, married and started families in Plantersville, Texas. Martin and these older sons farmed on rented land that had houses and some out buildings. I'm not clear on why they didn't stay because he never said. I was his last son and too young to ask him about such things. He died when I was fourteen years old. I suppose the income was poor and maybe the weather wasn't to their liking. The more likely answer was that Martin's three brothers and one sister were already on homestead land in North Dakota. The lure of getting his own land was probably the reason for Martin's migrating north."

"Moving that far north must have been quite an undertaking?"

"They had horses and wagons to transport food and household goods. They followed the harvest from Texas up through Oklahoma, Kansas and Nebraska into the Dakotas. John, one of Martin's younger sons, stayed in Kansas and married, starting another branch of the Hecker clan.

"But why didn't the older sons go on to Belfield and Dickinson?"

"I suppose the attraction of farm land didn't interest the older sons as much as it did Martin. Mathias and your grandfather found jobs on the railroad in Mandan and made their homes there. My folks and the younger children from both of their families went on to Belfield where I was born and where Martin's brothers helped us get established."

"Wow," I said, "talk about wanderings. Crossing oceans, visiting foreign lands, and migrating by horses and wagons just like the earlier peoples of the American westward movement."

"Yes, it was the pattern for our ancestral Heckers as well as for my dad. He wasn't a happy man at his end and suffered from his travels."

I was about to ask Adam about what he had just said when we heard a car door slam. Adam stood up and said Ruth was home. He went to the front door and opened it, saying as she entered carrying packages in both hands, "It looks like you had good shopping."

As I watched Adam addressing his wife and as I thought about his talk, I knew he was a Hecker, for most of us had a gift of speech.

Many Heckers could talk for hours and that was thought in some quarters to be a liability. For now I accepted Adam's accounts of what had happened to Martin and family in their journey to a new future. I wasn't practicing my seminar-learned skepticism, for I was swamped in new information that jarred my skimpy past knowledge of my family. I was also chagrined that I had known so little, but it wouldn't be long before I questioned what I was hearing even though I thought Adam very sincere and truthful in what he believed about our family.

Ruth, a tall, thin woman with gray hair and glasses, put her packages on the end of one of the sofas and said, "Yes, it was quite a day. I'm sorry I'm late, but our daughter and I shopped until we dropped as the saying goes." Adam introduced us to Ruth, and she embraced Helen and shook my hand. She looked at the coffee table and said, "I can see that all of you have been busy as well."

I said, "Yes, Adam has overwhelmed us with information about the Hecker extended family that I didn't know anything about, and I'm sure there's more to come."

"Well," Ruth said, "that'll have to wait. Right now, Helen and I have work to do in the kitchen. We're going to prepare a German dinner, and you guys have your part. The short ribs have to be grilled."

Helen said, "Oh good, I'd love to help. What can I do?"

The two women went into the kitchen while Adam and I went out into the backyard patio. We drank another beer while Adam started the grill and put on the meat. As we watched the grill, and Adam flipped the ribs and added sauce, we talked about living in the Pacific Northwest as compared to our old home state as well as other states we had lived in. Adam's work with the railroad had begun in North Dakota where several relatives had railroad jobs and continued from switchman to brakeman and later engineer in California. Helen and I had lived in Minnesota where I completed a master's degree at the University of Minnesota, and she taught elementary school at Bayport. After that we moved to Bremerton, Washington where we both taught and continued our academic educations until now. We heard the women in the kitchen talking and laughing about shopping and cooking. In about an hour we sat at table and ate short ribs, sauerkraut, green peas and mashed potatoes. The women drank wine while Adam and I continued with beer, now a German *Spaten* brand. Later we had coffee and apple strudel. We talked until ten o'clock about our families. Helen and I had a son and daughter, both in college, and Adam and Ruth had two daughters who were married with children. We agreed to turn in and resume our discussion in the morning after a breakfast at a local restaurant. Helen and I insisted that it be our treat.

We were all up early the next day and went to a nearby pancake house. Helen and Ruth were having fun exchanging information about German dishes that their mothers had prepared. Ruth also questioned Helen about the elementary classes her grandchildren were taking. Adam and I talked more about his years on the railroad before he retired. I answered his questions about my work as college instructor in English and American Cultural Studies.

Before long we were back at the Hecker house. The difference from the first session with Adam was that it was just the two of us now, for Helen and Ruth went to see an art exhibit at a local museum. Helen did watercolor painting and had taken classes from artists as well as at college, and she rarely missed the opportunity to see the work of fellow painters. I told her I would fill her in on what she would miss on our drive back home later in the day.

Adam lit up a cigarette and started by showing me another photograph. It was a black and white portrait of five men standing behind six seated women. The men all wore three-piece suits, white shirts, and a variety of ties. The fourth man from the left in the photograph I assumed was Martin Hecker because he wore a string tie that must have been a carry over from his Texas years. The women wore ankle length dresses with high necklines, full sleeves and necklaces with crosses. I looked at the picture carefully to be sure I had chosen the right man as my grandfather.

Adam anticipated my concern and said, " Martin is the fourth from the left. The picture I showed you yesterday was taken when he was fifteen years older and had gained weight." Martin continued and explained that this photograph was taken in 1914 when the youngest brother Leonard, on the left side of the photo, immigrated with his family to the United States. I glanced at the man and wife on that side of the photo, and they appeared to be more fashionable in clothing and hairstyles than the others.

"The two other brothers in between Leonard and Martin are Jacob and Frank. The younger man on the far right was standing in for George Hecker, his deceased father." I saw that the young man was well over six feet tall, thin, and broad-shouldered. His mother who sat below in front of him was large framed as well. There was variety in looks of these brothers although all of them were 5'10" or taller like my dad and myself.

"The extra woman, the second from the left is Barbara, the sister to the brothers. She immigrated to Canada with her family after living in North Dakota for a year or so."

— *PHOTOGRAPH OF ORIGINAL HECKERS TO IMMIGRATE TO NORTH DAKOTA* —

Adam handed me another photograph in black and white showing about forty people, all adults, standing and sitting in front of a modern looking one-story house. "This is Barbara's extended family as we met them some years ago in Saskatchewan. It isn't complete, for some moved west to Alberta and British Columbia. Children and grandchildren are also missing from the picture." I didn't recognize anyone, so I returned to the photograph of the brothers, wives, and sister, thinking that all of them probably had large families since they were Catholics and farmers. All of them, except Barbara, had lived permanently in the Belfield-Dickinson area, and I hadn't known or heard about any of them, until now! Adam interrupted my thought by adding, "Leonard made a quick trip back to Munchen in South Russia to sell off his farm and other property because he thought after a month or two in North Dakota that the war in Europe would probably lead to more trouble."

"What," I exclaimed, "old South Russia!"

"Yes, all of the brothers and sister immigrated to the United States from Russia."

I was startled and upset. Why didn't my dad tell me about my extended family? Why was I left in the dark? Maybe I had encountered a family secret? During the cold war years it was difficult to admit having German ancestry, given the tragedies of The Third Reich, but now I'm a fourth generation German American from Russia? "Are you saying, Adam, that we are Russian?"

"No, we're Germans from Russia. Our ancestors immigrated from Rulzheim, Germany to South Russia in 1809. Catherine the Great and Alexander the First made that possible. Germans and other Europeans were given free land and loans to build houses, start animal herds, and seed crops. They didn't have to serve in the Russian Army either. In other words they were Germans living in Russia."

I had graduate degrees in American history and literature, but I hadn't studied European history and literature except for a required course or two, so these comments came as a total surprise. I didn't know what to say, so I asked the obvious question, "So why did they leave Russia in the 1890's and later, since the generous terms they were offered in Russia were far better than those offered in our Homestead Act of 1862?"

"They lost most of these rights, one by one, by the third and fourth generations. When my dad decided to leave Russia, his sons, including your grandfather, were faced with a six-year Russian Army draft. Many young Germans in Russian villages who were drafted were never heard from again."

"Wow, I've got some studying to do!"

I didn't want to say so, but I was again embarrassed. I knew something about the Russian Revolution of 1917, but I didn't know what that meant to the various nationalities that had lived in Russia at that time. I had read some accounts of Joseph Stalin's reign, and the suffering of Russians under his rule, but I didn't know about these German colonists.

"I feel indebted to Martin Hecker for leaving Russia when he did, and I can appreciate Leonard Hecker's decision to sell off what he could in 1914, but did all of the Heckers get out of Russia?"

"No, I'm afraid not. Leonard sent packages of food and clothes to some of the remaining Hecker families, but they asked him to stop because the Russian authorities punished them for being in contact with "Capitalist pigs". After early 1915 Leonard and his brothers in North Dakota heard nothing more from family in Munchen."

"Has anyone been able to track down what happened to them since the end of the cold war?"

"I traveled twice to Germany during early retirement and asked questions about the original Heckers of Rulzheim. I found more ancestral names and added them to our family tree. My research also led me to some surviving Heckers from Munchen, Russia. I met with Johannes Hecker, Martin's nephew and son of Martin's brother John who had stayed in Russia. I located him in Munich, Germany, where he spent his last few years with his second wife. He and daughter Magdalena were the only survivors of a family of ten. The Soviet Army caught them near the end of WW II when they tried to cross the Elbe River into what would become West Germany. They were sent to the Gulag until 1974 when they were allowed to immigrate to Germany. Magdalena now lives in Hamburg, Germany with her husband and two daughters. I met them there during my last visit to Germany. Magdalena told me her family's grim story."

"But Helen and I stopped at Dachau on our way from Vienna, Austria to Western Germany in 1986. We didn't go into Munich because we only had an extra day or two, and we thought we needed more time to do the city justice. Had we known we could have met Johann and heard his story."

"It's probably just as well that you didn't. Johannes was blind when I saw him, and neither he nor his wife spoke any English. Fortunately for me the German dialect they spoke was similar to the one I learned from my parents."

"What about Magdalena and her family? Are they still in Hamburg?"

"Yes, Magdalena and Christian, her husband, live in an apartment in Hamburg. Their older daughter Irma is married and has a family. The younger daughter Maria just graduated from college and speaks English. The others don't. I'll give you their addresses, and maybe some day you can visit them."

"That'll be our next trip to Europe. Meanwhile I've got a lot of reading and research to do, thanks to you."

"I'm glad to hear that you are serious about the family. I've waited a long time for someone like you to show up. I'm going to pack up copies of this stuff and the family tree, including addresses of American relatives as well as those in Germany.

"Thanks Adam, I think I'm hooked. I enjoy doing research, and this looks like a formidable task."

"Well, don't be turned off by bumps on the rails. There are lots of them."

Ruth and Helen returned, and to our surprise they had purchased take-out dinners from a Thai Restaurant near the art museum. It was nearly three p.m., so they thought it best not to spend time preparing a meal. Helen and I had a four-hour drive ahead of us, or more if the traffic was heavier than usual as often happens on Sunday afternoons and evenings. Adam and I enjoyed another beer with the meal. Later Adam lit up his last cigarette of our visit. Helen and I both thanked our newly found relatives for their hospitality, and I gave special thanks to Adam for his preparations, discussion, and especially for the materials he handed me at departure. We agreed to meet again after Helen and I had time to absorb what we had learned and to do some other investigating. Adam said he was always available for questions.

— Photograph of Adam Hecker and his Dog at Age Seven —

− Chapter 3 −

On our return trip to Bremerton Helen and I talked in exclamations, questions, and in statements of disbelief. It was like getting lost in a section of Seattle where one-ways, dead ends, cul-de-sacs, and bodies of water block your passage. How could I not know that I have a great-grandmother buried in Texas? Really, I'm a German from Russia? I have relatives living in Germany who had been imprisoned in a Soviet Gulag! Forced migrations! Helen also wondered out loud about her family, the Blacks. She knew that Wendelin Black, Sr., her grandfather, had exited Europe with his family from the Port of Antwerp, Belgium in 1898. We had visited that port on our first trip to Europe. We sailed on a ferry out into the channel where his ship would have passed on its way to America. She had always assumed that Wendelin, Sr. and family had immigrated from a village somewhere near Karlshrue, Germany. Now she wasn't so sure. Maybe her family had also lived in South Russia. "Why," she asked, "if this is true, wasn't I told?"

As I drove, Helen paged through the box of materials that Adam had given us. She studied the photographs, looked carefully at the people, guessed at their ages, and commented on their clothes and hairstyles. She held up and waved a batch of stapled pages labeled family tree. She commented as she paged along through them. The first page listed the original Heckers from Rulzheim, Germany and continued on for several pages with many descendants living in South

Russia. The bulk of the pages added other Hecker families who grew out of the original brothers and sister who immigrated to Texas and North Dakota in the eighteen-nineties and later. "There are hundreds of them," Helen said.

The first Hecker families in Texas and North Dakota had six, eight and ten children. Martin Hecker's accumulation of children in two families topped them all with a total of twenty-five, although several didn't get beyond birth. Tracking them and their offspring must have occupied Adam for a long time. I shook my head in amazement. I certainly wouldn't try to duplicate Adam's travels. If I could just meet a few more like Adam in the United States, I would be satisfied. One thing was for sure. I had to give my ancestry research a high priority on my list of projects-to-do because of Adam's statement that the right person had finally shown up. I couldn't let him down. As explosive as the information was, he had expanded my knowledge of my family one hundred fold, and there was more to come. I already looked forward to meeting him again to share my research and to get answers to some of my future questions.

"How was your time with Ruth?"

"Just fine. We had fun at the gallery. There were several excellent exhibits, and we talked. Ruth told me she spends a lot of time with her daughters and grandchildren. She's glad, however, that the traveling by RV is over. She said they'd spent six long summers driving across the western half of the country and even into Canada looking for relatives."

"Yes, Adam said he'd met my parents in Minot. I don't recall any comment from mom or dad. Maybe they said something, but it didn't mean anything to me at the time, but I wonder why he searched so widely and diligently? I guess he needed something to do in retirement."

"Ruth said Martin died when Adam was only fourteen, and his mother had already passed away."

"Ah, that's one answer. At his young age he probably didn't ask many questions about ancestry. And Martin must have been at least sixty when Adam was born. He must have moved in with one of his older siblings when his dad died."

"Ruth didn't say anything about that."

"Could you believe how much Adam smoked?"

"Yes, Ruth said that was one reason why she got me out of the house."

"You were lucky, for he chain-smoked after you left and until you returned."

"Aren't you glad you quit smoking?"

"I'll say. I hope Adam's health is ok. I didn't like his pale skin color."

Helen continued to review the contents of the box. I drove on and thought about what I was getting myself into. The project appealed to me not only from a family perspective but also from a professional one. Since before I completed my Ph.D. in American Studies, I had been a member of the American Studies Association, a professional society that focused on both history and literature. The themes of its annual national conferences aimed at just such topics that I would tackle in my lineage research: ethnic, racial, and religious issues. The organization not only encouraged academic research in these areas but also sought political action to rectify deficiencies in the American promise in these areas plus others like gender and sexual orientation. In spite of my growing interest in this project, I would have to do much of it in my spare time and on vacations. My schedule at Olympic College was full. I lectured daily, worked on developing additional courses in American Cultural Studies, a program I had introduced through a National Endowment for the Humanities grant, and had my share of committee work in discipline, division, and institution.

This research in ancestry would involve letter writing and telephone calls to newly found relatives, archives, census bureaus, and immigration agencies. Reading Russian and German history, especially about the Russian Revolutions and Stalin's regime, would be major undertakings. I had read some novels by Tolstoy and Dostoyevsky and rejoiced particularly in the stories and plays of Anton Chekhov. The grand sweep of these literary works and the unusual psychological natures of their characters had attracted me. Solzhenitsyn's *One Day in the Life of Ivan Denisovich*, announcing the existence of the Gulag, came into my hands as soon as it appeared in English translation. I had read it with interest, but had no idea that the contents had a personal connection to me. With that thought in my mind, Helen finished with the materials in the box and said, "You've got a lot of stuff here. It's taken me almost two hours to just glance through it. I hope you'll be able to put names to all of these people." I nodded my head in agreement, thinking that there was much to do.

— Chapter 4 —

As was often the case, the first task I actively pursued was the one that intrigued me the most. Why didn't I know more about my German side of the family? In some respects I was hesitant about pursuing this path. Undoubtedly family secrets would open to scrutiny. As a cultural historian and professor, I knew about migration trends and the emphasis in America on rapid and complete assimilation. My grandparents and dad must have been influenced by these social demands. I knew that it was also true that second and third generation immigrants often shunned their elders and found their accents and manners embarrassing. Nativists, beginning with the Know-Nothing agitation of the 1850's and continuing with the Order of United Americans (1860's), and the American Protective Association in the 1880's, rejected minorities because of their possible foreign allegiance. In my own time I recalled how John F. Kennedy's campaign for President had to battle against the charge that his Catholicism would force him to obey the Pope in policy issues. Congress had passed an Alien and Sedition Act, Immigration Laws in 1882 and 1891, and had increased restrictions on the admission of minorities by adding head taxes and literacy requirements. Finally before the turn of the Twentieth Century, the Immigration Restriction League was founded in New England. By this time there were also racist and religious undertones to the nativist clamor. Italians were opposed both for religious and ethnic background as were Jews. The Chinese had been rejected as early as the 1870's and later Japanese-Americans would get their turn.

Contrary to all of this opposition, the railroads sent agents to Europe to recruit immigrants to the United States. They needed customers for their railroad towns and tracks they were laying across the West. They circulated advertisements throughout Europe trumpeting the availability of free land under the Homestead Act. Manufacturers of farm equipment and building construction materials, food processors and livestock sales yards were all busy calculating the per capita homesteader's value to the national economy.

An important aspect of the growing sentiment against German nationals living in the United States during the early 1940's was the use of Bismarck's Fort Lincoln. Originally a U.S. Army military post, the Immigration Naturalization Service now used the fort as an internment camp for both German and Italian seamen aboard commercial ships impounded in American ports when the war started in Europe in 1939. At first these individuals were allowed to find sponsors and jobs or other occupations like college attendance, but as suspicions were registered against these foreigners, the INS required all of them to report to its offices. Upon arrival they were booked and sent to various internment camps around the country. Over a five-year period until 1946 over two thousand German nationals were incarcerated at Fort Lincoln. Other internment camps were established in Montana, Texas, and New Mexico, but the one at Fort Lincoln was the largest. These men were not allowed visitors, and their mail was censored, but in general they were taken care of and allowed to work in the Fort's canteen, offices, and carpentry shop to help maintain the camp. Besides these activities they did theater productions, handicrafts, and various sports such as soccer.

Undoubtedly the existence of the camp at the State's Capitol was a factor in limiting the use of the German language and culture in North Dakota. At the beginning of the century there were about fifty-five German language newspapers in the State; by 1946 there were three. The antagonism against German-American newspapers had started much earlier during WWI when a Bismarck

German newspaper was admonished for using the German language since English was a more patriotic language for Americans. Other instances of anti-German attitudes were noted in the hallways of the North Dakota Capitol Buildings when monitors told people to speak English and not German.

Again, in my own time as I entered the world as a baby, Martin Dies, a Congressman from Texas, created the Un-American Activities Committee that directly targeted German and Russian immigrants as possible adherents to the German American Bund, Nazi spy rings, or supposed Communists infiltrating New Deal agencies. Father John Coughlin added his voice to the hysteria and later during my youth, Joseph McCarthy continued the fear campaign. I wondered to what extent these nativist activities impacted the rural reaches of North Dakota.

With this background of information on immigration and reactions to it, I probed my family relations to see why I didn't know much about my German side of the family. I was born in Mandan, North Dakota, at the end of the Great Depression in November of 1939, the second child of Adam and Lily (Peterson) Hecker. At that time we lived in the same neighborhood as my paternal grandparents, Frank and Veronica (Brucker) Hecker. My parents were of different ethnic backgrounds and religions, my father full German from Russia and Catholic, my mother Scandinavian and Lutheran. After high school graduation as salutatorian, mother took a job in the Land Commissioner's Office at the State Capitol in Bismarck, probably by arrangement of one of her older brothers, an assistant in Governor Langer's administration. My parents' marriage was representative of a slowly changing ethnic alignment in North Dakota. At one time one could draw a line from the northwest corner of the State to the southeast corner with a majority of German-Americans living below the line and the same for Scandinavian-Americans above the line. In our two families some of the ethnic German siblings married not only Scandinavians but also Protestants. The same was true of my mother's ethnic Norwegian/Icelandic family where roughly half of the siblings married German-Americans, some Catholic and some Protestant. Right from the beginning I entered an extended family with ethnic and religious variation and some friction.

— Photo of Adam and Lily (Peterson) Hecker —

An event took place that removed us from my birthplace and had this event not occurred, I would probably have been raised near my Germans from Russia-American family. World War II displaced us. My dad, who was thirty years old and married with three children in 1944, was required to either enlist in a branch of the military or go to work in a military production facility. Since my dad's sister and her family had already been confronted with this choice and now lived at Everett, Washington, my dad followed by train where he engaged in welding training and work at the Everett Naval Shipyard. After he found a rental house for us to live in, my pregnant mother, her niece, and my two sisters and I traveled over U.S. Highway # 2 in our 1934 four-door Chevrolet sedan. We crossed Montana, Idaho and much of Washington in a week or so of travel, stopping at cabins along the way.

Our stay in Washington was short-lived, about a year, but a few fundamental changes occurred while we were there. My brother John was born, making us now a family of six, and my mother's niece became pregnant but without husband. The free wielding ways of the war years near military installations took their toll. I learned much later from my father that he had not escaped without blemish. Apparently he had engaged in an extra-marital affair during the time he was alone in Everett and continued it off and on during the time we were living there. Many years later after he had retired and was visiting us at Bremerton, dad told me about that relationship. He and I had gone fishing in my boat on the Hood Canal when he began reminiscing about the times he had taken me salmon fishing as a five year old at Everett. This was news to me since I couldn't remember much about that time period at all. That recollection must have reminded him of his affair, for he suddenly added to his remarks, "I had a relationship then with a woman I met at a bar."

I glanced at him, and he had a pensive look on his face, gazing steadily at me to get my reaction. I was about forty years old and had survived the 1960's and 1970's without any infidelity although extra-marital affairs, divorces, and open marriages were commonplace at the time; thus his confession didn't stir any critical response from me. I was surprised, however, that I didn't know anything about the relationship. Mother must have known about it, but she didn't mention it to me or use it as a weapon in any of the few arguments that we children were exposed to while we were growing up.

Dad was apparently caught off guard by my silence, for he added, "She was a gym teacher at a junior high school." Just as he made this comment, I had a strike on my line, so I quickly took the outboard out of gear and began reeling in what felt like a small salmon. I said to my dad as I took these actions, "Things like that happen to people now and then," and quickly added, "Get the net ready!" He scooped the small salmon into the boat, and we both perked up at the catch, not mentioning his confession again. I did think about it though, and it didn't surprise me, for my brother and younger sister who lived at home with my parents had commented about his bar hopping alone in Minot during the years after Helen, Jeff, and I moved to

Washington. They said he was drinking heavily on weekends at clubs where he was seen dancing with women of questionable character.

That is why when we left Washington to return to North Dakota at the end of the war, the same family members plus John drove back in the fashion we had used to get there, but we didn't stop at Mandan, but went on to Devils Lake, North Dakota. Part of my mother's clan resided in this town. My mother's sister had a grocery store business, and her husband shared ownership of a car repair shop with one of my mother's brothers. This aunt had arranged for us to live in a small two-bedroom rental house that we would later buy. Within twenty miles of this small town lived the rest of the Peterson clan at Minnewaukan, North Dakota, a village named by the Sioux Indians to mean Spirit Water. My dad returned by train in about a month when he was discharged from the Naval Shipyard. These circumstances of war, displacement and my father's affair led to our separation from our German relatives and accounts for some of my lack of knowledge about them.

– Chapter 5 –

After my dad returned from Everett, Washington, he found a job as a warehouseman with Nash Finch Company, a national food distribution firm that had a transfer center in Devils Lake. Since he had worked in Mandan at a bottling plant after he dropped out of high school at age fifteen because of the Great Depression (another displacement for him), this seemed like a good fit. Over the years we lived in Devil's Lake, a town of about three thousand residents, dad advanced to city delivery, long distance delivery to small town grocery stores, and finally to salesman. Our family settled into our small, four-room house that had two bedrooms, a kitchen-dining room, a living room with coal burning stove as central heat and two enclosed porches, one at the back entry that served as laundry room on Mondays and a front porch entry that served exclusively as storage space.

I became well acquainted with the coal-burning stove since it was my job to empty clinkers (the remains of the coal after burning) and haul them out to a heap beside our coal shed. On return I would carry lignite coal chunks from the shed in pails and place them next to the stove. Often as I grew older, I would get up during the bitter cold winter nights and fill the stove full of coal to get us through to the morning. The stove would not have kept us warm during those winters had my dad and I not attached sheets of plastic with laths over the windows and banked up snow against lath attached curtains of thick tarp all around the base of the house. The house had no foundation, so we had to keep the cold winds from getting under the house and freezing the bottoms of the floors. I also became familiar with carrying water from our Aunt's water pump, a block away. During the summer I pulled a five-gallon can of drinking water on a red wagon. In the winter I hauled the same with a sled. If it rained, our gravel roads became slippery and rutted with car and truck tire tracks. When we had blizzards in winter, the snow could get eight to ten inches deep. Either situation made the job more and more arduous.

Once I complained that hauling the water in my wagon was too difficult for someone as young as I was, and I suggested that we hire the man who brought our clothes washing water to also bring our drinking and cooking water. My mother then told me the story about my first job at age four one summer when we still lived in Mandan. "Mom, I need some money," I had said. "Well," she answered, "if you want money, you'll have to get a job." "A job," I said, "what's that?" "You do something for someone else, and they pay you money for doing it," she answered. "But what can I do?" "Take your wagon to any of our neighbors on the block and offer to haul something. Maybe you can rake leaves and haul them to a pile in their back yard. Maybe they need wood moved from a stack to their kitchen stove. All of us need groceries from the store down the street, and you could get it for them." So I started my first business. Since everyone in the neighborhood had charge accounts in those days at the local grocery store, I took their lists to the grocer, and he or she filled the order, and I pulled the bags of bread, milk, vegetables and canned goods back to their houses. They gave me some change for the job, and I turned the money over to my mother. I followed the same process for other jobs for the neighbors, and finally one day my mother set a quart jar on the kitchen table and told me it was my earnings. "What do you want to buy?" she asked. I answered, "I want long pants." Apparently I only had shorts to wear in the summer, and I must have seen older boys in jeans. This story ended my complaints about being too young at age ten to haul water on my red wagon.

My life wasn't all work, for we children had a lively time at our home and neighborhood. During the summer months we played hide and seek, jump rope, and various games, including marbles, with other kids in the area. In the winter we had snowball fights, built snowmen, and enjoyed sledding, though we had few hills nearby in the neighborhood. We also practiced ice-skating at a downtown rink. During the evenings of both summer and winter, we kids huddled around the radio on chairs and sofas and listened to various programs like "The Shadow." When the program became especially scary, the youngest of us screamed, and we pulled blankets to our chins or over our heads. We enjoyed popcorn, taffy, and chocolate candy that our mother taught us to make. Mom was an accomplished cook who specialized in roasted chicken, Swiss steak, chili, and fresh baked bread with her homemade strawberry rhubarb jam.

Another variation to the normal condition of life in our town that excited all of us was the coming each summer of the Ringling Brothers Barnum and Bailey Circus. There was an open, flat field of many acres just down the gravel street that went by our house. On the other side of the street about two blocks away were railroad tracks. Our house was on the south side of those tracks, the wrong side, but it was in keeping with where I was born in Mandan, also on the south side of the tracks in a section of town referred to as *Houndstadt*. We were the first ones in town to know that the circus had arrived, for the circus arrived on the tracks in a long line of freight cars. They were filled with elephants, lions, tigers and many other such foreign creatures that we couldn't wait to see in the rings of the large tents that would be erected on the first day of their arrival. The elephants were the most notable to us since they couldn't be crated to the circus area like the wild animals. They were unloaded, and walked down our street to where the tents were to be pulled up into place by these giants. When they went past our place on the gravel street, the ground vibrated and shook our house. The ten or so of them were led by strange looking men with long, hook-ended poles in their hands that were used to direct and control the animals. Horses pulled wagonloads of animals and luggage to the circus area, but they weren't so exciting to our neighborhood kids because we were used to seeing them on farms and at rodeos.

One summer when I was a teenager, I got a job at the circus, helping to unpack crates, erect temporary tent shelters for circus performers and help with raising the big tents. Fifteen kids from town had been hired; our pay was free passes into the main three-ring tent arena where the big performances were given. It was quite an experience for a Catholic schoolboy, for I was mixing with the permanent roust-about employees of the circus. I had never seen black men or men who were obviously from foreign countries before. I heard their slang expressions, crude jokes, and foreign languages, but they always treated me and the other boys well, and they gave good advice about how to avoid accidents and how to get the job done with the least effort. I had to feign disinterest when some scantily clad circus women smiled and joked with me. For the first time I took real notice of the burlesque tent for strip tease performances that I helped put up when I realized that the women who were kidding me would probably be the performers on the stage that evening. The circus was an introduction of sorts for me to the larger world that existed outside our rural section of the country. Getting exposed to it probably led in part to my life long urge to travel, first around the United States and Canada and later to Mexico, Europe, Asia, and South America. I was always thinking of where to go next even as I'm typing now. Kyoto and Lhasa come to mind. I thought also that I hesitated to make negative generalizations about people of other races or ethnic origins because of the kindness of these men and women of the circus.

Now as I think back to these earlier stages of my life and family, I wonder about the circus workers and the care and attention they gave to me and other teens. Could it be that they had children and teenagers of their own in some distant town in Alabama, Texas, Michigan, or Illinois? Maybe they were originally from India, Africa, Brazil or Argentina. Hadn't they seen their families for six weeks or six months? Were they homesick for their wives, or husbands, and children? Did we serve temporarily as surrogate members of their families?

As we grew older, my brother John and I wanted our front porch turned into a bedroom for us. It was big enough for two twin beds along one side with room for a chest of drawers for our clothes. Our carpenter uncle from Minnewaukan came and looked the situation over. He concluded that the renovation was not possible, for the porch had too many windows and no insulation. In addition we would need to replace our coal-burning stove with a larger one to heat the added space. This alteration of the porch and the addition of a new stove were too expensive for our family's meager budget. So my brother and I were relegated to sleeping on a roll-a-way bed in the living room. The small bed was stored during the day against the wall in a corner. We shared our parents' bedroom chest of drawers and closet for our clothes. During my teenage years I never invited anyone to our home because I would have to explain the purpose of the bed.

My older sister Pat and I were enrolled at St. Mary's Academy, a Catholic grade school in September of 1945. I recall that we must have registered late because when I finally got into the first grade classroom, the room was already filled with pupils who were hard at work. Our mother had agreed to raise us as Catholics when she went through the rituals of the Catholic process of matrimony. This didn't set well with some members of her family. Our maternal grand-mother, an Icelandic-American of Lutheran affiliation, accepted the mixing of ethnic backgrounds, but Roman Catholicism was crossing the line. Bertha (*Thorvaldsdottir*) Peterson retaliated after the mar-riage when my family visited her home by singing and humming tunes from the Lutheran hymnal. My mother, grandma's favorite and last-born child, confronted my grandmother and forced her to accept the facts of her marriage. The ultimatum was that Bertha would either cease her resistance or go without further contact with our fam-ily. Grandma, a powerful force in her extended family, dropped the issue. She was the one who woke me up for Catholic Mass on Sunday mornings when I stayed at her home during the summers of my teens.

The only other resistance to our family's Catholicism to my knowledge was from another Peterson uncle. After he and family moved into Minnewaukan from a farm they had lived on for about fifteen years, they bought a small house on the outskirts of the village.

How the conversation shifted to religion I don't remember, but he was an opinionated person. He claimed that the local Catholic priest was having an affair with the housekeeper of the rectory where the priest lived. I was only about thirteen years old and just beginning to feel the demands of nature sexually, and so I wasn't aware of the adult world of sexual affairs and was skeptical to hear that a priest would engage in such a relationship. My experience for the most part was that nuns and priests were honorable and committed to both the education of youth and the spreading of the word of God.

This attitude was reinforced by three-day religious retreats for high school students at St. Mary's, given annually by a visiting brother, a member of a religious order who had not taken holy orders, from an out-of-state monastery. He gathered boys and girls separately in the school's chapel and gave talks about the importance of living rightly and respectfully, especially towards members of the opposite sex. He warned us about the sinfulness of masturbation and any mis-placed touching of girls. Sex with them was to be avoided until the sacrament of marriage was attained, and the goal was sex to create children. Each year at the end of the retreat the priest gathered all of us, boys and girls, together and again he spoke about the soul and spirit to be enhanced by prayer and devotion to God. He urged each of us to search our feelings to find out if we had vocations or callings to devote ourselves to the religious life. I was by this time a gregari-ous young lad with girlfriends and sexual urges, but I sympathized with the monk's warnings and thought it best to use restraint since pregnancy and venereal disease were at stake. On the other hand I thought he was naïve because a few couples that were going steady sat in the front pews of the chapel and held hands. They were well known for their sexual prowess, and they gave expressions of desire to partners right before the brother's eyes. This outward display of defiance by these couples placed them in a minority at the school, but masturbation and losing one's virginity were common topics for discussion and practice by many of the students.

My grandmother Bertha shared her strong feelings of devotion to God, and on occasion would read to me from her Icelandic Bible. This would happen generally on Saturdays after lunch. We would sit across from each other in the parlor, she in an easy chair and I across on a sofa. On one such Saturday when I was fifteen she invited me into the parlor. I was used to the regimen and was familiar with the same kind of proselytizing from St. Mary's Academy in Devils Lake. By this time I was spending my second summer at her home, and I had developed a sincere attachment to her. She was always kind to me and didn't impose any strict house rules for me to obey. As was my habit, I combined a positive feeling for someone with teasing whenever possible. As she read out loud to me in Icelandic, I took out a cigarette, struck a match and lit it. She was so absorbed in her reading that she didn't hear or see me do it. I sat back and blew smoke rings up at the ceiling and watched the smoke drift across the ceiling and down the opposite wall. When the fumes reached her face, she breathed heavily, coughed, and looked across at me with bulging eyes while yelling "*Fieda, Fieda!*" I hurriedly snuffed out the cigarette and apologized. I genuinely didn't want to upset her, and I was ashamed. She calmed down quickly and smiled, but closed her bible and set it aside.

In one respect this episode was prophetic, for gradually I separated myself from church affiliation. The process started later in high school when I couldn't go to confession and admit to masturbation and sexual intimacy with girls when I knew full well that I wouldn't stop doing these things. It would be hypocritical to confess and then continue these sexual actions. I also resisted the idea of praying for victory at basketball and football games. Shouldn't winning be based on the preparation and skill of the players? I also experienced an episode while serving morning mass that caused me considerable anxiety. My partner altar boy had worn a serving gown that was too long for him, and when he moved the bible from the epistle to the gospel side of the altar, he tripped and fell, shattering the bible across the floor. A visiting priest who served mass that day turned his head to see what had happened and said under his breath, "You son of a bitch." I was stunned to hear this from a priest, even though it took over ten minutes to get the pages back on the altar with all three of us working at it. Then when I brought water and wine to the priest and poured each into the chalice, he had me get more wine after I had emptied a full flask. Yes, he was frustrated, but I thought his profanity was too much. These high school happenings didn't stop me from practicing a limited form of Catholicism. I continued to go to church and did take communion on occasion, but I didn't believe in confession, so I dropped it, believing especially once I was in college that it was a matter of conscience and choice for me.

– Chapter 6 –

Going to a Catholic school gave my sister and me a dimension that I didn't notice then, but it kept us in some connection with the German side of our heritage. Although no one spoke German at the school, a significant number of the students were ethnic German-Americans. Hartmans, Krafts, Buckmeiers, Singers, Hagers, Kellers and Schells were among the many surnames on the school's roster. It may well have been that they were also Germans from Russia. The students made little of their ethnicity, as I recall, but it may have been that they chose to make little of it. The curriculum also made no notice of it. German was not taught nor was any other language except Latin. The mass was still presented in Latin at the time, and altar boys were needed to answer the prayers of the service. The teachers also didn't give attention to any ethnic heritage, but they did focus on religion

Nuns taught all of the grade school classes. They wore traditional black and white habits and started each day with prayers and a recital of the pledge of allegiance to the American flag. They were generally well received by students and were good teachers, that is they kept our attention, and we learned what was expected of us. Reading, writing and arithmetic were the central subjects of instruction. Over the years in grammar school at St. Mary's, I had developed strong impressions of the nuns as teachers. Three of them stood out. Sister

Concepta was my sixth grade teacher. A tall woman and at one time surely a beauty, she worked us hard at our writing and math skills. She nevertheless had a soft spot. One afternoon a week she gave us extra seatwork to do for the one hour she was absent from the classroom. I found out that she served the principal of the school, a priest, coffee during that time. When she came back on those afternoons, she gave us more seatwork. She then sat at her desk and gazed out the window at the trees and seemed to drift into a reverie. She obviously had strong feelings for the priest. Perhaps she noticed my awareness of her state of mind, for on occasion if I drifted off myself into dreamland, usually from lack of sleep, she would address me as her "Sleepy-eyed Susan."

The best teacher I had in elementary school was Sister Ursula who taught eighth grade. Her instructional techniques kept my classmates and myself on our toes and engaged in our subjects. She taught most lessons in a competition mode. She used flash cards for teaching both math and spelling. Boys were pitted against girls in these contests. Addition, subtraction and multiplication problems were flashed, and the first one of the two in line who answered correctly returned to the back of the line of those still standing to await the next challenge. The problems always became harder until only one student remained, the winner. I sometimes was the winner in math, but I couldn't beat a female student in spelling. She was a tiny, quiet girl who lacked feminine wiles, and had decided apparently that this was her realm. She always won, and for years went to the State Spelling Bee contests in Bismarck. Sister Ursula taught English grammar in the same competitive fashion. As many students as could fit would stand at the blackboards. She would give us a list of printed sentences, and we had to diagram correctly the contents of the sentence: subject, verb, object or complement on one line. A second line was drawn if the sentence was compound with a connecting line containing the conjunction or punctuation mark. Any error and you were seated. This process went on down the list with more and more complicated sentence structures until again only one student stood. I often won.

My favorite nun, however, was my ninth grade teacher, Sister Oliver. She became my teacher after the high school building was erected next to and connecting with the grade school. She acted as a mentor of sorts and hoped, I believe, that I would end up in the priesthood. She allowed me to skip English class in the first part of my freshmen year because I scored so high on the English grammar test she administered at the beginning of the year. I give thanks to Sister Ursula for this accomplishment. My job was to go to the school library and help out in any way I could, but mostly I browsed the stacks and looked at books. Sister Oliver would come in occasionally and suggest that I check out a book like *Huckleberry Finn* or *The Wind in the Willows*. As time passed, I became a steady reader, and she encouraged me to get a card at the downtown Carnegie Library. I did, and before long I spent evenings there studying and reading. It was much preferable to our cramped quarters at home. Thus I became a lifetime reader.

Large flakes of snow float down
under the glowing light of a street lamp.
I skip through the slush and spring up the steps
to the wide double doors of the library.

Inside, warm air carries the fragrance
of books and carnauba wax.
Draping my parka over a chair,
I stand with my back to a radiator,
feeling the heat drive out the chill.
Stepping into the stacks of books,
I thumb through photographs of art,
and visit the Sahara Desert.
Should I climb aboard the *Pequot* or visit
my friends Tom and Huck?

And for sure I can wander about the world unfettered
by such trivialities as money and transportation.
For this house is like a home should be:
cosmopolitan, all embracing, and civil.

After the high school was constructed, several new nuns were added to the teaching staff along with priests who taught courses in math, business, Latin, history and sciences. The priests also administered the programs and provided coaching in basketball and football. Some of us boys were selected to serve mass at St. Peter's Catholic Church near the center of town. Both boys and girls were encouraged to join the choir at the church as well. Since I couldn't carry a note and since Sister Oliver got me enrolled in Latin for my sophomore and junior years, I served mass on Sundays and later at early morning mass on weekdays. Studying Latin was a great asset since it helped increase memory capacity and with the study of English. I didn't do the morning masses until I gave up my paper route, delivering the Grand Forks <u>Herald</u> before going to school. This job was partly the reason why I took short naps in the sixth grade. I was out to pick up and deliver papers by 6 a.m. In the winter I slogged through the snow bundled up in a parka, and during the other half of the year I rode my second hand bicycle, both of which I purchased with my delivery earnings. I also picked up a habit that I financed also with my paper route job. I started smoking. Since I had spare cash, I would go into the candy store located in the basement of the school next to the cafeteria. Sister Oliver who was in charge during lunch hour would sidle up to me as I looked at candy bars and licorice, my favorite treats. She would sniff and say, "What brand are you smoking today?" Until then I didn't know how easy it was for non-smokers to tell that someone was a steady smoker. I owed much to my favorite teacher, especially her subtle way of guidance without recrimination.

— Chapter 7 —

During the eleven years from 1945-1956 that we lived in Devils Lake, we were close to the epicenter of the Peterson clan in Minnewaukan. This town was the seat of Benson County where the county newspaper was published, the administrative offices and courthouse were located and where the Benson County Sheriff presided. But more importantly this is where Grandma Peterson lived in a five-bedroom home that her husband and offspring built with their own labor. She was wife to the late Adolphus Peterson who died when I was two years old. Several of grandmother's children—Edwin, Lawrence, Ole, and Charlie—lived in this town with their families. Bertha and Adolphus had had thirteen children, five of whom died before he did. Adolphus was a second generation Norwegian-American, arriving in America at age three in 1869 with his parents Olaf and Caroline Peterson, all from Hallan farm that was located north of Trondheim, Norway. Adolphus and Bertha met and married at Vang, North Dakota in 1895 and moved to Minnewaukan with their large family in 1919. The Peterson's had a strong foothold in their village. As one relative pointed out, there were fifty-three Peterson's, counting spouses, children and grandchildren in this county seat of about 600 population, nearly ten per cent of the total.

Uncle Charley, who I worked for in part during the summers, was a carpenter who lived as a bachelor with my grandmother. He taught me how to drive when I was twelve and thirteen years old and regarded me as his chauffeur when I lived with them in the summer. He would make sure that I visited my family weekly in Devils Lake, generally on Saturday afternoons and evenings. That early training allowed me to get a driver's permit at age fourteen so that I could haul grain for another Peterson uncle on his farm. The permit was only good on County roads. I still recall the afternoon that Uncle Lawrence took me to the local County Judge's place where he was outside trimming some hedges. Uncle Lawrence introduced me to him, and the judge immediately went into the house and came back with the permit in hand. I was surprised to get the permit, but I have often thought that the judge was probably a schoolmate of my mothers. I particularly enjoyed my stays at grandmother's house since I was given my mother's former bedroom during my summer stays there. For the first time in my life I enjoyed a bedroom that I could call my own.

Bertha Peterson was a first generation Icelandic-American. Although married in the Lutheran faith, in her later years when I visited she was attracted to the tent meetings of evangelical churches. This shift agreed with a belief I came to in my middle years that Grandma Peterson had distant Celtic ancestry. The Vikings had raided the islands off of Scotland, inhabited then by Celts at this early time, for goods and women to help establish their encampments on Iceland. Grandma's fiery religious attitudes were consistent with what I knew about Celtic religious rituals that resembled those of the evangelicals of her later years. Politically, most of her offspring were Republican, although my mother, her only sister Aunt Lenore, and another brother Uncle Hans were Democrats. Two of the older sons married Norwegian-American women, and the rest of the sons linked up with German-Americans or in one case a Russian-American woman. Both daughters married Germans from Russia-Americans.

Most of the offspring of Adolphus and Bertha engaged in farming and blacksmithing. Gradually the sons added auto-mechanics, carpentry, car and implement sales and repairs, as well as mail delivery, barbering, watch repair and jewelry sales. Entertainment included playing cards (whist, and pinochle, in the evenings and Sunday afternoon), dancing, singing and family gatherings at homes for national holidays, birthdays and marriages. During the hot summers the extended family met at local lakes or rivers for fishing and picnics. It was a folk culture of a fairly close-knit variety. Some of my fondest memories of my youth are fishing trips on a Saturday or Sunday to the Cheyenne River or a nearby lake. The clan would gather by mid-morning, park and unload the cars of kids, picnic supplies and fishing gear. My dad, uncles, and older boys would set up fishing rods along the river or lake bank; some had bamboo poles and red-white bobbers. They used worms from home gardens as bait or minnows if we were at a river or lake with pike. Mainly they sought perch or bullhead. My Uncle Ole always said that the bullhead had the finest and best tasting white meat of any fish. They would sit on the ground generally and watch the bobbers for a strike. Some of my uncles wore bib overalls, long sleeved denim shirts, and straw hats. They would talk about local matters, politics (if my grandmother wasn't present), and the big one that got away. They ate sunflower seeds, and later in the afternoon when it got hot, they would drink canned beer, usually Hamms or Budweiser.

My aunts and mother would spread blankets on the grassy slopes, set out ice chests with pop and soda for the kids and wieners and hamburger for picnic lunch. A variety of fruits, usually apples from the store or fresh berries picked from nearby shrubs, were the fare for dessert. They would have other boxes with potato chips, cookies, bread and buns as well as a supply of candy bars. These women took charge of the youngest kids and sat around drinking iced tea and chewing sunflower seeds. Also, if my grandmother wasn't present, my mother and Aunt Lenore and one or two other women would smoke and perhaps even drink a beer or two in the afternoon.

I joined my brother, sisters and cousins for swimming in the river, much to the consternation of the fishermen. I would dive into the flowing river, swim underwater and occasionally bump into a fish. The collision would startle me into surfacing. After that I would swim to the shore and climb the bank, yelling to my cousins about the fish. They would in turn report their own encounters with fish under water. We would often play catch with softball or football or engage in games such as hide and seek, marbles or foot races.

We boys would eventually tire of the activities and go and sit beside our fathers and see what was being caught. If luck were good, we would join in and set up additional poles for perch and bullhead, or if a rod and reel were available, we would cast daredevils for walleye or pike. When lunchtime was announced, we boys would collect firewood and thin branches to roast wieners on. After starting a fire, a grate was placed over the smoldering coals. Frying pans were placed on the grill for hamburgers, and we children would roast wieners on the edges of the fire. Potato salad and cooked beans were prepared and bags of potato chips were available. We kids drank cool-aide by the quart, and the men drank their first cans of beer.

After lunch we kids, boys and girls, again played games and swam. If the fishermen had been lucky, we would stay for an early dinner of fried fish, baked potatoes, and more heated canned beans. The men and women alike now consumed beer, and we kids consumed more cool-aide but often of a different flavor. After much talking and resting the women would direct packing and clean up of the camp. Goodbyes were said and each carload headed for home. Dirty, tired children often slept all the way home. If that is, they didn't get carsick. In those days tires weren't as durable as now, and it was likely that a tire would have to be changed or repaired on the way home.

With this intense Peterson family life, especially for me with summers at grandmas, was it any wonder that I didn't learn much about the paternal side of the family? My mother kept an on-going correspondence by letter, especially during the Christmas season, with Grandma Hecker, her two daughters in North Dakota, and several others of my dad's siblings in California. Mom let them know in detail how our family was doing with special remarks about each of us children, now numbering five with the birth of my sister Nancy, the last child.

– Chapter 8 –

During the eleven years we lived in Devils Lake we made only two trips to the German side of our family. It wasn't avoidance that kept us away from them. Our family of seven simply couldn't afford the cost of gas, motel, and food for seven on a round trip of four hundred miles. One of the trips was a visit one summer for a weekend at Bismarck. My Grandfather Frank Hecker had died, and we couldn't get to the funeral, but we did make the trip later to console Grandmother Veronica Hecker and to visit with Aunt Marion, my dad's sister who lived in Bismarck. It was a short trip because of the expenses, but we did see grandmother's apartment where she lived after grandpa's death and the sale of their house. She lived near relatives on her side of the family, the Bruckers. Later in her last years, she moved to a basement apartment in Aunt Marion's home because she needed more care than she could manage herself.

— Photo of Frank and Veronica (Brucker) Hecker —

— HOUNDSTADT —

The south side of Mandan, North Dakota

Frank sat tied to his wheelchair
on his small front porch,
drooling on his shirt
staring out over a gravel street.
Dogs prowled along ditches,
skipped across lawns, barked
and deposited their scent.
Cars drove by, driving dust
over lawns and onto Frank's lap.

As a child I must have looked up at him
after getting out of our car.
Did I greet him as "grandpa" or peek
at him from behind my mother's dress?
Most of my recollections are from
photo albums and stories.

Old Mr. Kaiserslaughter, grandpa's neighbor,
hated dogs for defecating on his lawn and
pissing on his trees. He set out poison.
The next day nine dogs
were stretched out on his front lawn.

Frank's world had been reduced to his house
by an accident he had at the railroad roundhouse.
While on his knees beside a freight car,
blocking the wheels to keep it from rolling,
the car was nudged by another, and he fell,
wedging his head between wheel and track.

Frank sat in his wheelchair for about ten years,
not knowing he was disabled or how it happened.

The other trip of about five days was to visit another of dad's sisters, Aunt Angeline, who lived on a farm with family southwest of Mandan, near Flasher, North Dakota. Her children numbered twelve, and nine of them still lived at home. I was sixteen years old at this time. The George P. Schmidt farm was something to experience. The Schmidt's had a herd of cattle of about one hundred and fifty head, of which one hundred were milked daily. The family farm had hundreds of acres of land devoted to grain crops such as wheat, barley and oats. Haying was a major enterprise as well. The rest of the land was pasture for their cattle and horses. Some of the horses were kept in the barn across the way from the house for pleasure riding or herding milk cows. Many other horses were kept in a large pasture about a mile away. Uncle George had a soft spot in his heart and had released old workhorses into this place many years earlier after the haying and plowing operations were taken over with tractors, trucks, and other power equipment. He apparently appreciated their contributions to his farming business so much that he viewed this hilly land of ravines, trees, and creeks as their retirement haven.

When we first arrived at the farm, my male cousins took their town relative to look at the horses in the barn. Unknown to me they had kept an older horse there without exercise for several weeks before our arrival. One of my cousins saddled and bridled the horse and led it out into the barnyard and invited me to ride it. I climbed into the saddle and immediately the horse trotted toward an entrance road. In no time we were galloping down the road at full speed. I tried to get the horse to slow up by pushing my feet down and forward in the stirrups and by pulling the reins with all my strength, but the horse didn't slow down. I decided then to give the horse full rein and started banging my feet against its undersides as I had seen it done in western movies. It wasn't but ten minutes or so before we reached the pasture where the retired horses were located. I guessed that the horse I was riding wanted to join them. The gate was shut, and my horse was exhausted, so we rested for a moment, and I looked at the many horses in the distance, lazily grazing in some of the tree filled ravines of the pasture. Bernie, one of my cousins about my age (who apparently had some concern for my safety) then rode up and accompanied me back to the farmyard. Bernie took our horses into the barn and put them into stalls. I followed and another of my older cousins showed me their breeding horse, named King.

My next exposure to horses was about to begin. King was huge, and one other older cousin bridled and led him out of the stall. King was so tall that as he exited the barn he had to lower his hindquarters to slide under the doorway. Once outside, I was asked to guide the horse to the watering trough about one hundred feet or so away. I was told to hold the reins with one hand just below the horse's mouth. I did, and when King started to walk, he lifted his head high into the air and lifted me off the ground. I reached up with my other hand and grabbed the reins as he walked, shaking the ground as we neared the water trough. Obviously the horse had not been watered for a day or two. This was the last of my initiation into farm life. I had passed muster.

My cousins were the farm hands in many work situations that they called chores. For the rest of our visit, I paired up with Bernie. One of his jobs was to bring the cattle down in the morning from another pasture about a mile away from the farmyard. George P. called up the stairs at 5 a.m. to the second floor where all of the children in the family slept. I was eager to go, but Bernie told me to wait until my Uncle George made a second call. Ten minutes later he yelled up the stairs, "Get down here now, or I'm coming up there!" I imagined a sergeant in a military barracks barking at recruits. Bernie said to me, "Now we get up."

We saddled and rode horses up to the pasture. Since I had already proven myself to be a novice at horse back riding, I rode the same old mare as the event of the day earlier. I managed the ride without incident, and we delivered the milking cows to the corrals by 7 a.m. Older cousins and my sisters Pat and Carol met us there, but the youngest cousins and my other siblings were still in bed. The ones who were gathered for the work had brought milking machines, pails and stools. The older cousins hooked cows to machines and then milked others by hand. As pails of milk multiplied, several of the work force carried them to the milk room and started separating cream from the milk. I was amazed at the efficiency and rigor of the work. There was a reason for it. Bernie told me that no one ate breakfast until the milking was completed.

By 9 a.m. the Hecker and Schmidt kids were seated at an enormous table in the farmhouse kitchen. Aunt Angeline had plates of bacon, sausage, fried and scrambled eggs, fried potatoes, pancakes and toast lined up and down the middle of the table. Pitchers of milk and orange and apple juice were also placed at intervals on the table. Everybody dug into the food. Even the smallest of the children ate several eggs with meat and either pancakes or toast. The pitchers of milk and juice reached bottom quickly and were refilled immediately. Empty serving plates were removed and replaced as fast as they were drained of food. I was astounded at the appetites and even more so since none of my cousins was heavy. Bernie noticed my attention and leaned towards me whispering that no one had to go to work as long as they were at the table eating. Finally, however, Aunt Angeline took off her apron and threw it on the floor, announcing, "No more food!"

As if a cue had been given, Uncle George came into the kitchen from the living room where he had been visiting with my parents. He stopped next to the table, giving work orders for all of the Schmidt kids. The older boys, including Bernie, were assigned to summer fallowing or haying, some mowing and others stacking. The younger girls, and one older one who supervised the others, had immediate kitchen chores. They cleaned the table, washed dishes and dealt with garbage. After that they had clothes to wash and iron and house cleaning. Other children, including several older daughters, had to do garden work, canning of vegetables, and fruit picking. Some of the younger boys had to feed the hogs and chickens, pick eggs, and do other chores that their dad assigned them, as he needed it, while he repaired equipment. Uncle George did all of the maintenance work on tractors, trucks, mowers, plows and combines. This included lubrication, tune-ups, and repair of broken or dull equipment. My dad and I went and watched him do this work, and I helped when I could.

My cousins received rewards for this labor, including Saturday nights in town with allowances. The older of them, boys in a pickup and girls in a spare car, went to dances and drank beer with the understanding that they had to get up for milking chores and Catholic Mass regardless of their condition. The younger kids went to movies and bought popcorn and candy. Aunt Angeline and Uncle George took them home after Uncle George finished his discussions with neighbors about prices, animals, and local news in saloons. On these evenings that sometimes got very late, so the kids roamed the streets or sat in the car with Aunt Angeline.

A larger reward for my cousins was a couple of days each year at the Fourth of July rodeo in Mandan. The older ones were allowed one riding horse apiece. If they didn't like their current horse, they could take it to the rodeo, sell it, and buy another with Uncle George supplying the difference within certain limitations. All of the family members went to the rodeo to watch the grand procession, roping events, and bull and bronco riding. It was the only vacation they got during the year, so they all played it to the hilt. Kate, one of the middle cousins, was a true horse person. On the weekend we were at the farm, she rode her horse, a palomino, bareback into the farmyard and then stood up on its back, balancing perfectly as the horse galloped out the other side of the yard past the barn. She was as good as any rider I had seen at rodeos in my time in North Dakota.

These two trips to the Heckers and Schmidts were memorable, but they didn't allow for anything bordering on a good understanding of the German-American side of my family. Grandma and the Schmidts spoke some German, but English was the standard fare. Nothing was said about any Russian connection or even a German connection to my knowledge. They seemed well assimilated into the American Way, at least the American Way of North Dakota farm life. Their lives were hard, and they had few luxuries beyond a lot of hearty food, horses and good clothes. The kids slept in barracks style upstairs in the second floor of the house. The beds for the boys and the girls were lined up along one wall of the lengthy, narrow room with a curtain separating the two groups of beds. The other side of the room held chests of drawers. In between the chests and beds was a pathway that led to the stairs down to the kitchen below. The washing room just off the kitchen had several sinks lined up along one wall. The only toilet was a three-seater outhouse about fifty feet from the farmhouse. Undoubtedly they used portable potties for indoor use during the freezing cold winter nights. Uncle George and Aunt Angeline slept in the huge front room that held a heating stove, sofas, chairs and tables as well as two beds at different ends of the room.

I did learn on this trip that my dad had worked one summer on the Schmidt farm. He stacked hay, rode the header box on the threshing machine, and shoveled grain. His pay for the summer's work was an adult pig for Grandma and Grandpa Hecker. They would have it butchered and packaged for meat throughout the winter. This pattern by my German grandparents of collecting the wages of their offspring continued after my dad quit high school at age fifteen in the late fall of 1929 at the beginning of the Great Depression. Dad worked at a bottling plant and gave his weekly check to grandma in exchange for an allowance and free room and board. This practice continued until he was twenty-one when he received a brand new four door Chevrolet from his parents who had saved his earnings and returned it in this gift. Hecker relatives told me that since dad's older siblings moved (many to the west coast) out of the parental home at their first opportunity, Grandma Hecker wanted to keep her youngest son at home. Unfortunately, the gift of the car led my dad to the "Strip", a nightclub area on the highway between Mandan and Bismarck. Dad's cheerful, gregarious nature, love of dance and drinking led to a riotous nightlife. Since he had no experience at budgeting money, it wasn't long after he married that mother had to take over his wages, less the amount he wanted for entertainment.

Dad also had his first experience with home made beer at the Schmidt farm. That was the time he tried to walk from the farmhouse to the outhouse, but he had either walked sideways or backwards and couldn't reach the outhouse in time for the eruption. This initial bad experience with alcohol did not cure him of his later tendency to frequent and sometimes heavy drinking throughout his adult years. Fortunately for our family he had inherited the easy-going and friendly nature of the original Hecker families who settled in North Dakota. At least this was my experience with him except for one or two unsavory episodes. I also learned from relatives that the sleeping arrangements in my grandparents' two-bedroom house in Mandan were similar to the ones on the Schmidt farm. In that case all remaining children (They had twelve in all.) slept in a large room in the basement with a curtain separating the boys from the girls. This visit then to the Schmidt farm taught me that our cozy sleeping arrangements in Devils Lake were not unusual to the Germans from Russia-American side of the family. I also learned that these relatives were not only hard working, but they were also regimented. Some of this parental authority came, I would learn later in my investigations, from the conditions they experienced while living in the villages of South Russia and continued after they arrived in the United States.

I couldn't find you in the faces of older men,
in books, movies, or even dreams.
It was no use. I had to invent you
since your residue was everywhere.

Arriving on a late night flight,
I found you waiting at baggage claim.
You drove because you knew a shortcut
through residential streets, but stopped
half a block away from a traffic light—
Were your eyes that bad?
You, who once could cast a lure
eighty feet to sink where pickerel hid,
or brought down a pheasant on the wing
at sixty yards, not for sport or pleasure,
but food. The next day when I drove
you told me where to park at Miracle Mart—
To avoid a search for your pickup truck later?

At your favorite watering hole,
you drank boilermakers
and asked about children and grandchildren.
And then repeatedly sang a tune,
If you don't do it when you first have a chance,
You won't get to do it at all.
You won't get to do it at all.

II

Giving up another
for your family's sake—
not knowing it would contribute to your forlorn
nature when binging on wintry nights—
you tried to end your life,
alone in your pickup,

engine running, headlights shining
against the blank apartment wall.

Another time and place,
you raged against life,
including me, in the foulest language.
Howling and weaving about,
your eyes flashed red.
And the flesh on your forehead
protruded into two horn-like bumps.
Your mouth ceased moving,
and smoke steamed from your nose.
I stared into your eyes
until you whimpered and collapsed
into a lawn chair.

Your forehead felt clammy, cool to my hand.
"Damn it, don't touch me."

A nurse's call pulled me from sleep.
You had slipped out of your lounge chair to the floor.
You didn't call out for help
but just lay there.
When she entered, you said,
"I suppose I should get up."

"No real harm, just bruises,"
she told me from that distant time zone.
"He's survived many slips to the floor," I said.

III

Burn, rave, and *rage*
shadowed you at every turn.
These words, written for another, suited you,
so I thought to read Dylan Thomas at your bedside
among the mourners.

You, however, didn't wait
didn't storm and bellow,
but chose to just slip off,
leaving me to recall your measures:

> A serious drinker, flushing your dentures down the toilet,
> A non-voter, holding forth like a political zealot,
> A newspaper skimmer, telling wry stories,
> An old man, sallying forth to bump and grind.

I laughed and laughed—
the response you preferred—
until tears scalded my heart.

– *Chapter 9* –

The road I traveled to learn about the paternal side of my family had a few bumps and gallops but lack of contact was the central cause of my scarce knowledge about them, along with the nature of American Society in the 1940's and 1950's. Ethnic variations sometimes vanish into the shadows when political realities strike. Third generation Americans, such as my dad, often sought acceptance and assimilation into their new society and ignored the standards and values of their old-country forebears. Learn the language of the new country and avoid accents that identify you with the archaic past. Popular culture forms like motion pictures presented figures like Cary Grant, Burt Lancaster, and Clark Gable for young men to identify with. And these models would lead one into the rising middle class with its good employment and material benefits. When I looked at pictures of my parents in the early forties before the move to Washington State, I could see these movie idols in my dad's clothes and hairstyle, so he must have looked to the screen icons for his models of behavior. In music he favored Lawrence Welk, a German-American from southwest North Dakota, who popularized polka and waltz dance music. Even in his last years he always insisted on watching the Lawrence Welk show on television.

The next route I followed was to get data from government agencies and other institutions that kept and circulated records. I started at the entrance of my Hecker great-grandparents into the country at the Port of Galveston, Texas in 1891. The first detour wasn't long in coming. The immigration records for the period from 1890-1900 were missing because of a hurricane at Galveston in 1900 according to an archivist at the Rosemary Library of Galveston. I couldn't then find out the name of the ship Martin Hecker and family had arrived on or where they had stopped in route to America. Adam Hecker of Salem had told me that his father had gone to Argentina first but hadn't stayed there for very long. The first census for Texas that applied to them was the 1900 one, a full nine years after they had entered the country. By then the original family had changed. A year or so after Christine (Schmidt) Hecker, my great-grandmother had died in childbirth, Martin re-married. His second wife, Christine (Dillman) Hecker was a twenty-six year old widow with a young son. Since Martin had nine children, two older sons moved out of the household and started their own families. My grandfather Frank Hecker was one of them. His and his older brother's families showed up in the 1900 census separately from Martin Hecker's second growing family.

I wanted to know where my great-grandmother was buried. I had information from Adam Hecker of Salem that the Hecker families had settled and farmed at Plantersville, Texas, a small village located about thirty miles north of Houston. Another of my family tree sources, Selma (Hecker) Schmidt of Dickinson, North Dakota, had informed me that my great-grandmother was buried at Anderson, Texas in Grimes County. I contacted the county's District Clerk and found no record for the Heckers from the early 1890's to the early 1900's, not exactly a surprise since this time period was over a century ago. The Martin Heckers were Catholics, so I contacted the Catholic Diocese Archives at Austin, Texas. No records were available. I then contacted the administration of the Texas State Library's Genealogical collection, also at Austin, for an obituary, but none again was located. Even the census data for 1900 was incomplete. Census records are collected from individuals, not documents, and the human memory is a fickle thing. Combine that wobbly mental faculty with the fact that immigrants often don't know much about their lineage, as was the case with my dad, and you know that I braced myself for the many potholes and alternate routes that I would encounter ahead.

These failed efforts to get information didn't stop me from setting aside these unanswered questions to a later date. Instead I reviewed the detail I had received from Adam Hecker of Salem about the exit of the Heckers from Texas. They left Texas, not because of a forced migration this time, but because the prospects were better in North Dakota. Martin's three brother's had emigrated there from South Russia after Martin had gone to Texas. Homestead land was still available in the Upper Plains and Canada, so that must have attracted Martin. Employment in the expanding railroads of North Dakota was another attraction that had already been secured by some of Martin Hecker's relatives. As it turned out, this was especially attractive to the older sons in the Martin Hecker branch of the family. The prospects in Texas were limited because they were renting land on a shared-crop basis. How to finance their move was a question they answered in the early summer of 1903. They had horse drawn wagons to transport themselves and possessions. The wagons served also as bedroom and kitchen. To earn money they followed the harvest north. Since the harvest season was earlier in the South and later as one traveled north, they had a guaranteed source of income all the way to North Dakota. As they worked the harvest through Kansas, John Hecker, one of the younger sons of Martin Hecker's first family met a sweetheart and decided to stay and set down roots. Thus another branch of the Hecker clan was started and grew during the Twentieth Century. At this time in my research this information from relatives seemed logical, but as I would find out later in my investigations these stories were not correct.

The next stop was at Mandan, North Dakota, a main hub for the Northern Pacific railroad. This corporation had a roundhouse for repairs and many sidetracks for loading and unloading freight. My Grandfather Frank Hecker and some Brucker men, of my Grandmother Veronica (Brucker) Hecker's family, took jobs in this growing industry rather than continue in farming as they had done in Texas. This work opportunity created employment that led to my dad's birth as well as mine in Mandan. Martin Hecker and family went on farther west to Belfield to join his brothers in the only work he knew, farming. Since Adam Hecker of Salem had provided accurate family tree information after this time, all I had to do was establish their first appearance on the Census and naturalization bureaus.

I used the 1900 census to verify the original Hecker brothers who immigrated to North Dakota in the 1890's, and the 1910 census for Martin and sons who didn't enter North Dakota until 1903. I was able to get documents on four of the original brothers—Martin, Jacob, Frank, and George—but not on the fifth brother Leonard who didn't emigrate from South Russia until 1914. In addition to census data I was able to locate naturalization papers plus obituaries on three of the brothers. The census agreed with what I had, except for omissions of some names of children and slight variations in age of some of them that could be attributed to memory failure or miscommunication due to language barriers. The three brothers had naturalized as citizens at various dates between 1898 and 1907, suggesting that these brothers didn't coordinate their civic lives. Two renounced any allegiance to the Czar of Russia while one was more specific and identified Nicholas II, Emperor of Russia. Their obituaries showed they survived into their 70's and 80's, a fairly long life span for the times. Frank Hecker of the originals lived the longest to age 84 while my Great-Grandfather Martin lived to be 77. He died in 1930 at the beginning of the Great Depression and nine years before my birth. I also acquired naturalization papers on Mathias Hecker, my grandfather's older brother who filed in 1904, and for my Grandfather Frank Hecker who filed in 1906. They both denounced the Czar of Russia. My grandfather died at age 75 after a long convalescence from a head injury suffered at the Northern Pacific roundhouse. My dad Adam Hecker of Minot lived to age 88. Since I am seventy years old, I took special note of all of these death dates, which tended to enhance my prospects for more years of writing and travel.

I took pleasure and reassurance from reviewing these documents because they were official confirmation of what I had learned from family correspondence and meetings. At least I could definitely affirm data from these sources so long as they agreed in content. These documents also verified the persons who appeared in the original Hecker family group photograph taken in 1914. I now could recognize my paternal family members and had documents proclaiming their existence. I extended my sense of who I am and where I came from as well as an enlarged connection to the broader world. I also noted the detail in the naturalization papers that required an immigrant to renounce any allegiance to any "foreign power, prince, potentate or sovereignty whatever and particularly to the Czar of Russia." These pledges must have stuck in the minds of these brothers and had impact on their desires to assimilate as quickly as possible. For them the past was over and done with and probably led to the forfeiting of language and cultural patterns of the old world.

– Chapter 10 –

As it happened, other Hecker clan members also sought contact with their larger families, and they organized reunions. These gatherings provided many isolated individuals with contacts who gave them knowledge of family heritage. Fortunately for me a group of Heckers in Tacoma, Washington, a city only about an hour away from Bremerton put together a reunion at Spanaway Park in July 1987. I received information about it and the names and telephone numbers of planners from Selma (Hecker) Schmidt of Dickinson. I telephoned one of them and received by mail a handout, detailing the time, place, and preferred plates of food, for this event was a potluck lunch. Helen and I went and talked with a few members of the various branches of the original Heckers to emigrate to North Dakota as well as some individuals from the John Hecker branch of Kansas. Again I received names and addresses of other Heckers who weren't in attendance. Oddly enough my investigation into my roots was bringing me together with extended family that I might have met in North Dakota in my youth had we stayed in Mandan.

This reunion put me in contact with Heckers from Washington, Oregon, California and a few from Kansas and New Mexico. I was indeed surprised at the extent of the fanning out of Heckers across the western half of the United States. Most of them in fact were connected to the Belfield/Dickinson clan. Three Californian brothers—Frank, Joe and Albert—were quite tall and stongly built and were from the George Hecker branch. Another George Hecker from Eagle Creek, Oregon, resembled closely my own father. He had to be from Martin Hecker's second family, but I wasn't able to get direct confirmation from him. He, like my dad, didn't take a vital interest in lineage. Since the picnic included anyone who was from Belfield or tied by family to Belfield, I did meet a Norwegian-American at the picnic who had met and knew my Great-Grandfather Martin and Martin's brothers. He said all of the Hecker brothers were talkative and easy going, but none of them spoke English. Whether these statements were fact or not I didn't know, but the comment about being sociable seemed likely from what I had heard from relatives and from what I had experienced, but the statement about language usage I wasn't sure about although it wouldn't have surprised me since they were first generation and middle-aged when they arrived in the United States. This man also related that the youngest of the brothers, Leonard, had brought his mother with him in 1914. This older woman who lived to be nearly one hundred was very energetic and spoke only German. When on an outing, such as berry picking in the Dakota Badlands to the west of Belfield, she would chatter incessantly without bothering to get responses. After meeting some of these new Heckers at the reunion and from my earlier experience with my immediate family, I confirmed what I thought were traits of the Heckers; they were sociable and very verbal. I was thankful for this because it made my life as lecturer easy and enjoyable.

Although I was busy writing more letters to new Hecker contacts, to government agencies and to historical societies, especially in North Dakota, the second family reunion at Tacoma in July of 1988 brought me into direct contact with Selma (Hecker) Schmidt of Dickinson, someone I had corresponded with for about a year. Selma was in her sixties, short and petite with short cut, graying hair. She spoke rapidly as she showed me her chart of the members of the original Heckers to enter the country. When I said I had met Adam Hecker of Salem, and he had given me 96 pages of family tree that probably included some of her work, she bristled a bit and said, "Are you putting together a book on the Heckers?" I sensed there was a bit of competition between some of the researchers in the family, so I assured her that I was only trying to put together a family tree of my great-grandfather's line.

During our discussion she told me about her visit with Johannes Hecker at Munich, Germany in 1982. Johannes and his daughter Magdalena were the only survivors in their family of ten and had suffered greatly in a Gulag in the Ural Mountains until 1974 when the Soviet government allowed them to immigrate to Germany, the place they had tried to reach thirty years earlier. Johannes was blind from excessive exposure to the rays of the sun reflecting off snow while felling trees in the forests. The Soviets sold these logs on the international market. He lived with his second wife and spoke German and Russian. This report was the second from a Hecker about other related survivors from Russia who hadn't immigrated to the United States. Adam Hecker of Salem had visited Johannes in 1983, and he reported to me that Johannes was critical of his American relatives for not coming to his aid. Johannes didn't know anything about the agreement at Yalta by the Big Three that made it nearly impossible for the Allies to intervene on their behalf. If the Allied military couldn't help, then how could ordinary Americans do anything?

At this time Selma didn't add much more knowledge about the Heckers in Germany, other than to state that they had suffered greatly under the Stalinist regime. Her information along with Adams, however sparse, made me more eager to travel to Hamburg to visit Johann's daughter and family who were alive and well. Both Selma and Adam had informed me that Johann had died in October of 1987. I knew that I had to travel to Hamburg soon if I wanted to gather with a Hecker who still had memories of life in South Russia. My letters to Maria, Magdalena's daughter, who was fluent in English, were answered, and I had invited her to visit us in Bremerton on a proposed visit she planned in 1988.

Selma Schmidt's conversation at the Hecker picnic also gave me a name and address of another Hecker who lived at Yakima, Washington. I contacted Leonard Hecker, Jr., and Helen and I visited him early in 1988. Leonard was short, wiry and full of energy even though he was retired and in the process of selling his house since his wife had died. He talked rapidly and nearly non-stop. One almost couldn't get into the conversation. I immediately recalled the comments of the Norwegian-American from Belfield who had described Leonard's grandmother's speaking habits. A friend was helping Leonard with getting his house ready for sale; he quipped that Leonard was also a devotee to the spirits of the bottle, primarily whiskey.

Leonard gave information about himself and family, but not much about his father's family line. He was a son of the original Leonard who came to North Dakota in 1914. Leonard, Jr. was born in Munchen, South Russia in 1911 and immigrated with his family to North Dakota at age three. Later he took up farming in his early manhood, but the drought and the Great Depression of the 1930's forced him off the land, and he migrated to Yakima. There he tried working in the orchards, but ended up in building construction. He and his wife stayed in Yakima and raised three daughters. I was particularly interested in his journey from Munchen to the United States in 1914, and he told me to contact his sister, a Sister Reinhardt of the Annunciation Priory at Bismarck, for more detailed information. She was an older sister who would have better memories of the travel. Helen and I were grateful to have met another Hecker from a different branch of the clan who linked us yet to another Hecker, and we invited him to attend our only daughter's wedding on June 18, 1988. Leonard agreed to attend.

Leonard had given me his sister's address in Bismarck, so I wrote asking for information about her family's travel to America. Sister Reinhardt Hecker was a founding member of the Benedictine Sisters of Annunciation Priory of Bismarck. She, the oldest of nine children, had entered the convent of St. Benedict at St. Joseph, Minnesota at age twenty, and had taken vows in the summer of 1923. She had served as a cook at missions in Minnesota and North Dakota, but most of all she was remembered as cook and housekeeper at the residence of Bishop Hacker of the Diocese of Bismarck.

Sister Reinhardt responded by letter and said she remembered the trip well as she was thirteen years old when her family made their journey. Not only did Leonard's family make the passage, but Leonard's mother and sister Barbara and family also were along. They traveled by train from their village of Munchen to Odessa and then on to Warsaw, Poland. "There we crossed the city, passed the beautiful cathedrals. I still remember the big, colorful funeral of a certain archbishop. Our taxicabs were drawn by beautiful black horses, and the enclosed carriages were decked out with red velvet." From Warsaw they went by train to Berlin and finally on to Hamburg. Sister Reinhardt wrote that she remembers two German military officers at the Berlin station. "They wore beautiful light blue uniforms, black shiny boots up to their knees and their special fancy helmets. They also had a variety of decorations on their coats. It made a permanent impression on me to have seen them thus." Once the families arrived in Hamburg they boarded a steamer, a ship named <u>America.</u> "It was quite new. We spent 11 days on the ocean. When we reached New York we were taken to Ellis Island for the inspection and then to the City of New York. We then boarded a train for Dickinson; we stopped once at Chicago." It was clear from Sister Reinhardt's letter that their passage was not in steerage.

Since three of Leonard, Sr.'s brothers—Jacob, Frank, and George—had arrived in Dickinson and Belfield in the 1890's, they were well established and were helpful in aiding him.

"Uncle Frank took us to his farm where we stayed for three weeks. After that we moved to a Belfield farm that was located one mile from your great-grandfather Martin. Uncle Frank's son, Mike, lived two miles from our farm; he was a great help to my parents. He took them shopping because we had to buy everything from dishes to furniture. His advice always was 'Get the best of everything. It will last a lifetime.' At that time my dad also bought six horses and two cows to start with. Our relatives gave us chickens and a large variety of garden vegetables since we were unable to put out a garden that year."

Sister Reinhardt also provided information about what happened to Leonard Hecker, Sr.'s sister and family. "Uncle George took Aunt Barbara and her family to his farm, and they stayed with him for three weeks at which time they moved to Canada. She had three married daughters in Canada."

A second letter from Sister Reinhardt arrived about one month later. It answered additional questions that I had asked about life in Munchen at the time that they left it for America. She portrayed a healthy village that was the center of their lives with its new elementary school built of stone where both German and Russian were taught. Three Hecker brothers played prominent roles in the village. "Ludwig was the most important man in that village; he was a farmer like the rest of the people. My dad and John were also farmers." She continued by describing her family's situation. They lived in the village as all German farmers did and had house, three barns, vineyards, and a large garden. They also had two outdoor brick ovens that could bake eight and twenty-four loves of bread respectively. They had cows, horses, goats, chickens, geese and ducks. In addition Sister Reinhardt explained the particulars of grain farming.

"During seeding and harvesting time they left the village late Sunday afternoon with enough food supplies for the week; they returned on Saturday evenings every weekend. However, all the hired help stayed on the farm until the threshing season was over. It was customary to let all hired help go on that day, September 29. Most of the men were Russian, and there were a few Polish men; my dad liked the Poles better because they were the best workers. There was a large house on that farm so the three brothers hired three German ladies to do the cooking for all the men—about fifty of them."

Sister Reinhardt added information about Munchen's social life. In the winter these villagers made visits to friends and relatives to taste the wines each family had distilled. During these occasions Leonard and others played accordions and enjoyed lively conversation. They also played cards and smoked pipes around kerosene lamps. "The women provided the goodies with a lunch of ham and potato salad; they never missed the black olives and that favorite morsel, halva." They enjoyed name-day's celebrations, large weddings, and generally enjoyed life in these times. When Ludwig's daughter Theresia got married in 1909, Sister Reinhardt, at age eight, witnessed the largest wedding she had ever seen. She described the event after the marriage and mass. "Ludwig put up an extra frame building for the dance hall.

The reception and meal were held in their large reception room. The menu usually started with chicken noodle soup, veal, roasted brown potatoes, tubs of cole slaw decorated with pimento specks and green peppers. Cole slaw was served because they could prepare it ahead of time. It was a blessing they had those large brick ovens."

Since I had asked her specifically about how the original German colonists had lived after they were well established in Munchen, she provided the following paragraph:

"Each family received one block of land to build his house and barns on it. The buildings were of stone with red tile roofs such as you see in Italy and Germany. Some houses had green glazed roofs. My dad had a large cistern to save rain water for washing clothes. Also, every family had a well. The front year [sic] had a flower garden next to the house. Then there was a three-foot wall to divide the back yeard [sic] from the barns where they kept the livestock— horses, cows, chickens. My mother always raised geese and ducks since the river was near by for them to swim. It was also a necessity that feathers be gotten for feather beds and pillows. Roast goose and duck were special for feast days. They stuffed them with rice, raisins, and apples. Delicious enough for a king!"

I will always be thankful to Sister Reinhardt for her letters, for they are the only eyewitness written accounts of life in Munchen in the early period of German colonization that I've received in my research. The letters contain much more than what I've quoted, but I have provided a good general sense of the contents. The Leonard Heckers left Munchen because of the advent of World War I and because of the strikes by workers in Moscow and St. Petersburg that looked likely to cause nationwide trouble. The workers also threatened to overthrow the government, and these eruptions did lead to the Russian Revolution of 1917. Little did Leonard know at the time how important his decision to immigrate to America in 1914 was. Had he stayed with family in Munchen, it is likely that his whole family would have perished.

– *Chapter 11* –

Our daughter's wedding finally arrived, uniting Michelle Hecker and Shannon Coddington in holy matrimony. Both had attended and graduated from Washington State University with degrees in interior design and architecture respectively. Some members of my family arrived from Wisconsin and Arizona, and some of Helen's from around the Puget Sound. The Coddington's also came from various parts of the country. It was a happy affair with much celebration before and after the service. One notable absence from the wedding was Adam and Ruth Hecker of Salem. Adam had died in April of 1988 just months before the wedding. Ruth sent me the funeral notice and a double image photo of Adam as a middle-aged man and as a seven year old, living on the farm near Belfield. The youth half of the picture showed him in ragged clothes standing beside a sturdy sheep-herding dog. I recalled his smoking habit and pale skin and was saddened not just by his passing but also because I wouldn't have his further collaboration on my search for roots. I became more resolved now than ever to continue with the lineage project as he had suggested.

One cautionary note occurred at the Sons of Norway dance hall in Bremerton. One of our new in-laws, or at least a member of their entourage, was an officer in the American military. Somehow this man had found out that Leonard Hecker, Jr., a Russian born German-American, was present at the wedding. I recognized Leonard and guest at the church ceremony and invited them to the dinner and dance. I especially wanted him to meet other Hecker's who were present for the ceremony, especially my sisters and families. Leonard and his guest arrived, but they didn't do more than sit and watch although I knew that he liked to dance at his winter retreat in Southern California. My sister told me the next day that the officer had made a stink about a Russian born guest at the dance hall. The incident was minor to the overall event, but it was out of order and I would have intervened had I known about it. As strange as this attitude may seem today, the context of the incident was the Cold War. Ronald Reagan had delivered one of his many addresses against the Soviet regime at the Brandenburg Gate in West Berlin in 1987, just a year before our daughter's wedding. In his speech he said, "Mr. Gorbachev, tear down this wall." He was referring to the wall that had been erected to separate East and West Berlin. No one, especially myself, was against the downfall of the Soviet Union, but to extend that wish for that collapse to include all immigrants from there who were now truly American was a stretch. So the general climate of opinion was against everything Soviet even in this case a German national from old South Russia who had entered the United States as a child. The long established American nativistic attitudes and xenophobia raised their ugly head at our daughter's wedding dance.

At about the same time as the wedding episode, I had told a Hecker relative that I was researching the Hecker family heritage and had discovered that our family had immigrated directly from Russia, not Germany. She had graduated from UCLA and remained in Southern California throughout her adult life, but she had been raised in Mandan, North Dakota where her father was an engineer on the railroad. She must have remembered her teenage years when there was antagonism against Germans and even using the German language during World War II. She thought it would be better for me to leave well enough alone. In other words she was afraid of some retribution or social ostracism if one admitted to this type of German from Russia legacy.

As I was following the destiny of the Heckers, I became more and more aware of how the vagaries of history and the personal histories of individuals impact our paths of life. As fate would have it, Helen's father, Wendelin Black, Jr. died in the summer of 1989, so Helen and I drove back to Karlsruhe, North Dakota, for his funeral. He was a widower—Anna Black had died the Christmas before, and we had attended her funeral on a short visit by train—and as his wife had, he lived into his nineties. Both had led fruitful lives as I illustrated in eulogies I gave at each of their funerals. Since we were on summer vacation from teaching at the time of his death, we had the opportunity to visit both Sister Reinhardt in Bismarck and Selma (Hecker) Schmidt in Dickinson.

Helen and I were delighted to visit both of them, but I was particularly drawn to Sister Reinhardt because she had actually lived in Munchen, my ancestral village, from 1901-1914 and had favored me with letters about it. She was in her mid-eighties and was recovering from knee surgery when we saw her. A true Hecker, she was sociable and articulate, and welcomed us to the Priory. Sister Reinhardt was short with a medium stature and wore glasses. She was dressed in an all white habit with curly hair showing under a head veil. We met in a reception room and were served coffee and pastries. She added some additional detail about village life that she had not given in her letters, and I paid special attention to her description of how her family traveled from Munchen to Odessa by railroad to shop or to get medical care. These were important details because the German settlements beside the Bug River and throughout the region had contributed greatly to making the Port of Odessa the chief exporting center of grains to the outside world. The fact that these colonists could travel the roughly ninety miles from Munchen to Odessa to shop for clothing, manufactured goods, and other supplies suggested their relative wealth and the importance of the railroad. Ninety miles by horse and wagon would have taken several days each way, especially on coarsely built dirt roads.

The picture she painted in words, sprinkled throughout with "Yes, Yes", "Yah", and "Oh yah, oh yes" revealed a prosperous and progressive German national presence that greatly benefited Russia of that time. Unfortunately as time passed these German folk were viewed as wealthy outsiders who had considerable control of land and money. In other words there was jealousy and ethnic ostracism.

Helen and I were delighted to visit with Sister Reinhardt and to see the fine complex she lived in with other sisters, some of whom were also retired. I thought she deserved such a fine place for her last years after her many, many decades of dedicated service to her religious order. I also felt fortunate that she hadn't inquired about our religious life, for I didn't want to offend her with my usual response to that question which was "We are retired Catholics." If she had asked, I would have explained my views on religion and how I had arrived at that position.

I would have started with my college education. I was exposed to many ideas in my literature and history courses that gave me doubts about the teachings of the Catholic Church. For instance some of Robert Browning's poems challenged the sincerity of some priests, bishops and cardinals. Did priests and monks hide their true feelings behind the robes that they wore? Did cardinals have sons and daughters that they referred to as nieces and nephews? The few European history courses I took as an undergraduate made the papacy to be just another powerful nation vying for domination. The popes who took the name Innocent, almost to a man, battled for supremacy over kings and other monarchs. Since neither of my parents attended church with any regularity, it wasn't an issue at home, but when Helen and I got married, we married in the Catholic Church, for she was from a family of Catholics. Helen and I continued to attend church for some years and had both of our children baptized, but only a few years afterwards we moved to Washington where I taught English to college freshmen and sophomores. I grappled with my disagreements with church doctrine. I found the infallibility of the Pope, celibacy, virgin birth, and sainthood faulty doctrines.

As I worked towards a Ph.D., I studied the Enlightenment Period and found that some of our founding fathers were Deists who questioned the divinity of Jesus Christ, a prophet to them whose life deserved emulation. Our Deist leaders such as Benjamin Franklin and Thomas Jefferson believed in a benign creator that established the universe under the principles of natural law and gave humans the intelligence to discover these laws and use that knowledge to improve the lives of people. In other words we could use our wits to solve our problems; praying for solutions seemed ineffectual and a denial of our responsibility. As my understanding grew with study, I wondered what these two national period leaders would have thought about a benevolent creator had they been confronted by the writings of Darwin, Freud, and Einstein or the scientific studies of quantum mechanics and chaos theory. Existentialism had also taken the stage by this time, and its tenets on individualism, with free choice and responsibility for one's actions in an indifferent and perhaps hostile universe at the core of its message, fit my expanding knowledge at the time. Sartre and Camus became important sources of information on this philosophy. I also heard a chorus from my students to "Tell it as it is."

When the final break came, I agreed that being honest with oneself and one's beliefs was more important than observing standardized family traditions. If a family or clan is Democrat-Catholic, it is psychologically trying to separate oneself from that tradition. I had become an agnostic and quit attending church. On the Sunday morning that I stopped going, Helen and the kids had gone to church. I was extremely nervous, and decided to get out of the house, so I went for a walk in the neighborhood. As I crossed a nearby street, tears started rolling down my cheeks. I continued walking for several blocks, and I started sobbing. I stumbled along and made my way back towards our rental house. Apparently I didn't pay any attention to the traffic light because as I started across the street, a car's brakes engaged and a horn blasted into my ears. I could hardly see, but I was alert enough to back up to the curb, and I watched a heated driver slowly drive past, shouting at me from within his car. I looked at the streetlight and saw that I had been crossing against a red light. I realized that I could have been seriously injured at the very least. This potential fatality shocked me into stability. I also recognized that I couldn't continue to give token attendance at church, for I risked facing a nervous breakdown. Helen also had conflicts with church doctrine, especially the rigid stance against the use of birth control pills, so she couldn't confess and receive Holy Communion without being hypocritical. It wasn't long before our family stopped attending Sunday mass, but it wasn't that we didn't have our own spiritual lives. We believed in leading moral lives and hoped that there was a creator and eternal life although my reading of history and science left me with strong doubts on the matter.

I learned later how hard it is to move away from established patterns in a family. One circumstance at the beginning that made it easier was when Helen and I moved to the State of Washington, away from the constant contact of extended family. But even then we attended funerals for Helen's relations, who lived in the Puget Sound, and we couldn't justify receiving Holy Communion, and it must have looked like we didn't have love and support for the person who had died. We probably should have discussed it with the relatives involved for better understanding. It wasn't that I dismissed their right to faith and belief in their church and its doctrines, for I truly believed that each should follow his or her conscience in these matters. I must say that I did break this position when both of my parents-in-law passed, for I was asked to give eulogies for each of them at their respective masses. I felt that my role in the proceedings, their lifetime commitment to their faith, and my respect for them justified taking Holy Communion. Later my parents also passed, and again I gave eulogies for each of them as well as made the arrangements for their funerals. My mother's was especially difficult since I was left on my own to decide on the rituals. All of these situations occurred before I knew fully the specific details of three centuries of Hecker family traditions.

Fortunately for me I didn't have to tell my story about religion to Sister Reinhardt because I truly didn't want to question her lifetime of devotion to her church and God. Perhaps she would have surprised me by being sympathetic to my plight. Maybe she would have suggested some readings that I hadn't encountered in my studies, or perhaps she would have narrated her own concerns and changes of mind over her long life, hoping no doubt that I also had enough years left to change my mind.

On our trip to North Dakota we also visited Selma (Hecker) Schmidt for the second time, but now on her home ground in Dickinson. It was my ancestral ground as well since Martin Hecker had farmed near Belfield a few miles to the west on I-94. Selma was a descendant of one of the original brothers, Frank Hecker. Selma's father Mike Hecker was the second son of Frank and Elizabeth Hecker, out of a brood of thirteen children. Mike was the relative who provided much assistance to Leonard Hecker, Sr. when he settled on his farm near Belfield. Selma married John Schmidt, and they had four children. She worked for the U.S. Postal Service, but was retired when we visited. Selma met us for lunch and brought along a friend who was old enough to have known the original Hecker brothers. I didn't gain much new information, but both confirmed that the original brothers were sociable and easy going.

After lunch Selma escorted us to the local cemetery, and I saw the grave and headstone of my great-grandfather for the first time. Selma then gave me a map of the Belfield area, so Helen and I drove west, stopped and walked the ground where my great-grandfather and family had lived from 1903-1928. None of the buildings that had been built on the property now existed, but it was enough to see the flat fields and wide open spaces. Martin spent the last two years of his life in Dickinson after his wife died, living with one of his older sons, another Martin. His youngest son from his second family, Adam Hecker of Salem, accompanied him.

So after all the years from my birth in Mandan in 1939 to the summer of 1989, that is fifty years later, I finally had a look at my great grandfather's grave, his ancestral homestead and the Belfield area where the original Hecker brothers had lived. The land was much like the land that I would see myself at Munchen later in my life although the Belfield area had fewer trees and seemed less fertile. The homesteaders of North Dakota lived on farms miles from the nearest town unlike the pattern in Munchen. Here there was an isolation that my great-grandfather had not experienced in Munchen where farmers lived together in small villages, each with house, barn, farm animals, sheds, root cellars, vineyards and gardens. These structures, animals and vegetation were possible on farms near Belfield, but they were segregated from their rural towns by miles of pasture and grain fields. One had to travel by horse and wagon as Martin Hecker did to get to town and meet with others at the local hardware or grocery store. This isolation lead to emotional breakdowns, especially for women living on these farmsteads. Trains did run from Dickinson and Belfield to Mandan, but apparently my great-grandfather did little or no travel.

On our drive back to Washington we stopped at Yakima to visit Leonard Hecker, Jr. again. We told him about visiting his older sister at the Priory, our visit with Selma Schmidt in Dickinson, and seeing for the first time the grave and farmland that Martin Hecker, Sr. had worked. After hearing our information, Leonard launched into a lengthy commentary about my statement that the original brothers were easy going and sociable. He agreed with that assessment but gave his explanation of it. He said they were that way because they were landholders in Russia with cheap, available labor. Poles and Russians, he said, could be hired for little or nothing. He went on to add that his mother had three maids to help in her house at Munchen. When they came to the Belfield region and took up farming, the children in the family had to labor hard since they were the new servants. The fathers supervised their children, but didn't work much. His mother, he went on, cried continuously about being on the prairies of North Dakota with the lack of help and isolation and wanted to return to Russia.

Fortunately Leonard Sr.'s wife didn't get her demand, for the conditions in South Russia got much worse than anything in North Dakota, Kansas, or even Texas. I did check my notes upon arriving at home in Bremerton and found out that Adam Hecker of Salem had also commented about the hard work that his older siblings and he had done on the farms in Texas and North Dakota. These visits with relatives who share my concern about lineage and the collected education we were receiving about immigration and the historical events that drive the fates of people, including the ever-present nativism and its harm to society and people, made me all the more determined to continue my quest. I was feeling more and more like a world citizen than I had before. Little did I know just how deep that association would go. I would learn much more in the next stage of my journey by meeting other extended Hecker family members who now lived in Hamburg, Germany.

– Chapter 12 –

Mid-June 1990 finally arrived. The teaching year was finished, and Helen and I were off to Europe to continue our exploration of family roots. We flew from Seattle to Detroit and on to Frankfurt, Germany on a DC 10. Since we were flying "heavy" as our pilot noted upon taking off, we ended up refueling at Shannon, Ireland. Our journey this time had no bumps in the road or potholes, but making an unscheduled stop because of excessive luggage was a risk although in this case it had a benefit. As we approached the Irish coast, the sun rose, allowing us to see the countryside. It was a beautiful pastoral land, green and partitioned off by hedges, not in grid formation but in various shapes and sizes. From the air the houses, churches, and castles appeared as in fantasy, well kept, dreamy, and idyllic. Some of the enclosed fields had cattle, grazing lazily in the golden rays of the sun. The land laid flat like central North Dakota.

Since our first trip to Europe in 1986, I had contacted Maria (Reiswich) Kreiser in Hamburg by letters in the summer of 1988. She was the younger daughter of Magdalena (Hecker) Reiswich. Adam Hecker of Salem had provided me with Maria's address and fortunately she was fluent in English as was her husband Kai-Uwe Kreiser. By now I knew my extended Hecker family well and was anxious to meet German relatives who were separated from my branch of the Hecker family since 1891. These Heckers we were visiting had stayed in South Russia after my great-grandfather left and had somehow survived the Russian Revolution of 1917, Stalin's collectivization program, World War II and the Gulag in the Ural Mountains. They had emigrated from the Soviet Union in 1974 to West Germany. Magdalena (Hecker) Reiswich's grandfather, John Hecker, and my great-grandfather were brothers. I was delighted that I was finally going to meet these long lost relatives.

After landing at the Frankfurt *flughaven*, we caught a shuttle to our nearby airport hotel, stored our luggage in our room and grabbed a couple of hours of sleep. We then caught an airport train into Frankfurt where we visited the Goethe House. I was eager to see where the author of *The Sorrows of Young Werther* and *Faust* had been raised. His father had required that Johann learn how to read and play music as well as draw in perspective at a young age. I wondered to what degree this had prepared his mind for the great literature he would produce. The Goethe House, now a museum, displayed many of Goethe's journals and notebooks. The portraits of the Goethe family included individual family member silhouettes. Satisfied that we had accomplished one goal of our current travel, seeing a great writer's home, we walked about the center of Frankfurt, looking into the boutiques of the Veil, Frankfurt's magic mile of shopping, gazing at the river, churches, and Opera House. We watched the evening promenade from a sidewalk café where we sipped refreshing tall glasses of weisenbier. Finding an Italian restaurant up the street, we had carbonara and tortellini pasta dishes along with a plate of scampi. We then returned to our hotel by train, noticing the well-maintained streets, well dressed Germans and upscale BMW's and Mercedes Benz's on the streets.

Also during the train ride, we sat across from two Germans who were apparently returning home from a visit to the city. By their ages, size and facile bones it was certain that they were father and son. They had similar leather jackets of a suede texture, and both brushed particles of dust from their clothes. They seemed slightly nervous and apprehensive. Perhaps their traditional dress and life style seemed slightly off balance from the cosmopolitan milieu of Frankfurt. Or maybe they were reacting to two Americans who were eyeing them from head to toe.

The next day was June 28, and we checked out of our hotel, rode to the airport and met our son Jeffrey on his incoming flight from Chicago where he worked as an architect. He also wanted to meet our German relatives in Hamburg. He was about the same age as Maria and Kai-Uwe. Like the two of us Jeffrey was also looking forward to some sightseeing on our detour to Berlin. We met him at luggage and went immediately to our car rental and picked up a BMW 321 i, an upgrade from what I had scheduled at the expense of the rental agency. They didn't have the closed trunk vehicle that I had ordered and tried to give us a hatchback, but they finally offered the BMW.

Jeff and I shared driving duties on the autobahn. Both of us had limited experience with this brand of driving. Trucks and slower vehicles like an occasional car pulling a small camping trailer stayed mostly on the far right lane, doing about seventy miles per hour. If needed they passed on the next left lane. Faster cars like ours traveled on the third left lane, cruising at about ninety-to-one-hundred miles per hour. When we wanted to pass a vehicle in our lane, we did so in the far left lane but not before checking carefully to see if traffic was approaching from behind. When clear, I pushed the accelerator to the floor, passing the obstructing car, trying to get back into our lane as quickly as possible. Rarely did I make it without having a car approach with headlights blinking to within ten feet of our back bumper. After getting back into our former lane, the following car would accelerate to speeds of up to one hundred and fifty miles per hour, judging by their rapid disappearance ahead. Speed became the bump on this trip.

As I drove, I recalled a conversation I had with an Englishman on our first trip to Germany in 1986. He and wife had stopped at the same hotel in Speyer where we were staying. He and I were chatting in the parking lot, and he told me they had driven from England to Italy and were now on their way back home. He confided that a German driver would only pass on the left while an American would pass on either side. An Italian, he added, was unpredictable entirely. Another experience I remembered from that earlier trip was when I decided to stop for fuel at an off ramp station. Having been driving fast for almost two hours, I had grown accustomed to the high speed, so when I exited, I hadn't slowed enough and couldn't stop at the back of the queue. I finally came to rest beside the first car in the line. I was relieved to have avoided any contact with other cars, but before I could turn the auto around, I heard a tapping on the back of my car. I opened my door, and an attendant asked me if I wanted high test. I saw that he had pulled a gas hose across the back of the car beside us. I said "Yah, fill it up." He began filling my tank. I learned later from Kai that the attendant was accommodating us because he thought we were in a hurry.

One thing I noticed for sure was that the farther north we drove in Germany, the faster the pace became. Porches, large sized BMW's and Mercedes Benz's whizzed by us as if we were standing still. We passed by Kassel and Gottingen without seeing anything but the speeding traffic. There was an energy that was perhaps a trademark of Prussian Germany. We noticed this speed in restaurants as well where two or three waiters would serve many, many tables of guests far beyond anything possible in Seattle, Washington. I actually preferred the slower pace in the Pacific Northwest and thought that perhaps the pace in northern Germany was related to maintaining a certain standard of living. Maybe the rapid efficiency was also related to the need for individual productivity in recovering from the ruins of World War II. Jeff drove faster than I did and even suggested that he open up the BMW to compete with the cars that were passing us on the left. I told him to pull over and let his mother and me out first. He didn't, and we arrived at our hotel in West Berlin by 10 pm. After a few beers and pizza we turned in by midnight, a long day.

The next day we took a bus tour of West Berlin, lunched and visited the National Gallery. During the bus tour we spotted a Hecker Hotel on Grolmanstrasse, so in the evening we went there for supper at the hotel's restaurant, Hecker's Diele. My uncle Adam of Salem had told me there were Heckers in northern Germany, but he didn't find any evidence that we were related to any of them. He was relieved that it was so, as he had checked out one of them who had been a Captain in the SS. We ate heartily on pork, steak, and wiener schnitzel. After dessert I introduced myself to the headwaiter. He said the Hecker owner was on vacation, so I didn't have the chance to find out if maybe this one was related. We strolled the magic mile of West Berlin, the Kurfursten-Damn, and saw many boutiques with the latest fashions. Most of all, we enjoyed seeing West Berliners, walking the streets, laughing, and drinking beer at sidewalk bistros.

On the following day after breakfast we took a train to East Berlin. I was anxious to see the remains of what had been the heart of prewar Berlin. I felt for the German civilians who had faced the fierce onslaught of the Soviet Army, just as I felt for my own distant ancestors who had suffered the invasion of Napoleon into their homeland on the Rhine River in the early 1800's. They had immigrated to South Russia in 1809 rather than to stay under the control of the Confederation of the Rhine, established by the French. We found in East Berlin a combination of the old and the new. Some buildings still hadn't been rebuilt and stood vacant behind fences with floors missing and crumbling brick walls. Other buildings were occupied but still had bullet riddled brick exteriors. We visited two museums and saw classics of German art, but we also saw museums that were still battered from bombing. Ironically, we witnessed a reunification ceremony of East and West Berlin on one street. Chauffeured limousines, mostly Mercedes Benz's except for one Rolls Royce, were parked along an adjacent avenue. Television crews filmed the proceedings. I thought it curious that the politicians wore Italian suits and shoes in juxtaposition to the ruins about us. We exited East Berlin via Checkpoint Charley and took pictures of people chipping off parts of the short section of remaining wall that had divided the city. In the late afternoon Jeff went to the Bauhaus, and Helen and I went to a museum exhibiting German Expressionism. We met Jeff later for a German supper.

On the third day we drove to Neu Wulmstorf, a suburb of Hamburg, and Maria and Kai-Uwe invited us into their home. It was a three bedroom duplex, filled with the latest in electronic devices: radio, stereo, television, and camcorder as well as quality furniture. Maria had some of the features of a Hecker with high cheekbones, long face and deep-set eyes. She was reserved, but that was to be expected since we were almost total strangers, excepting for our correspondence. Uncle Adam of Salem had visited Magdalena and Christian as well as Maria in Hamburg nearly ten years earlier when Maria was still single. Maria also knew that Helen and I had spent some time with Adam and his wife. Maria was now expecting her first child. Kai-Uwe was a lean, dark haired man of about thirty. He was dressed in jeans and shirt and wore fashionable glasses. He was energetic, well-organized, and exhibited impatience with any unscheduled activity. As I was to learn, Germany relied on its export industries for a large portion of its gross national product, so I saw why speed and efficiency were not only evidenced on the autobahn but also in the behavior of its citizens. Kai-Uwe explained that he worked for a manufacturer of adhesive tapes and other packaging materials similar to the products of the 3 M Company of Minnesota.

Maria served us coffee and pastries and during our conversation told us we would visit her parents tomorrow. She went on to say that all of her family had arrived in Germany from the Soviet Union by airplane at Frankfurt in 1974. All of them had been living now in Germany for sixteen years. Christian had worked as a machinist until recently when an accident resulted in a back injury that forced him into retirement. The German government had admitted the family into the country with full citizenship rights, so he had compensation and retirement funding. Magdalena still worked as a nurse's aide in a local hospital. Maria also explained that Magdalena had insisted that her daughters receive better opportunities such as were available in Germany than they could get in the Ural Mountains. After finishing coffee Maria and Kai took the three of us for a hike on the dike of the Elbe River. We then returned to their house for supper. After dessert and cognac Helen and I presented them with some gifts—an American Indian print, a bottle of vodka and some American cooking spices.

After breakfast the next morning we left early and stopped at a farmer's market on the way to Magdalena and Christian's home. Kai and Maria wanted us to see something of Hamburg while we were visiting. Many venders sold fruit, vegetables, and fish (both smoked and fresh). A few venders from the Netherlands had driven through the night to sell their fresh bouquets of flowers and potted plants. It was quite a show, with aggressive selling and many bargains. Next to

the farmer's market an older warehouse was the stage for a pop con-
cert. Young Germans danced riotously, pausing briefly to drink beer.
Just another short stroll away rested the wharf area of Hamburg's
harbor, so we walked over to see the ships. On the way we passed
by a church where a Lutheran service was in progress. We looked
in and saw a minister standing on an enormous pulpit made out of a
light violet and grey variegated marble. He was delivering a sermon,
emphasizing certain expressions, probably passages from the bible.
We stopped for lunch at a whareside fish café.

– Chapter 13 –

On the drive to the Reiswich home, I asked Kai to stop at a liquor store so that I could contribute to the occasion. Kai suggested a bottle of Russian vodka as that was Christian's favorite drink. I bought it and also a bottle of white wine. The Reiswich's lived in a one-bedroom apartment in a multi-unit structure with concrete exterior finish. We entered their flat and were escorted into the front room, a large space with cloth-backed sofas and an oblong oak table. Magdalena and Christian stood together next to one of the sofas. She was small and slender with short pepper black hair swept back from the face to behind the ears. I recognized her Hecker facial features, the high cheekbones and deep set brown eyes. She wore a white, short-sleeved blouse with high round neckline and a knee length white and light grey skirt. Magdalena's appearance surprised me since I knew she had suffered an immense amount of family loss and hardship in the Soviet Union, but she smiled brightly and had an alert, keen expression in her eyes.

Maria had sent photographs of her parents in a holiday letter some two years earlier. One picture, an older one, taken when Magdalena was still living in the Urals, showed her with thick neck and shoulder muscles like those of a gymnast. Her expression in that picture was emotionless. I was told then that she had worked in the forest camps of the Urals, cutting off limbs of fallen trees and dragging them through snow into piles for burning. The remaining tree trunks were transported to ports for selling on the international markets. The other photograph was one that was taken a couple of years after they arrived in Hamburg. Her hair had grayed, and her body was fuller. Christian had also changed from the earlier photographs where he appeared gaunt, thin, and wore an expression of exhaustion. Now he looked taller and had a stocky frame. He wore glasses, had graying dark hair and a broad face. Wearing a white dress shirt with light blue vertical stripes over light blue dress slacks, he exhibited a full smile.

— *Photograph of Magdalena, Christian, Helen and Me* —

Helen, Jeff and I shook hands with our long lost relatives, and I handed Christian the two bottles of liquor I had bought. He looked at the vodka bottle label and smiled broadly, saying, *"Danke Schen."* All of us settled into the sofas while Maria talked in German to her parents, and they suddenly broke out in laughter. Maria explained to us that they were surprised that we looked so young. Uncle Adam had been retired and in his sixties when he visited them. I handed Magdalena a gift we had brought along for them. She immediately opened the package that contained two framed photographs. One was of Adam and Ruth Hecker of Salem, and the other was of the Heckers who had immigrated to America from Russia. Maria explained to her parents that the members of the large group picture were Magdalena's great aunts and uncles who had lived in Munchen and had left old South Russia before she was born. I pointed at my great-grandfather Martin Hecker and then at my chest to indicate my personal relationship. Both Christian and Magdalena said, "*Danke Schen.*" Christian examined the frames of the photographs by running his fingers on their edges. He gave me a smile of approval at the fine workmanship.

Christian got up and walked across the room to a hutch that nearly filled the opposite wall of the room. A crystal decanter and matching wineglasses sparkled in the light from a nearby window. Other glassware, photographs, and Christian's cache of liquors and drinking glasses neatly lined the three shelves. I admired the highly polished walnut wood and the bright, clear glass doors in that piece of furniture. In fact I was impressed with the quality of all the furniture in the room. Christian and Magdalena must have fared well in Germany even though Maria played down their circumstances. Christian poured drinks for Jeff, Kai, me, and himself. He then motioned the bottle towards the women, smiling wickedly. They all declined, but did pour themselves glasses of soft drinks that were on the table.

Christian raised his glass and said in German what Maria repeated in English, "David, Jeffrey, and I will get to know each other better if we drink together."

I raised my glass and said, "*Prost.*" I was glad to see that the bottle of vodka was only half full. Maria had told me that her father had learned to drink with the Russians in the Ural Mountains. In other words he could drink a lot. I thought how fortunate I was to be sitting with Magdalena who had lived in my family's ancestral village in old South Russia. She was born in Munchen in 1928 and had lived there until 1944 when the Soviet Army attacked. They drove the German Army, in control since 1941, and the German farmers out of their villages to western Poland. The German farmers could not stay because they would have been sent to the Gulag, ostensibly for collaborating with the enemy. With passports obtained from the SS in western Poland and the loss of her older brother Anton to his induction into the German Army, Magdalena and her parents and two other younger siblings traveled to Brandenburg but not for long. The bombing of Brandenburg by the Allies killed her mother and the two younger sisters. Magdalena and her father had then fled deeper into Germany to escape the advancing Soviet Army, but they were unable to cross the Elbe River to safety. Instead they were captured and transported to forest work camps in the Ural Mountains.

Christian had a similar but different fate, for he had been a Volga German. Catherine the Great had invited his ancestors to Russia at an earlier period than the Black Sea Germans of Magdalena's family. Christian had lived with his parents and other siblings near Kiev. Early in World War II he and family were transported by the Soviets to the Ural Mountains to work in the forest camps. The Soviets had anticipated that the German Army would aid these colonists in returning to Germany, so they decided to act in advance to secure the free labor of these people. When Magdalena met Christian in the forest camps, he was living with his mother and working as a blacksmith. He repaired wagon wheels, shod horses, and built fences, gates, and other useful items out of metal. Magdalena and Christian married and later had Irma and Maria.

After the toasts Maria made a few comments to her parents. They smiled at me as Maria talked.

"I told them, Uncle David, that you have the same intense interest in your ancestry as Uncle Adam had when he visited us in Hamburg. They say that they're ready to answer any questions that you might have."

"Tell Magdalena that I would like to hear her story about life in Munchen during Stalin's collectivization program in South Russia."

After Maria translated, Magdalena winced and fell back into the sofa, collecting her thoughts. She spoke slowly and didn't smile, but she seemed intent on telling the story. Speaking at some length, Magdalena's eyes grew cold as she spoke, and at other times she gestured with her hands in a short hacking fashion. She seemed both frightened and angry. Then she stopped and reached for her glass of soda.

Maria translated and said that Magdalena's family misfortunes began after the Russian Revolution of 1917 before she was born. In 1919 Bolsheviks executed John Hecker, her grandfather, in a raid on their village because he was a Kulak, a rich German national who had lots of property. They shot John in the face with his son Johann, eighteen years old at the time and later Magdalena's father, standing right beside him. John Hecker's infraction was that he refused to give them tax money because they had no taxing authority. Magdalena found out later that the assassins had mistaken her grandfather for his brother, Ludwig Hecker, the richest Kulak in the village.

I gasped and Helen put her hand to her mouth in disbelief. This was the first we had heard of this murder. Jeff put his arm around his mother.

Maria gave us a second to gather ourselves and continued, saying that the raiders robbed many families in the village on that day and that some women were raped. As time passed and the Bolsheviks became more organized, they returned and confiscated all of the land of the villagers, most of their livestock and horses, and gave the villagers what they called a head right, a small acreage per family in equal sizes. They were allowed to keep their houses and outbuildings, thus Johann and his mother became the heads of their family. This arrangement lasted only two years when Johann was drafted into the Soviet Army for four years, leaving his mother and her six younger children to fend for themselves. Johann survived the Army and returned to Munchen in late 1924. He added an orchard on the head right land, upgraded the farm buildings and married Margarete Metz who would become mother to Magdalena four years later.

Magdalena listened to Maria as she explained to us what her mother had said. She looked pale and tired. All three of us expressed sympathy to her. Christian looked frustrated at not being able to add or reinforce what his wife had said. He, of course, didn't come into Magdalena's life until much later when they met in the Ural Mountains.

"Please, Maria," I said, "ask Magdalena to describe her childhood under these circumstances."

Maria spoke again in German, directing her question to her mother. When she finished, Maria looked at the three of us and said that worse things were now to come.

Magdalena grew even paler as she started to speak. She would pause at times and shake her hand, sometimes down at the floor and at other times at the ceiling, especially when she uttered the name, Stalin. Sadness came over her as she mentioned the names, Eugenie and Filomena, two of her younger sisters. At other times when she mentioned the name of her older brother, Anton, she would smile, but her overall tone was subdued. Magdalena continued for some time until she uttered the names Johannes, jr. and Olga. She then broke down in tears. Remembering became too much for her.

Christian put his arm around his wife and drew her to his chest, but she pulled back and wiped her tears with a handkerchief that Maria handed her. Helen, Jeff, and I were dismayed to see Magdalena in this state, and we looked to Maria for reassurance.

Magdalena noticed our concern, and she said something to Maria.

"Magdalena wants me to translate what she just said, now without delay."

Maria started by saying that Magdalena was born in 1928, the second child after her older brother Anton. Her birth year was the year that collectivization of the Steppe's agrarian land was proclaimed by Joseph Stalin who had seized control of the Soviet government. Since he viewed the German colonists as a threat to collectivization, Stalin called for the "Liquidation of the Kulak." Johann and Margarete had no alternative but to join the collective even though that meant the loss of the head right land. Meanwhile the family had grown by the birth of Olga and a set of twins, Eugenie and Filomena.

By 1932, four years later, things got worse. The governmental police came and confiscated everything of worth from all the villagers. From the Hecker family they took the few farm animals they had, including chickens and geese, and all their furniture, dinnerware, and extra clothing. The only item of furniture that was left was the crib that held the twins. Johannes had to take a job on road construction to get money for sugar, salt, and flour, as well as other necessities. Margarete had to work on the collective, and it wasn't long before the twins died of malnutrition. Magdalena, Anton and Olga walked to the field at noon each day where their mother worked, and Margarete would give them her daily ration, a large bowl of hot soup and bread, her only pay. This was the only daily hot meal the children received. Anton and Magdalena gathered any grain or other harvested crops that remained in fields after threshing crew's left. They did this at their peril, for it was considered to be theft by the authorities. They also gathered straw from the fields to place on the floor of their house as mattresses. Deaths were frequent in the villages, especially of newborns and young children. Margarete had another son, Johannes, jr. named after his father. He lived only a few weeks and finally Olga died, leaving only the two older children alive out of six children. In spite of these hardships and deaths another daughter was born. Katharina somehow survived.

To say that I was dumbfounded was an understatement. Helen dabbed at her eyes with a Kleenex. Jeff looked at me with apprehension, nodding to end this discussion.

I looked to Maria for relief. She also was emotion laden and said, "Let's take a break. Mother needs to recover from her memories." I agreed, and we all stood up to comfort Magdalena.

— Chapter 14 —

Kai-Uwe then suggested that we go to a nearby Pioneer Farmer's Museum. Maria said she would stay and help Magdalena with preparations for supper. Helen offered to remain also, but Maria insisted that she go along to see the exhibit. We drove in Kai-Uwe's company car. Only a few comments were made about Magdalena's recollections. We were all emotionally drained. The walk along the Elbe the evening before and now the visit to a farmer's museum showed me how our relatives and perhaps Germans in general felt attached to nature and history. The museum was laid out as a small village with thatched roofed, single story dwellings. These cottages were built of wood with stout posts at corners and along the outside walls with thick beams across the ceilings. All were carved out of tree trunks. Displays showed two man saws laid beside axes that were used to shape the framework for the houses. A few windows and short narrow doors provided light and entrance/exits to the houses. A blacksmith shop was also featured showing scythes, single bottom plows, and tines for forks and metal attachments for oxen harnesses. Barns were made similarly to the houses with post and beam construction. A few cows and horses stood in stalls with milking equipment and harnesses displayed on walls.

Young men and women guides at the museum wore costumes of the Nineteenth Century and offered answers to questions from visitors. Women wanted to know who made the clothes and where the materials were purchased. They were also interested in sleeping arrangements. Straw filled mattresses filled recesses in the walls of the kitchen and living room, and drapes covered access to these bedrooms for privacy. These compartments could sleep an adult couple or several children. Clothes were stored in chests that were placed under and next to these cubbyhole bedrooms. Some visitors complained about lack of privacy and poor ventilation with fireplaces on opposite walls that were used for cooking and heating.

The grounds of the Farmer's Museum had pathways between buildings bordered with bright flowers and shrubs. Open spaces around barns had deciduous trees that were fully in blossom for the season. The theme was to admire these ancestors and their closeness to nature. The purpose was accomplished for our group, for we were all smiling and commenting on this agrarian past that was familiar to all of us. We purchased some soft drinks and beer at a local beer garden before we returned to the Reiswich home for supper.

On the drive back, I thought of my 18th century ancestors at Rulzheim along the Rhine River before they immigrated to the Odessa region of Old South Russia. Our Hecker family name came from the root Hacker and indicated that my male antecedents were woodchoppers or foresters, taking care of the forests and providing wood for construction and heating in the Palatinate, a separate principality before Germany was unified as a country. These ancestors must have used daily the tools that were displayed at the museum we had just left. Later, when these Heckers reached the land that would become the villages of South Russia, they built houses, outbuildings, churches, schools, and civic buildings using these same tools. They also engaged in farming, so the skills in blacksmithing and agricultural activities had to be learned.

We entered the Reiswich apartment and were greeted warmly by Magdalena and Christian. Magdalena looked well and offered a bright smile even though she had been through an ordeal just an hour or so ago. I came to realize now and later that she had the resilience of a powerful person and had survived experiences that would topple the faint of heart. The oak table was arranged with place settings for each of us with beautiful China plates, dinnerware, and wine and water glasses. The middle of the table had bottles of sparking water, juices, and beer. After we sat, Christian went to the cabinet and fetched another bottle of vodka, this time the one I had given him earlier. He opened the bottle and poured each man a shot in liquor glasses. Maria had meanwhile poured Helen and Magdalena glasses of juice. We all toasted each other, and we men followed Christian's example and drained our vodka in one gulp.

Maria and Magdalena brought in platters of sliced pork roast, sauerkraut and boiled potatoes. They then filled our wine and water glasses. The dishes were passed around, and we all proceeded to eat, expressing delight at the food and the wine. We talked in English and answered Kai-Uwe's questions about German food in America. Helen carried the conversation since her family had prepared many such dishes on their farm in North Dakota. Helen talked about *dampfnoodla*, *halupsie* (pig in the blanket), *sauerkrautbrot* (ham, pork and sauerkraut), borscht, and *Kaseknepfla* (cheese buttons). These names brought smiles from Magdalena and Christian. The meal ended with cherry torte and coffee. We were all in a comfortable mood.

As Magdalena and Christian cleared the table, I asked Maria if it would be good to continue our discussion about life in the Soviet Union. Maria said yes and commented that the day was still early, actually only five o'clock. After Magdalena sat down, Christian offered beer to those that wanted it. After he finished serving us bottles of beer with glasses, I asked Maria to get her mother to comment on World War II in Munchen. Magdalena started talking quite happily, and the reason why would become apparent in Maria's exposition later. After a few moments she grew more pensive and expressed herself rather rapidly with movements of her hands and body. At times she raised her voice, expressing her feelings with looks of exhilaration, distress and even fear. This pattern continued for some time. Maria had a sheet of paper and was making notes for her translations. Christian added a few comments as Magdalena continued. Finally Magdalena pointed at the ceiling with both hands and covered her ears with both hands and gave out some gasps as she started crying.

I quickly asked Maria if this wasn't enough, but Magdalena dabbed her eyes with a napkin and motioned for Christian to fill our glasses with beer, including her own. He did so.

Maria translated. She said that a new beginning came to Munchen when the German Army arrived in 1941. For three years the German villagers returned to the prosperity they had known prior to the Russian Revolution. The villagers were given back their lands that were confiscated during the head right system and during Stalin's collectivization program. The villagers planted and sold crops, acquired farm animals and furniture. For the first time in years they had nutritious food on the table. During these years of the German Army occupation Magdalena's mother became pregnant and gave birth to another daughter, Hildegard. After this period, the Soviet Army regrouped and returned in great force. The German Army was being defeated on many fronts, and so a retreat was made towards Poland and Germany. Margarete took her two youngest children, Katharina and Hildegard, who were too young to travel over land, by ship up the Danube River. After they were close to their destination in Poland, they traveled across country by train. The rest of the Heckers and other German colonist survivors at Munchen and other villages traveled by foot and by horse and wagon ahead of the retreating Army, for remaining in Munchen was not an option. The Soviets had already sent many colonists to work camps in Siberia. In western Poland the march stopped and the German refugees were placed temporarily in abandoned Polish farmhouses. The SS then interrogated them to determine their rights to visas to enter Germany. Because they had preserved the German culture and language and hadn't intermarried with Russians, many colonists, including the Johannas and Margarete Heckers, were given visas and sent to Brandenburg.

The Hecker's thought they were safe, but events proved them wrong. The Soviet Army came into western Poland and Germany with a vengeance. The Allies also softened the German resistance with bombing raids over many of the cities of Germany including Berlin, Dresden, Hamburg, and eventually Brandenburg. The final blow for Magdalena came on Easter Sunday, 1945 when she and her father were at church and Margarete, Hildegard, and Katharina were home at their apartment building because of illness. The bombing was so severe that Magdalena and Johann sought refuge in the basement of the church. The bombings went on for hours, leveling entire sections of Brandenburg. When Magdalena and her father could leave the church and finally arrived at their former neighborhood, they found total destruction. Eventually they located their former apartment building and found mother and daughters dead in the basement where they had sought shelter.

I was appalled by what I heard. We Americans had participated in the destruction of part of our Hecker family! I looked at Helen and Jeff, and they too were alarmed. I told Maria we were sorry that our bombs and those of the British had caused this blow to our distant relatives.

Maria showed sympathy for our predicament, and she said something to Magdalena and Christian. They reacted and showed sympathy for us. Maria said that her parents didn't blame us. The German Army had caused such dreadful damage in Europe and the Soviet Union that no one could blame the Allies for punishing Hitler's Third Reich. Maria then said that she hadn't finished with her mother's commentary, and she directed her father to pour more beer for everyone. It was easy to see that Maria had her mother's resilience and determination. Maria continued by saying that her mother and grandfather found themselves in a far more serious situation. After hastily arranging for the burial of the three dead family members, they fled to try to get to across the Elbe River, the point where the Allied Armies had agreed to stop their ground assault. But they weren't able to cross the river, and the Allies couldn't help the refugees because of agreements made with Stalin at the Yalta conference. The Soviet Army arrived and most of the refugees were captured and transported to the Ural Mountains to work in the forest and mining labor camps.

— *Chapter 15* —

Maria allowed Magdalena and Christian to relax, and she, from her personal knowledge, explained the conditions of the forest camps and work that captive refugees were expected to do. The German refugees had to build new barracks out of logs that they felled and trimmed for the thousands of other refugees of all ethnic backgrounds that were yet to come. There was little privacy and drafty conditions in these barracks. The outside work was laborious and dangerous. Magdalena worked in the forests with her father. She also worked on road crews to clear passageways for hauling logs to train tracks. Maria noted that Russian truckers made advances to these women with gifts of food. Magdalena never cooperated. Later she was selected to get nurses training because the Soviets didn't want to use their medical staffs for refugee injuries. After she finished training and took up nursing, she met Christian, a Volga German, who was a blacksmith with many skills also in woodworking.

Although Magdalena was reluctant to leave her father and step-mother, she and Christian married. Stalin had died in 1953, so circumstances improved for refugees, and they were allowed to build their own home if they did the work on their own time and at their own expense. They were allowed to use trees from the local forests so long as they did the cutting and fashioning of the lumber themselves. At this time Magdalena and Christian struggled with the task of building a house while also doing their shifts of regular unpaid work. Then they helped Johann and his wife build their house. All of their spare time was given to building houses and acquiring kitchen-ware and furniture. Christian was able to barter his blacksmith skills for hinges, doorknobs, windows as well as stoves, clothing material, linens, and furniture.

Occasionally Maria would interrupt her translations and turn to her parents to tell them what she was telling us in English. On one of these pauses Christian got up from the sofa and went over to a corner cabinet and returned with photographs. One was of him and Magdalena. He told Maria to tell us that he thought the photograph would tell us more about their condition at these trying times than words. The first pho-tograph showed the two of them standing in snow in a cleared parcel of land in the forest. They looked ghostly. They were skeletally thin, wiry and gaunt. A blank look filled their faces. The snow and dark forests enhanced this appearance of near destitution. After I passed the photograph to Helen and Jeff, we all expressed our sympathy. Christian then proudly handed us the second photograph that showed a house, pointing at himself and Magdalena as the builders. Maria identified it as the house Christian and Magdalena had built, and where Irma and herself were born and were raised until they left the Soviet Union in 1974.

The photograph revealed a log house that was square in shape and had a metal roof. The roof extended over eves about one foot from the sides of the house, but there were no gutters or downspouts. A chim-ney stood high on the front of and above the peak of the roof. Four windows were evenly spaced across the front of the house at about shoulder height. They added a stylistic feature to the front as well as interior light for the building. The house was painted a dark maroon color except at the corners where the log abutments where painted in white, giving another appealing aspect to the house. There was an entry door on a flat roofed extension to the house on one side. A picket fence about waist high stood across the yard just in front of the house. Four deciduous trees, leafless in the photo, stood outside of the picket fence about equally spaced across the yard. A pile of snow apparently shoveled out of the driveway, indicated that the flat exten-sion portion of the house was a gateway that lead into a backyard.

There was no vehicle in the driveway. The house also didn't have running water, sewer system, or central heating. An outhouse, Maria explained, was behind the house and didn't show in the photograph. The house actually didn't look much different than some houses in North Dakota where I was raised. The difference was that not many North Dakotans had built their own houses and only a limited few had hewed the logs out of tree trunks. The labor that Christian and Magdalena had endured must have been excruciating.

— *Photograph of Magdalena and Christian's House in the Urals* —

Once the house was livable and refugee status improved to include small wages for their work in the camps, Magdalena and Christian started their family. First came Irma and four years later Maria. Magdalena was determined to maintain her German cultural inheritance as well as Catholic religion by teaching the girls German, how to cook German dishes, and the principles and prayers of the Catholic faith but in the home only.

This cultural transmission was difficult and dangerous because it was prohibited by the Soviets, thus the girls were told to speak only Russian outside the home and in the school they attended at Karpinsk, USSR. The girls were brought up between two cultures and adapted, especially after they started school, but it wasn't easy as Maria testified.

Maria and Irma continued as students in the Soviet schools until they immigrated to Germany. Since Irma was older, she had progressed to the end of special training in mid-wivery by this time. Her fellow trainees severely criticized her. Some even labeled her as a traitor and a few went so far as to call her a Nazi. Maria at age thirteen didn't get such abuse. Maria went on in her commentary to tell us a few details of the difficult two years Magdalena and Christian had in applying for immigration to Germany. The process had large fees for each step of the procedure. Fortunately the German Chancellor Conrad Audenhower had worked energetically to make it possible for German refugees to get visas and for the Soviets to recognize their validity.

Maria deferred to Magdalena and Christian to tell about the physical and economic conditions imposed by the Soviets for their immigration. Magdalena talked rapidly and showed considerable sorrow. She again used her handkerchief to wipe off the tears on her face. Christian interrupted at times and waved the photo of the house they had built. He showed anger and frustration. He pulled out his wallet and emptied it of money and then tipped it upside down to indicate its emptiness. Maria stepped into the display of emotions at this point and explained that her parents had to give away their house and all contents, including kitchenware, furniture and Christian's work tools. Fortunately Christian had a nephew who decided to stay in the USSR and occupy the house. They had to pay for their own air flights with the little cash they had, so when they arrived in Frankfurt, they were nearly penniless and only had clothes in their suitcases. Nevertheless Magdalena spent their last few marks on Solzhenitsyn's latest book that she had heard about in the forest camps.

At this point in the commentary, I was so gripped by the story that I blurted out that the plight and journey that Magdalena and Christian experienced was exactly what Solzhenitsyn said was needed to fill in the details of the slave labor camps of the Soviet Union. I had read The *Gulag Archipelago* when it was published in the USA in 1973. I felt sorry for the forced laborers in these camps at the time, but I never imagined that some day these facts of slavery would pierce to my emotional depths, but they did now when I was in the presence of extended family members who were real survivors of this brutality. I noticed that both Magdalena and Christian reacted to the name Solzhenitsyn, and they turned their heads to Maria for an explanation. Maria told them what I'd said, but Magdalena shrugged her shoulders as if to say, "Who am I" to compare to this mighty author.

I again said to Maria, "Tell her that Solzhenitsyn had her in mind when he called for the witnessing of this terror by refugees. Magdalena could present the point-of-view of someone who had lived under Stalin's collectivization program and later in the labor camps. Importantly she could present the journey from a woman's angle and from tragic family losses. The cumulative effect of her view and other views by Poles, Jews, and other nationals would present to the world the essence of this monstrous scheme of using slave labor for government economic objectives. Perhaps my argument was too academic or too extreme, for no one responded.

Later after coffee and German chocolate cake, Helen, Jeff and I said *Auf Wiedersehen* to Magdalena and Christian. We drove back to the Kreiser home and had a nightcap of cognac and ice cream. I again brought up the importance of getting Magdalena and Christian's story out to the world. Maria said she would look into it, but it would be difficult since Magdalena was still working, and their schedules were tight. Maria was also expecting and would go on to have two daughters in the next few years. After breakfast in the morning and more good-byes we drove Jeffrey to the train station for his trip to Amsterdam, and we headed for Lubec and our next destination, Copenhagen.

After visiting with Icelandic relatives who were employed in Denmark, we had two additional weeks of travel left in Europe before we boarded our flight back to Seattle. We viewed the Van Gogh Centennial Exhibition in Amsterdam and spent a week touring in Paris, but I felt that the highpoint of the journey was the expansion of my knowledge of Hecker ancestry and lineage. Historically it placed my extended family in another dimension. To me it was not just family; it was history, as I had never experienced it before. Surely I sympathized with victims of such horrors as our American Slavery and Civil War, the near genocide of American Indians, Hiroshima, Nanking, and the bombing in Europe during World War II, but when I lectured on American History and our participation in some of these events, it was still just factual events to be considered and questioned. But when your own blood relatives sit in front of you and retell their journey, it chills one to the bone, causing amazement, regret, and a lot of soul searching.

PART II

August 1990

– Chapter 16 –

Before the start of the fall term at Olympic College, I had time to reflect on what I knew and didn't know about my Hecker family's past. I was satisfied that I finally had a good understanding of my roots. I accepted guardedly that I am ethnically a fourth generation German from Russia. I use the cautionary note because I found out that the first generations of Heckers in America had concealed their full ethnicity or just ignored it. I now understand the migrations of my family from Rulzheim, Germany to South Russia in the early 1800's and finally to the United States in the late 1800's. I now also possess a family tree showing the names of male Heckers and spouses and children extending over three countries in three consecutive centuries. The dispersal of Heckers from North Dakota to much of the Far West of the United States was extensive, but I didn't care to add to Uncle Adam of Salem's work in that arena. I felt satisfied that I had the line of descent from the beginnings in Germany in the early-1700's to the early Twenty-First Century in the United States. The Heckers had their beginnings in forestry work and carpentry in Germany and later took up farming in South Russia. In the United States they expanded into the trades and professions although their beginnings were in agriculture. For most of this time span they were family oriented, working class folk who were Roman Catholic, rural and provincial, and possessed German-American attitudes and culture.

I had gained a sense of family, but my academic training didn't allow me to be satisfied with my limited knowledge of the specific historic circumstances of the Hecker family moves from country to country. I didn't know the history involved in each of these migrations. I had heard a lot from relatives, but I didn't have the historic facts and the understandings of scholars about the roles of political leaders, social movements and wars in these moves. Since I had time to gather references and search out scholars and data on the various time periods involved, I decided to use the main branch of the Seattle Public Library in downtown Seattle, a convenient one hour ferry ride from Bremerton. The first research was to check into the bombing of Brandenburg by the Allies during World War II. When Magdalena told us about the air strike that occurred when she was sixteen years old and that caused the death of her mother Margarete (Metz) Hecker and two sisters, Olga and Hildegard, she had expressed the most emotional state in her remarks. My response was disbelief at first since the bombing was on Easter Sunday, 1945. Could Americans have conducted these air raids on this Christian Holy Day? I located a Combat Chronology for 1941-1945, issued by the Center for Air Force History, and it reported that 1300 heavy bombers that were supported by fifteen fighter groups had dropped bombs on Brandenburg beginning on March 31 and continued into April 1, 1945—the official day of Easter Sunday for 1945.

I had hoped that my German relatives in Hamburg were wrong about the date, but the evidence was clear from this official Air Force publication. I was aware that the recollections of my German from Russia relatives in America had contained errors in dates of birth, death and marriage. These showed up occasionally in census records and other "official" documents such as obituaries. Now, to the contrary, I gained confidence that my relatives in Hamburg had accurate memories since their words were substantiated by public documents.

Since I had little knowledge of German history other than an undergraduate course or two on general European history, I felt I needed to explore my German ancestral land in at least a few texts. I checked out two German histories for background reading, and in the next month of evening reading I finished W. M. Simon's *Germany:*

A Brief History and A. P. Taylor's *The Course of German History.* These two books gave me some understanding of the slow progress the Germans made from principality status to that of a sovereign nation. What I didn't know twenty years ago was that these two books were just the start of many more books that I would read on German history and literature leading up to the time that this writing began in early 2009. Those first two books also revealed the authoritarian nature of German society and the domination of the working class by the elite. The goal of the German leadership was to one day rule the countries to the east of Germany, namely Poland and Russia. More importantly to my study of family history, I learned from these books why my distant relatives decided to leave Rulzheim and to trek to South Russia. The reason was Napoleon and the Confederation of the Rhine (1806) that he set up to govern what was formerly German territory. Georg Hecker and his family left for South Russia in the spring of 1809 just before Napoleon's Army marched across southern Germany and crushed Austria.

My question when I read these first books was why go to South Russia when other countries like the United States and Canada were available to immigrants from Germany. Part of the answer came from reading three more books during this period of research: John Alexander's *Catherine the Great: Life and Legend*, Robert Bartlett's *Human Capital: The Settlement of Foreigner's in Russia 1776-1804* and Adam Giesinger's *From Catherine to Khrushchev*. The proclamation by Catherine II (1763) that was reaffirmed by her grandson Alexander I (1806) granted immigrants the right to set up villages and operate their own civic, educational and religious institutions. In addition ample loans were granted to give these colonists funds to start building homes and outbuildings in their villages, to purchase farm animals and agricultural equipment, and to begin tilling of the farmland that they had also been granted. These documents also allowed reasonable loan repayments on start-up costs and the guarantee of the right to buy additional crown land. Finally tax-free status for ten years and freedom from the Russian Army draft were contained in these proclamations. The lure of acquiring land and the benefits set forth in these documents far exceeded anything available at the time or later in the United States or Canada. The fact that Catherine was formerly a German princess who ascended to the throne of Russia also had its attraction for German colonists. Thus my question was answered why I had become ethnically a German from Russia.

Of course there were specific requirements of reporting and repayment of these loans and final authority still rested with the Russian government, but overall the conditions of colonizing were extremely attractive, especially in the context that the Russian peasants were still serfs. In the first nine years of the Nineteenth Century over six thousand colonists came to what was then called New Russia at the cost to the crown of 3,000,000 paper rubles. By 1818 a hundred German villages were established in the Black Sea region. Some difficulties were experienced by these colonists such as illness and loss of life from travel to the areas north of Odessa, and there were setbacks in loss of livestock in the winter of 1812-13, but overall the conditions were ripe for prosperity.

– Chapter 17 –

The first Hecker family to immigrate to Russia in 1809 helped found and settle the village of Speirer. Georg Hecker and family built their house and farmed the land they had been granted. Descendants of this first family moved to Munchen, another German colonist village in the area, and built their homes and outbuildings and stayed there until my Great-Grandfather Martin moved his family to the United States in 1891. These early Heckers had made the right decision. They prospered for several generations and had large families and holdings in land, livestock and orchards. They used their skills as craftsmen and built sturdy homes much like those in German villages that Helen and I witnessed with Maria and Kai-Uwe in a museum near Hamburg, Germany.

The Georg Heckers immigrated from Rulzheim in the Palatinate, a former principality of South Germany. The name Hecker derived from hacker or forestry workers who cut down trees for firewood or lumber they used in carpentry. Other villagers brought skills in bricklaying, stone masonry, blacksmithing, weaving, tailoring, shoemaking, butchering and milling. Since these colonists brought these skills from Germany and had the right to set up and manage their villages, the end product had such a distinct German village look that when the German soldiers arrived in 1941, they immediately recognized the dwellings and outbuildings as Germanic and weren't surprised to hear these villagers speak German. These Heckers and other colonists in New Russia also built barns and other outbuildings to house their horses, cattle, sheep, goats, chickens and pigs. They established extensive gardens and fruit orchards, especially grape vines for wine making. Root cellars were dug and assembled to store potatoes, corn, carrots, beets and other fruits and vegetables. Jars of preserves such as berries and honey were also stored to provide food for the long, cold winters in the region.

One of their first lucrative commercial activities was sheep raising. Russian peasants preferred sheepskin coats and hats. Merino sheep flourished on the pastures of the Steppe. The other moneymaking activity was growing grains such as wheat, rye, and oats. Huge surpluses of these grains not only made the colonists wealthy enough to buy more land and cultivate more crops, but the surplus grain made the Port of Odessa a center of grain exportation to countries accessible through the Dardanelles via the Treaty of Adrianople signed by Russia with Turkey in 1828. Access to Odessa for exporting grain from Munchen and other villages was made easy by extensive railway construction in the region. New farming techniques advanced by Mennonite villagers such as summer fallow and crop rotation also increased grain production. As a result of these conditions much of the 19th Century was a time of pastoral bliss for many of the Heckers as verified by letters I had received from Sister Reinhardt Hecker of Bismarck. So why didn't prosperity continue? Why didn't my Great-Grandfather Martin and his brothers—George, Frank, Jacob and Leonard—and their sister Barbara stay in South Russia? And why was it that the ones who remained—Ludwig and John—suffered so much starvation, death and terror? That was my next task for evening and weekend reading. There turned out to be several reasons, but gradual dismissal of the provisions made by Catherine II and Alexander I, the advent of the Russian Revolution, Civil War, and the rise of Joseph Stalin to power were the main factors.

— Chapter 18 —

Although the conditions provided by government proclamations led to considerable expansion of land holdings for some German colonists in the Black Sea region, other historical facts slowed down progress for other colonists. A provision in the Colonization Law of 1764 determined that a family's holdings were to pass from father to youngest son. This put my Great-Grandfather Martin Hecker and the other older sons in a difficult position. The land that was provided to the Hecker family originally passed on to a younger brother, Ludwig. He then collaborated with the other younger brothers Leonard and John to manage his holdings, thus giving Leonard and John income to further their own accumulation of land, vineyards and livestock. But in the end these advantages became their downfall. Leonard saw what was coming in 1914 at the advent of WWI and sold out his holdings and immigrated to North Dakota to locate near his older brothers. John and Ludwig stayed, probably purchasing Leonard's property.

Any colonist could also purchase additional crown land at the local price, but without crops or livestock, one couldn't set aside savings to buy more livestock or land. Those who had the resources quickly bought up the Crown land. The result was that some German colonists became quite wealthy while others were just able by their labor to buy or build a home and outbuildings. They could raise vegetables and keep livestock and thus maintain a subsistence living. Another provision in the Colonization Law allowed the landless to acquire or rent "sheep land," land set aside by the village to raise sheep and obtain wool for sale, but this provision had a minimal effect on the landless colonists. Another proclamation, this one by Alexander II in 1861, freed serfs from their slave status. This left wealthy Russian landowners with property they couldn't work for lack of labor. German colonists, who had excess money or land they could mortgage, did buy property from the landed aristocracy, especially during the 1860's, 1870's, and 1880's. In another Alexander II proclamation that resulted in out migration to other countries by German colonists, including my great-grandfather who had older sons, was the abolition of the exemption from military service for colonists. This 1874 law ruled that all male Russian subjects, aged 20, had to do six years of military service.

Other changes by Alexander II also led to more outward migration. The Zemstov legislation of 1864 provided for district (not village) assemblies to control schools, public health, prisons, and tax levying. Later in 1871 a decree abolished the old methods of operating German villages, thus removing self-control of German colonies. These changes caused the less wealthy Germans to look to immigration. Argentina, Canada, and the United States all vied for these farm people to come and occupy their open lands. Enticing promises of land were made by each of these countries with special privileges guaranteed just as they had been in the Russia of Catherine and Alexander I. America's Homestead Act of 1862, Canada's Dominion Land Act of 1872 and Argentina's Land Act of 1876 all led to immigration by German colonists in Russia. Corporations in these countries, especially railroads, often sent agents to recruit immigrants, sometimes even providing for their transportation expenses.

— Chapter 19 —

When I first researched this history back in 1990 and a year or so later, I didn't find all of this information. I located some of it later when I decided to write this memoir starting in early 2009. At that time I also decided that I had to answer the question of why Martin had moved to Texas rather than other states that had land grants still available like Kansas and North Dakota. Partly the reason was that his economic circumstances were less than desirable, and he and Christine had nine children with a tenth on the way. They had little money, and the transportation costs across the Atlantic and the eastern half of the United States were significant to them. Also there were start up costs such as housing if one did apply for Homestead Act land. In addition their family would have to eat until crops could be tilled, preserved or sold. Agents had been sent to Europe and South Russia by railroads and other companies that sold merchandise to newly arrived immigrants. These recruiters primarily touted the availability of land. In the case of one county in Texas where Martin and family located, there was an additional recruiter sent by a cotton plantation owner who needed farmers to share crop on his land. He offered to pay passage and relocation costs to those who didn't have funds. The cost to these farmers was agreement to work until these advances were repaid. There was also the guarantee of some farm animals and housing. The reason the plantation owner was offering these incentives was the lack of workers caused by the slave freedom act and out migration by former slaves. The Baker plantation was located in Grimes County just north of Houston. The nearest village was Plantersville and that became Martin Hecker's families new home in the United States.

Getting to the new location in Texas was by train from Munchen to Odessa and on to Hamburg, Germany. From that port they sailed by passenger ship to New York and finally by train to Plantersville, Texas. What they actually found there was less than desirable. They had to live in cramped quarters until they could build some kind of shelter. The requirement for repayment of transportation costs obligated all family members, so young children and older siblings had to work alongside their father in the cotton fields. As one member of another family in the same circumstances at Plantersville remarked, "We were indentured servants." Martin Hecker and family arrived in late May 1891 and stayed until 1903. The first year was devastating for the family because Christine and her newborn died in childbirth. The family carried on and Martin remarried within a year to a young widow with the same ethnic background.

Martin Hecker made the decision to move from Russia when he did, not just because of a crop failure that year but also because of the changing political conditions. Alexander II was assassinated in 1881, and his son Alexander III succeeded him. This new czar was anti-German and determined to Russify the Germans, Poles, Finns and Jews. In 1892, a year after Martin left, all schools were placed under Russian school inspectors. Russian became the language of instruction. German villagers still paid the taxes that supported the schools, but they lost what little voice they had left in running them and in curriculum choice. Thus the two Alexanders, II and III, accomplished their goal of reducing the influence of the German colonists in their villages. This attitude was in accord with the Russian peasantry who envied and resented the special privileges that the German colonists had held. These two czars also promulgated propaganda that described the German colonists as supporters of the Kaiser of Germany who was intent, as the Russian Czars saw it, on fostering a German State in Russia.

Circumstances did improve for Martin Hecker's brothers, Ludwig, John, and Leonard as well as other German colonists after Alexander III died in 1894 at age 50. His son Nicholas II was much less anti-German, but he was inexperienced at statecraft and didn't provide relief measures to the German villages that had suffered earlier the 1891 and 1892 crop failures and subsequent famine. Again Martin Heckers 1891 departure was fortuitous. There were strikes and riots in the streets of Russian cities. Another mistake was Nicholas II's agreement to wage an aggressive foreign policy, as his ministers wanted, that led to war against Japan in 1904. Even Nicholas's Manifesto in 1905, giving new freedoms of expression and plans for a constitutional monarchy were misplaced and unfortunate. More riots broke out in the cities, and the scene was set for the Russian Revolution of 1917.

Although Nicholas did have the support of German colonists and his leadership led to some additional German secondary schools in the Black Sea region and to some German participation in his government, WW I destroyed much of this acceptance and led directly to the Russian Civil War and clashes between Red and White armies, representing the old regime and the new arising political faction. These changes during Nicholas II's reign caused difficulties in the Black Sea German villages for my relatives who had not immigrated. The younger Hecker brothers who had inherited land and buildings felt the impact directly. Ludwig and John Hecker experienced the loss of control of their Catholic churches, the village's schools, and the civic government that they had instituted and managed for generations. The German language was forbidden in the schools that the German colonists had built and paid for. Russian teachers replaced all teachers of German origin.

The outcomes of World War I were partly responsible for the changes in attitude towards German colonists. The German Army had ravished Russia and had left millions dead. The German colonists were blamed for and were accused of aiding the Kaiser in his quest to defeat and subjugate Russians to German authority. It didn't matter that most, if not all, of the German colonists were loyal to the czar, and since the repeal of special privileges for German colonists as many as 250,000 German colonists had served in the Russian Army against the German Army. Many of these died in battle for Russia. The situation was similar to the reaction against Japanese-Americans who lived on the West Coast of the United States and were placed in internment camps after Pearl Harbor. In Russia the Czar ordered the removal of 150,000 German colonists from one province, placed them on trains and sent them to eastern Russia, causing them to lose farms, crops, personal property and villages. In these instances Russian peasants moved in and took over the vacant properties without paying for them.

In the Beresan District of the Black Sea region where Heckers lived in Rastadt, Speirer and Munchen, the impact was serious. In February and March of 1917 the czar's regime ended. The Bolshevik faction of the Russian Democratic Party that was led by Trotsky and Lenin executed a successful coup and started the Communist era of Russian history. By decree Lenin abolished landed proprietorships and ordered the confiscation of landed estates. Rural land committees, made up of peasants and deputies from the Bolshevik government, ordered land seizures by roving bands of peasants. The Cheka, the newly organized secret police, arrested and imprisoned or executed thousands of what were called "class enemies" without regard to guilt or innocence. Since German colonists had long ago been labeled "Kulaks," or privileged outsiders, they felt the impact directly. John Hecker, Magdalena's grandfather, met his fate by one of these armed bands of peasants who in this case were led by anarchist revolutionaries. These men had been political prisoners, but peasant Russian soldiers had released them from jail. When this motley crew demanded money from John Hecker, he refused. Many of John's fellow Munchen villagers had left the area and were hiding in the woods. Without hesitation the leader of this group shot John Hecker in the face, killing him instantly. The band of marauders left John's son, Johann, a teenager, who had stood beside his father, and Johann's mother and his siblings to grieve John Hecker's death and to carry on without him.

— Chapter 20 —

I recalled our 1990 meeting with Magdalena, Christian and family in Hamburg when she told about this episode. She couldn't provide the information about the Communist Party takeover, or the new government's orders for the takeover of estates and villages. All she knew was that her grandfather had been murdered for his refusal to comply with their demand for money. I can still see the sorrow in her eyes and the pain of loss in her face for a grandfather who was dead before her birth. How many times had her father, Johannes, told her about how he had witnessed his own father's death by a bullet to his face by thugs? Magdalena had also heard about how the bands of peasants returned in following months and years to confiscate land, horses, and farmyard animals until finally they took even their household furniture and spare clothes. In subsequent years after her birth in 1928, Magdalena became aware of how these same Reds had requisitioned all stockpiles of grain in the Odessa region and shipped them out to other parts of the country. These yearly gatherings of grain left the German colonists with no reserves when droughts set in, so there were famines in which many died of starvation. Magdalena saw her twin sisters die in this fashion. No wonder she cried at the telling of these facts even though more than fifty years had passed since she had experienced them.

For many years after John Hecker's murder, Johann and his mother led the family except for a few years when he was drafted into the Russian Army. He survived and upon his return he rebuilt what they had left, married Margarete Metz and started his own family with Anton, the first born, and two years later Magdalena. Now Johann led one of the few Hecker families left at Munchen. The circumstances of their lives were brutal, and several more newborns died of starvation. Only with the coming of the German Army in 1941 would these German colonists get back to a normal existence, but then for only a short three years before the German Army retreated back to Germany near the end of the war. What a dreadful existence they had faced! Magdalena and her father Johannes would subsequently suffer the loss of the rest of the family in the bombing of Brandenburg, get captured by the Russian Army and be sent to the Ural Mountains to serve in the work camps of the Gulag.

— Chapter 21 —

Yes, the German colonists suffered greatly in South Russia and had promises broken by a succession of czars and later by the Soviet government, but as I now study the history of my family's past, I also think about the Russians who also suffered. The serfs were freed by proclamation in 1861 and were later rewarded by Lenin when he ordered the division of estates into small farms for these people. They had little experience in managing farmland with its grain crops and herds of farm animals, both of which needed to be prepared for sale at markets. They quickly became subsistence farmers with little hope of progress later as workers on the collective farms that Stalin established. Many of them died of starvation or freezing because the collectives didn't work and little food was harvested. Finally Stalin drove many of them out of their homes onto roads in the middle of the winter to freeze to death. They didn't fit into his plans of establishing an industrialized nation with products for the international markets.

Another group that I thought about were the Cossacks. They had been on the Steppe since the time of Ivan the Great. These people had first lived in the general area of Moscovy, but they refused to become a part of it when Ivan redistricted his realm to include their farms. They held their independence and way of life to be more important than anything else and moved farther out onto the Steppe away from the reach of Ivan. Gradually they congregated along rivers like the

Dneiper that flowed south of Kiev to the Black Sea and the Don that flowed south to the Sea of Azor. It became clear to these groups that although they were primarily farmers and herders, they had to protect themselves, so they formed military units. The Dneiper River Cossacks set up a fort at Zaporizhia on an island. Some men stayed there year round, but most of the Cossacks remained in their villages and continued to seed their fields in the spring and harvest the crops in the fall. They raised cattle and sheep as well as other farmyard animals, especially horses and bullocks, but they were on call as Cossacks at any time during the year for military purposes.

When I read about them in Gogol's *Taras Bulba*, I visualized a highly disciplined militaristic set of men, proud and defiant and not given to subjugation. The Czars largely left them alone, but they answered the call for military service to the crown if Russia was attacked. The Cossack showed up with regiments of men on horseback, ready and willing to do battle against an enemy of the national government. Gogol's book reminded me of the Japanese Samurai. Taras Bulba fought against the Polish invaders of Russia in this book by his name. He ended up sacrificing his two sons and himself rather than to accept defeat by the enemy. Taras Bulba owned land and farmed it, but his passion was liberty.

The other book that I read about the Cossacks was Mikhail Sholokhov's novel *The Don Flows Home to the Sea.* Sholokhov was a descendant of Cossacks of the Steppe country bordering the Don River. He wanted to give his ancestry their due and chose to write about their involvement in the Russian Civil War of 1919-1920. These Cossacks formed their own brigades of horsemen and supported the White Army of Russia against the Red Army of the Bolsheviks. In the novel, which exceeds six hundred pages in length, Sholokhov chose to follow one family through the two years of war. The Melekhov elders have two sons, Piotia and Gregor, and one daughter Dunia. These three children have spouses and several children are born, but by the end of the novel only Gregor and his two children and his sister and spouse survive to face a world shred of the proud Cossack way of life. We readers experience the characteristics of their former lives through glimpses of the seeding of the soil, harvest, hut kitchens and great rooms, meals of soup and bread, lamb, and pails of homemade vodka. We see the members of the family as human beings with all the flaws and virtues of normal people, suffering long absences of spouses, illicit romances and the conflicts involved in the politics of Civil War.

I thought of them as being similar to Native Americans of 18th and 19th century America. They too were proud advocates of their way of life. Invading foreign peoples dogged them, and they established armies to protect themselves; but also like the Cossacks their way of life was reduced to reservation conditions. Other Russians also lost their normal life styles during the turmoil of the Russian Revolution and Civil War. Not least of which were the aristocrats whose estates were confiscated. Some of this class had seen what was coming and had transferred money to banks in Europe and escaped there for refuge. Others didn't have the foresight and ended up in collectives or waiting on tables in Parisian restaurants. The talented that had the benefit of higher education found jobs in countries where they knew the languages. Many opposed the Communist State and were imprisoned or sent to work camps in the Gulag where they were given the lowest form of work in kitchens and latrines. In many ways my great-grandfather fell into this same category. He too had poor prospects in South Russia and didn't want his sons and family to endure the political changes, so he moved his family to Texas where they suffered near servile circumstances, but at least he gave his descendants a better life in America than those of his family who stayed and suffered or perished under the rule of the Bolsheviks and Stalin.

– Chapter 22 –

What can one make of all this sorrow and turmoil? Those who seize or inherit power seem to set destinies for others. Rulers tend to demonize ethnic minorities in their countries and other nationalities outside of their boundaries to give their own angry citizens a way to vent their pain. Depending on circumstances and goals, one ruler frees people like the serfs from slavery while the next governing group use ethnic minorities as slaves in their work camps to further their goals of industrialization and power. Where does justice fit into these schemes of government? When are promises kept or at least when broken paid for? One thing is for sure that rulers always pay themselves well even in so-called egalitarian societies. Didn't Orwell write about this in *Animal Farm*? Perhaps we are just an extension of the animal world where territorialism, dominance and instinctive behavior rule. An alpha male of a lion pride invades another pride and drives off or kills the adult males, kills the pride's cubs (to rid himself of the blood line) and impregnates the lionesses. We certainly have the vision to transcend these primitive instincts! We set up churches to aid us in this endeavor, but even many of these institutions ended up in rivalries seeking domination.

At least for my part, I am satisfied that I have come full circle. I have the basic facts about my ancestry. I know where I came from and what my ancestors faced and dealt with in their lives and movements from country to country. I understand what forced migration means and understand how changes in governments and rulers bent or destroyed the lives of my people. I have met my relatives in Germany who survived the Soviet Union and the Gulag, and I feel thankful that they lived to tell me their story. I can now get on with my own life. I also gained something invaluable that I dreamt of last night. I have gained more sympathy for my fellow human beings because of the directness of this knowledge. It happened to me through my ancestors. I now feel and empathize with those who have suffered under the subjugation of rulers like Hitler and Stalin. I can now extend that sympathy to my countrymen the native Americans who suffered near genocide, to Black Americans who experienced slavery, to Chinese who at one period were forbidden entry into the United States, to Japanese-Americans who were incarcerated in internment camps and to every other ethnic American like Italians, Irish, Germans, Russians, Mexicans, Vietnamese and so forth who have felt the pangs of ostracism, the threat of xenophobia, and have survived the cauldron of the American melting pot. I feel empathy for future American ethnic groups like Muslims who might be shunned because of religious and cultural differences. I feel more able to return to my life as educator and to lecture on American history and literature and to give a more balanced understanding of my society and its benefits and potential. I feel more acceptant of my mixed ethnic background. Now the exceptionalist destiny of Americans is more in reach for my students and me. One Scandinavian tour guide once said to me about his experience with Americans and Europeans: in America people ask what you do; whereas in Europe they ask where are you from?

Chapter 23

Thus I returned to Olympic College at Bremerton, Washington, to my primary work as Professor of American Culture where I taught three sequential courses, covering American society from the colonial period to the national and then to the modern era, that I had created and coordinated with the collaboration of several other faculty members in theater, music and art disciplines. I felt better prepared to lecture on my country in the respect that I could present a more critical and sympathetic view on issues of race, ethnic backgrounds and immigration than I did before my ancestry studies. I think I also understood better how xenophobia and nativism functioned in American culture now that I had stories from relatives who had been affected by these patterns of thought in Russia when they were stereotyped and robbed of their assets and in some cases their lives. I would now be able to deal with these issues on a more personal level. I wouldn't just be lecturing and presenting facts, but I could add a sympathetic dimension to those groups who had been treated likewise in American History.

American Indians, for instance, were the first to feel the pressure of racial bias. They were driven to near genocide by European settlers and their military, all largely Caucasians, because of their race and because they occupied coveted land. As colonization of America spread across the country from Massachusetts through Pennsylvania, Michigan, Indiana, Ohio and on to Missouri and Iowa, tribes of

Indians who hadn't been defeated or placed on reservations moved themselves to the Upper Plains. They joined the tribes of that region, but they all soon felt the encroachment on these ancestral lands with the coming of the Lewis and Clark expedition of 1803. By 1862 and the Homestead Act, the incursion grew more intense and the battles between the Indians and the American Army multiplied, leading to the near disappearance of Native Americans.

My Scandinavian relatives became a part of the incursion when my Great-Grandfather Olaf Peterson, a blacksmith and farmer, moved his family from a farm near Oslo, Norway, into the Dakota Territory in about 1870. He settled in the northeast corner of the territory near the Red River and present day towns of Mountain, Vang, and Walhalla. He and other immigrants made claims under the Homestead Act on land that Indians believed to be part of their ancestral territory. I know of no direct conflict between Olaf and Indians in the region, but I did hear of Olaf's solitary defense of his farmhouse and outbuildings during what was called an Indian uprising in the area. He was alone because he had sent his wife Caroline and young children to a military fort for protection.

The same sequence of incursion and removal that happened in the north occurred as well in the Deep South of the country to the Indians in Florida, Georgia, Tennessee, and Alabama. The Trail of Tears affair was the removal of tribes from these states to the Oklahoma Territory. As in the Upper Plains, Indian land had been invaded, removal of most of them (Those, that is, that didn't die on the forced march.) was accomplished and only a few remained behind, assimilated or on reservations. Later that same pattern of pillage and destruction continued in the Far West, Southwest and Pacific Northwest. At the base of this carnage were land hunger, railroad expansion, and race. American Indians did not generally speak English and had religious and cultural ceremonies that were anathema to prevailing Anglo-American religions and cultural mores.

I was aware of these biased attitudes in my own upbringing during the 1950's at Devils Lake, North Dakota where I was raised as a teenager. Indians, some Sioux and some Chippewa, lived on the fringes of the town and largely kept to themselves. Other Indians lived on or near reservations like Fort Totten that was about twenty miles away. Indian children generally attended reservation schools although the few who lived in Devils Lake attended public school. Several of them who were Catholic went to St. Mary's Academy, the school I attended. My direct experience with American Indians was limited although my family lived on the south side of town where several Indian families had modest homes. In one case, a Chippewa teenager who attended the local public high school invited me into his family's tiny, old house. I was amazed when we entered a side door into a room with dirt floor and a webbing of tree branches that crisscrossed the space from wall to wall. It turned out to be a room for drying out meat from deer, rabbits, and upland game. Although I didn't see his dad, he must have been a hunter.

I did encounter some Indian boys and men at a local pool hall on Saturday afternoons and evenings. The older ones that I saw quite often sought out people who could buy alcoholic beverages, for State Law at the time forbid the sale to them directly. Those Indians who came to town on Saturdays for alcohol or other stimulants, like vanilla extract, would often be intoxicated by evening. At these times a few white teenagers would gather to witness the parade of drunken Indians, often found pushing their cars by hand to roll them to a start in the frigidly cold weather. On occasion a few of these unruly teenagers would use these staggering men as punching bags until police intervened. Rarely was any charge brought against these thugs. Even at my young age, I realized that a distinct minority of Indians did these displays of drunkenness. Maybe there was a total of twenty or twenty-five of them, and they were perceived to represent the majority of area Indians as sots.

Not all assaults on Indians, however, went unchallenged. I recall an incident that I witnessed which indicated the contrary. One afternoon I sat at the lunch counter of the local pool hall, a gathering place for teenagers as well as pool players, including Indians who generally sat in the back of the poolroom. I was drinking a soft drink and talking to a high school classmate's mother who was serving customers from behind the counter. As I talked, she caught sight of someone walking the aisle behind me towards the poolroom. She nodded for me to look. I turned on the swivel stool and saw a short, broad-shouldered older Indian man who was walking quickly towards the first pool table. A taller, white man in his early twenties stood at that table, holding his cue stick while waiting for his turn. As the Indian approached the younger man from behind, he tightened his leather gloves over his fists. He then tapped the white man on the shoulder. The man turned, revealing his face and upper body. The Indian swung his right fist, connecting with the man's jaw, and sent him sprawling onto the pool table. The man who was hit shook his head and tried to push himself up with both hands. He was stunned. Meanwhile the Indian had already turned around and was walking by us towards the front door of the place. I was astonished at the scene, for it reminded me of a movie about Geronimo that portrayed Indian attacks as quick, silent and effective.

I glanced at Mrs. Schell, and she said, "That'll teach that punk a lesson." I said, "For what?" She told me that the young man who was decked was a student at the local junior college. He was a veteran of the Korean War and was attending the school on the G.I. Bill. The Indian had two very attractive daughters who also attended the college. The young man drove the college's bus to nearby towns and Ft. Totten where the girls lived with their family. This guy had hassled the young women repeatedly, asking for dates and more. They wanted no part of him, and they made that clear, but he continued to badger them. For some reason he felt entitled to favors from these Indian women. That was what led to this assault and battery. The Indian father, a potato farmer with a large family, handled conflict on his own terms. Some years later I learned that one of the Indian's sons finished law school and practiced law for the reservation. The two young women graduated from the University of North Dakota and became teachers. Another son, a warrior like his father, excelled in all sports, especially football, and eventually served three terms of duty in the Vietnam War.

Even at my young age, I didn't approve of the violent encounter, but there didn't appear to be any alternative. The local police and County Sheriff didn't respond normally to the complaints of Indian women, and the Ft. Totten police had no jurisdiction off the reservation. The young man who was slugged didn't press charges, so he must have accepted the consequences of his actions. Another flagrant example of womanizing on the reservation that I heard of while attending high school in Devils Lake resulted in the castration of a white man. Although these two instances of Indian violence were tiny in comparison to what had been inflicted on the Indians over the years of settlement, none would have happened had there been a higher standard of justice and less xenophobia and nativism. I feel moved to add that I was very fortunate in my upbringing and education. My parents never spoke negatively of persons of other races or ethnic backgrounds. They didn't object if any of us associated with children of other races, religions, or ethnic backgrounds. Our Catholic school teachers, where we had different ethnic backgrounds as well as a few Indians, held us to a high standard of values and emphasized the importance of "doing unto others as you would have them do unto you."

— Chapter 24 —

After the fall term at Olympic College was in full swing, I told my colleagues in the Humanities Division of my meeting with relatives in Hamburg, Germany. Although I had gained confidence in my need to speak out on the issue of discrimination and nativism, I was still somewhat reluctant to share my past with them. We were still in the dregs of the Reagan Era with his Star Wars initiative and the Berlin Wall encounter. Bremerton was also the location of the Puget Sound Naval Shipyard where aircraft carriers, destroyers, and other military vessels were docked for repairs and upgrading. The Bangor Trident Submarine Base and Keyport Naval Station were nearby. In other words the area was chock full of military personnel and thousands of civilian employees who made their living at these facilities.

The word got around, and one day I received a call from a Bremerton *Sun* reporter, asking for an interview about my meeting in Hamburg with Germans from Russia relatives. I hesitated, but I agreed to the interview at my office on the campus. The interview resulted in an article titled "Local man's family had Russian Branch." The short piece covered my family's two hundred year past from Germany to Russia and finally to the United States with some comments about the Heckers who stayed in Russia and ended up in the turmoil of the Russian Revolution, Stalin's collectivization, WWII, the Gulag and finally immigration to Germany. The reporter tied the narrative together with the sentence "Just because they were German."

A map accompanied the article, showing central and Eastern Europe on one side and the Soviet Union and the Black Sea on the other. The capitols of Germany, Poland, and other eastern block countries were labeled, and over a vacant Soviet Union rested a world globe with an arrow pointing across and part way around the globe, presumably showing the immigration route of my family.

Instead of propelling me into the limelight with discussions of my family history and invitations to give talks on the topic, the news article wasn't mentioned to me by anyone. It was largely ignored, except by one colleague who was Japanese-American and taught English in my academic division. Since the article's title used the phrase Russian branch, it was easy to believe that I was Russian or at least had Russian relatives. In fact I had some distant German relatives who married Russians in the Ural Mountains and stayed in the Soviet Union or Russia as it is now named. Also, the use of the word German as a propeller of privilege or expulsion didn't help. I was being confronted head on with the complexities of ethnicity in my pursuit of my family's history. I was feeling in the early 1990's what had existed in the United States since the 1850's. John Higham, an American historian, called it nativism. American nativists feared that foreign newcomers would have allegiance to a foreign power and that assimilation for them would fail. In my case there were three factors in this circumstance. I was raised Catholic (a continuing concern in some circles). I also had German from Russia ancestry, and finally I had relatives who had not only lived in the Soviet Union but had survived the work camps of the Gulag in the Ural Mountains. Fear of outsiders or xenophobia was still alive and well in the United States.

I immediately added new topics to my course syllabus and added more notes for lectures on this topic. Pearl Harbor was just such an incident that students needed to hear about, but not only as a justification for entering WW II, as it is presented in American History courses, but also for how the reaction to the incident encouraged nativism and the incarceration of the innocent. Japanese-Americans who lived on the west coast of the United States were placed in internment camps because it was feared that these people would honor their past affiliation with Japan through ancestry and that past association would overpower their allegiance to the United States. 150,000 Japanese-Americans were given ten days to settle their affairs, that is to get rid of their homes, businesses, vehicles and household goods, and show up at specific points for transportation to prisons. How did they deal with health problems and medications? How many dollars were lost in quick transactions? How many chose suicide or died of separation from their familiar surroundings and friends?

– Chapter 25 –

So I continued my work at Olympic College, adding material to my courses that gave voice to what had been missing in my lectures. I understood the misfortunes and tragedy that some of my family had faced, but I was also aware that the second and third generation Heckers had fared quite well in the United States. Overall they had been given a fair chance to achieve according to their talents and had not been stripped of any privileges available to Americans in general. There had been, to my knowledge, little ostracism, no overt employment restrictions and few, if any, barriers to success. There was, however, an unwritten understanding that English was the accepted official language and that the American way of life was the norm. Certainly there was no Gulag. Many of my cousins on both sides of my family had attended colleges and had taken degrees; some in engineering, pharmacy, and medicine; and others in theology, law and various academic disciplines. Relatives had also fared well in commerce, the trades, and agriculture. This is not to say there weren't shortcomings in family circumstances that held some back from realizing their full potential. Lack of family income stopped some although a few overcame this obstacle by using the G.I. Bill. A few didn't meet their potentials because they attended primary and secondary schools that had inadequate coursework, teachers, and counseling. My father lost his trucking job with a wholesale food distribution company because he advocated unionism in North Dakota, a right-to-work State.

I continued in my position as Professor and Coordinator of the American Culture Program for seven additional years. I added and revised courses in American Culture that I taught myself such as the Culture of the American West, Arts in the Pacific Northwest, and Technology in American Culture. During these and in preceding years, I had the benefit of attending professional conferences arranged by academic organizations. These three and four day meetings had many sessions that dealt with issues that I was engaging in my lineage studies. These conferences were held in cities in various regions throughout the United States and Canada that I had not visited personally, so I had the opportunity to mingle with local people and visit their clubs, cafes, and museums. I was thus afforded many anecdotes about various life styles in these places that I could share with students and colleagues that gave added character and variety to my lectures.

As early as 1975 I attended a biannual American Studies Association meeting in San Antonio, Texas. This was my first venture into a southern state, and I met with academic peers from Alabama, Mississippi, Georgia, and the Carolinas. During sessions and afterwards in breaks I first experienced the story telling capacities of southerners from different ethnic backgrounds. I also spent time roaming the streets of this city and visited museums that featured the Alamo and Spanish heritage before Texas separated itself from Mexico. Various cafes and nightclubs provided other aspects of this culture, especially the music and food of Hispanics. Other ASA conferences gave me the same benefits for other regions of the country. I attended one at Minneapolis, 1977; another in Philadelphia, 1983; San Diego, 1985; New York, 1987; Boston, 1993; Nashville, 1994; Pittsburgh, 1995; and Kansas City, 1996. One early meeting in New Orleans that the Organization of American Historians sponsored in 1979 stands out as an example of how these meetings provided substance for educators of all stripes. As I hadn't traveled in Louisiana, Mississippi, or Alabama, this was an opportunity I couldn't bypass for many reasons. These states had multi-ethnic and racial groups that had evolved over the centuries from American Indian enclaves with Spanish and French pioneers to Plantation cultures with a variety of

European immigrants and African slaves. New Orleans itself was a mixture of all of these influences. In addition there were writers in the region like Eudora Welty and William Faulkner among others that I had read and taught. By attending this conference I could arrange to visit a broad swath of the region and drive the roads and walk the streets that these authors had portrayed in their writings.

Helen and I made arrangements with our respective institutions to take a full week off for this venture. We flew on Saturday morning of the preceding weekend to New Orleans, rented a car and drove northwest into Cajun country. We stopped for an early dinner at a restaurant where we ate jambalaya, crayfish, and other local specialties. We sat among Cajuns who spoke the local patois and were aided graciously by a waitress who translated the menu for us. We received friendly nods from people who sat at adjoining tables. We continued our journey, relishing already the experience of a foreign language, exotic food and a natural environment that varied considerably from what we knew from the Upper Plains and the Pacific Northwest. We drove into Baton Rouge, stayed at a local hotel, and enjoyed visiting antebellum plantation houses the next morning. After lunch we headed east towards Jackson, Mississippi to take in Eudora Welty's locale.

A narrow, two-lane paved highway offered the first startling experience for both of us in this part of the country. We drove through this heavily forested landscape, spotting occasionally a few people walking, sometimes east and sometimes west, along the road. They were mostly older black women in dresses, carrying bags, either in hand or slung over the shoulder. I thought about some of Eudora Welty's photographs that she took for the WPA guidebook to Mississippi in the 1930's. As we were miles from any town that we knew of, I wondered where the walkers were going. As Helen and I talked about these women, we cleared a short hill and came upon a scene that nearly caused me to stop the car. We had driven into what must have been former slave quarters. These log cabins, on both sides of the road, were elevated about three feet above the ground and were supported by tree stumps. These old, weather-beaten dwellings were situated among trees, fairly close together, and in several rows; but there were no streets, just pathways. I noticed that there were no poles carrying electricity or telephone lines and also no evidence of water or sewer lines. More noteworthy was the fact that Black Americans occupied these cabins that we saw through cabin windows and outside on the paths, but there were no cars, trucks, or even bikes. Since there were no signs indicating that these were museum models, I had to assume that these were permanent dwellings, apparently lived in by the women and their families that we had seen walking along the roads. I now thought they were probably headed to work at former plantation houses in the woods.

We drove on into Jackson and looked for a restaurant for a late lunch. This small city was unusually well kept. The streets were paved and without cracks or other blemishes. The sidewalks were brightly clean with no debris in the gutters, not even a cigarette butt, scrape of paper or empty candy bar wrapper. The stores were built of bricks and mortar with wooden doors and window frames that were freshly or recently painted. The doors had brass handles, and the windows were brightly clean. The restaurant we found was equally polished. Black American waitresses and busboys served us, and the food was delicious. An oddity was the lack of people in the restaurant or on the streets. After we returned to our car and drove around the downtown of Jackson, admiring the buildings and parks, I noticed the many late model cars parked on the streets.

Again I thought the lack of people strange, so I decided to cross a bridge that spanned a river to see what was on the other side. As we turned off the bridge, I pulled the car over to the curb and stopped. In front of us were old wooden structures on both sides of the street. Some leaned precariously to one side or the other and were in danger of collapsing. Others had missing or cracked windows, but all were being used as grocery stores, barbershops, apartments, auto-repair and hangouts of one kind or the other. One thing I noticed for sure was that the many people (Black Americans of all ages, sizes and gender who walked the sidewalks and streets) were enjoying life. They were talking, laughing, even dancing at times and generally having a good time. I could hear music from cars and from hand carried portable radios. Some of the cars that were parked along the curbs had been abandoned and stripped of mirrors, windows, and perhaps even engines. Other autos were newer, customized and painted in bright, sparkling colors. These vehicles were occupied or had individuals sitting on fenders or leaning their upper bodies into the vehicles through door windows.

What was clear to me was that we were on the other side of the tracks or in this case the river. These were the streets of the lower orders of this city. But I thought to myself this is 1979, and this looks like segregation. I was shocked since the Civil Rights Movement of the 1960's had left most Americans, at least many of us who lived in the north, thinking that things had changed. Of course I had once accidentally driven into the south side of Chicago and refused to even stop my car as we drove back to the freeway entrance, and I had driven through American Indian villages in South Dakota, Montana and Washington that were equally shabby, but then the entire section of that city or village were the same. I thought again of Eudora Welty and her focus on social prejudice in her narratives.

We drove north to Oxford, Mississippi where we cruised the streets before we located a place to stay. The motel was close to Rowan Oak, the former Faulkner home, now a museum, so we walked to it. We toured the house and entered his study in an adjoining structure, and I immediately thought about scenes in *As I Lay Dying* and *The Sound and the Fury*, two of my favorite Faulkner novels. We then walked about this university town and saw many people of all colors and ethnic backgrounds on the streets. I thought about this locale and sights we had seen on our drive into Oxford as what became Faulkner's fictional Yoknapatawpha County. We strolled about the grounds of the University of Mississippi and then investigated the Student Union Building. Here we saw photographs of elegantly gowned Homecoming Queens in a large room and adjoining hall-ways. None were Black-American Queens, but it was obvious from the students we saw on the campus that it wouldn't be long before one would appear on these walls.

We spent the next day driving around the city and surrounding area and walking the streets, stopping for meals whenever we saw a café or restaurant that looked interesting. We must have looked like outsiders, but everyone we met greeted us hospitably. We didn't notice any prejudice. We drove south the next day to visit Biloxi, Mississippi and Mobile, Alabama. We stayed in Mobile and enjoyed the beaches and museums, absorbing as much of the culture as possible, but we were by now anxious to get back to New Orleans, so we drove to this famous city, dropped our rental car and checked into the conference hotel.

New Orleans and the OAH conference met all of our expectations. We toured the city, visited the French Quarter and took an afternoon cruise on the <u>Mark Twain</u> paddleboat. The cruise took us into the bayou country, and as we floated along, we saw cabins that were elevated several feet above water level on poles embedded into the inlet river floor. Small boats were both attached to these dwellings or were occupied by Cajuns who netted for crayfish and crabs or fished.

The real purpose of the journey came for me next in the many invigorating and challenging sessions. Helen skipped these and went shopping, relaxed in our hotel room or enjoyed the swimming pool and exercise rooms. She always joined me for dinner, and we did dine at several gourmet restaurants. On the last evening we attended the concluding dinner of the conference and heard the presentation of a noted academic scholar. I took notes as I had at all of the sessions I attended. It would take me some time to process all of the information I had accumulated and find answers to some of the questions that were posited at some of the sessions. My students would benefit as much as I did, once I had this material entered into my lectures.

A dance had been scheduled as the last event of the conference, and Helen and I decided to participate, but we needed a breath of fresh air and exercise after sitting for so long. We followed others who had decided on doing the same and took an escalator to the rear exit of the hotel to walk around a small park. On the way down at the last floor above the exit, Helen noticed some boutique store windows with displays, so we detoured for a look-see. Two men who were just behind us continued the descent. After we returned to the escalator and were about half way to the bottom floor, we heard what sounded like a gunshot. As we descended, I peered at the exit doors and noticed that a man was lying face down on the sidewalk and another person stood beside him. As we reached the ground floor, I saw several hotel security guards approaching the two men. I walked over to the sliding glass doors and saw that the man on the sidewalk had blood all around his head. We didn't exit the building, but we heard the story later that evening (from an account given by the witness accompanying the murdered man) that the deceased was an academic from the East Coast. The witness further stated that the killer appeared to be deranged and under the influence of drugs. He had demanded the man's wallet and then shot him in the face when he thought the victim was going to defend himself. The man who was shot had actually reached into his sport coat pocket to get his wallet. The thief had apparently spooked, thinking the man was reaching for a gun. The gunman then ran off down the street.

I told Helen that I would never complain again if she wanted to window shop, for had we not stopped for that purpose we would have been the first people to encounter the shooter. I would have been asked for my wallet. Since I carried my wallet in my back pocket, maybe the outcome would have been just robbery. A front-page newspaper article the next morning reported the capture of the gunman; he was a Black American in his late teens. I wondered if he was from Jackson, Mississippi where segregation might have poisoned his mind into this kind of criminal behavior. I hoped not, for that would make this death even more senseless and tragic.

I also engaged in additional projects that broadened my horizons during these seven years as well as in a few earlier years. In the spring of 1985 I promoted the arts in general by coordinating the Regional Conference of the Pacific Northwest American Studies Association at Olympic College. The theme of the conference was "The Artist in America," and I moderated the concluding session of the conference under the title "Artist and Audience in American Culture." I continued my work on this topic and was appointed four years later as a Washington Centennial Scholar and Lecturer on the Impact of the New Deal on Arts in Washington State. I gave presentations on this topic in the summer and fall of 1989 at Whitman College, at the annual conference of the Board of Trustees of Community Colleges for Washington State and at Cheney Cowles Museum in Spokane. By the spring of 1991 I had published an eight-page article in *Columbia: The Magazine of Northwest History* under the title "The Impact of the New Deal on the Arts of the State of Washington."

I also continued doing projects related to my doctoral dissertation on John Steinbeck. Since a number of his early stories and short novels had community as theme, I wrote about it and presented my findings to colleagues at regional and national conferences. Since Steinbeck focused on the 1930's in America, I followed up the ASA conference on the Artist in America with a study on the artists who created murals for United States Post Offices in Washington State under the auspices of the WPA. I focused on how these jobs under government sponsorship gave work to painters who were in financial need. I also dealt with the WPA sponsorship of State Guidebooks. Again the jobs gave work to journalists and creative writers. In both cases the painters and writers were able to continue in their creative arts rather than to undergo a gap in their chosen fields that might have altered or damaged their ability to create permanently.

− Chapter 26 −

A significant aspect of most of my writing was that it was evaluative and critical, just as my many years of teaching had been. I enjoyed lecturing and then evaluating student essays, research projects and exams. It was my way of contributing to their understanding of their culture and to aid them in skill mastery. From another point of view my work on the role of artists in American culture showed me how important their arts and writings were to the creative side of mental development for everyone. My students and I needed our imagination's stimulated. I encouraged them to keep journals and to take courses in the creative arts regardless of their majors. I took my own advice to them. I enrolled in creative writing workshops during the summers beginning in the late 80's at Centrum in Port Townsend, Washington. Each summer for three years I worked in turn with Leonard Michels, Craig Lesley, and Douglas Unger. After that I attended Mary Blew's creative nonfiction workshop at Yellow Bay Writer's Conference at Flathead Lake, Montana, sponsored by the University of Montana. I found pleasure in the process of creating stories and found that my knowledge of American Culture was helpful in creating characters and following their motivations and values. Since I had also met and heard readings by poets at these conferences, I began to write poems as well. Wanting more advice on the craft of writing poems and more interaction with other creative writers, I enrolled in and completed a three quarter certificate program in poetry at the University of Washington during the 1994-95 academic year.

Since I attended many venues in Seattle where authors read their poems and stories, I continued to read widely in contemporary publications. I also started reviewing readings for a local newspaper in Seattle, *The Belltown Messenger*. Gary Snyder and Donald Hall were two writers I reviewed among others. I also began reviewing novels for publications like *Western American Literature*. I was, of course, applying my critical academic skills, but instead of writing papers for conferences on American Culture and critical essays on academic themes, I was writing about current authors of creative literature. I also started reading my poems and stories at various venues in Seattle and on the Kitsap Peninsula. Finally my poems started appearing in local publications like *Exhibition, Paper Boat,* and *Poets West.*

A signal characteristic of my creative efforts was that they often concerned my roots. The stories I wrote were about my adolescent years in North Dakota. One of them was titled "The Hunt" and was about visiting my uncle's farm. While there I went deer hunting with him and two of my cousins. My uncle sat on an old sofa that occupied the front part of the truck's box. My cousins and I rode in the cab of the vehicle, and when we spotted a deer, my older cousin who drove, would stop the truck and lean out his open window and point his arm and hand in the direction of the deer. My uncle would stand and fire. He rarely missed, and we would have venison for dinner that evening after we had skinned and butchered the buck or doe. The same subject matter informed many of my poems. Many were about my ancestors, including both of my great-grandfathers and other members of extended families that I had learned about in my ancestry studies since 1987.

Even the creative nonfiction course I registered for in Montana brought me back to my ancestry. On the first morning of the conference I wrote my name on a sign-up form for a nonfiction workshop. It wasn't three minutes later that I heard a female voice ask of the gathering writers, "Who is David Hecker?" I turned and saw a young woman looking about the room. I walked towards her and said, "I am." She was trim, of medium height and had a short blonde hairstyle. Dressed in light-colored slacks and blouse, she identified herself as Therese Uri, a former Hecker in her single life from Kansas. She had married Larry Uri, an attorney, and she taught school in Kansas. Larry wasn't at the conference, but he also wrote fiction, and they had plans to publish their collected writings.

Therese wanted to know if we were related. My genealogical studies told me immediately that she had to be from the John Hecker branch of the family, one of the younger sons of my Great-Grandfather Martin Hecker's first family. I told her I had obtained this information from Adam Hecker of Salem, Oregon. She didn't know him, but for the rest of the conference, we told each other about our branches of the family. Over the next few years we visited on occasion in Seattle where she was working on a master's degree. The Kansas branch of the family would become an important part of my research later in my studies although at this time I thought I was finished with it.

I was more and more drawn to my imagination as I attended conferences and wrote fiction and poems, and it wasn't long before I thought about establishing a writers' conference at Olympic College, especially since none existed on the Olympic Peninsula. I involved Art Wicks, a colleague who was our only creative writing instructor. He agreed to join forces with me on the project if we produced a chapbook of student writing from enrollees at each annual conference. He accepted the task of publishing the chapbook if I did the organizing and coordinating of the conference. I concurred with the proviso that the leaders of sessions at the conference select the writings, poems and stories for publication in our chapbook. After some deliberation we named our chapbook *Signals*. I met and arranged with the Extension Division to supply the clerical support needed for promotion of the conference, met with the registrar who agreed to handle enrollment and room assignments, met with the financial administrator for contractual and accounting services, and finally with the cafeteria management for food service at the annual conference.

My last but most important job in getting this first writer's conference off the ground was to select a date for the conference and contract for a keynote speaker and writing workshop session leaders. I felt that I needed a prominent writer to accept the lead spot on the conference schedule. With that writer in position I could then expect others to flock in to fill the session leader roles. I immediately contacted William Stafford who had read his poems at Centrum in Port Townsend. I had also met him earlier at a Western Literature Association meeting in Portland, Oregon where he was a speaker. I offered him the keynote speaker role, and he not only accepted but agreed to lead a poetry workshop session as well. Since I knew many of the poets and fiction writers from the Pacific Northwest from my attendance at writing conferences and from reading of their works as preparation for the course I created on the Writers of the Pacific Northwest, I had a full component of other writers within two weeks. Thus in 1992 the first creative writing conference at Olympic College was staged on a Saturday in May.

Writers of all skill levels from Kitsap County and the surrounding areas of the Puget Sound responded avidly, and we had the first of five successful conferences. The appeal of the conferences was because of several things. First, since a former Poet Laureate of the United States had served as the first keynoter, it was easy to attract the next four lead speakers—Denise Levertov, Craig Lesley, Madeline DeFrees, and Marvin Bell. With leading writers like these at the top of the program, session slots filled rapidly. Since our college bookstore agreed to sell publications of the keynoters and session leaders, there was that added benefit for these participants as well. A distinct advantage for conference registrants was the potential they had to get published in *Signals*, and enrollees responded avidly to that feature of the conference, especially when they found out that the session leaders would select the pieces for publication.

– Chapter 27 –

Another direction that my lineage studies inspired was an intensi-
fication of my reading of German writers during this time. I read
Goethe's *Elective Affinities* and *Wilhelm Meisters Apprenticeship* as well as
Nicolas Boyle's biography *Goethe: The Poet and the Age.* Rilke's *Letter
to a Young Poet*, the *Duino Elegies* as well as his *Notebooks of Malte L.
Briggs* became late evening reading. Thomas Mann also caught my
attention, and I read *The Magic Mountain* and *Buddenbrooks.* I felt that
these varied literary activities that were consuming my time were
linked, and even though I wasn't sure how, I was delighted that my
creative side was emerging.

On the other hand the demands of full time teaching, my creative
writing efforts, advising and supporting our two children through
college, following and giving advice and support on their subsequent
lives, and coordinating the writers' conference, there were other additional responsibilities. My extended family needed attention as well,
and this took a lot of my time. My parents were in their dotage and
required care. Both parents had problems that required hospitaliza-
tion and surgery. My sister Pat moved them to an apartment complex and into a two-bedroom ground floor unit that had easy access
to parking. I then made arrangements to sell their home. There
were also final arrangements that had to be considered. I persuaded
them to agree to legal wills and living wills, to purchase burial plots,
and to contract for funeral services and coffins. I made all of the

arrangements for these items as they had made me executor of their wills. My dad's health gradually failed until there was no option but to admit him to a nursing home. Each of these family matters required either travel to Minot, North Dakota, or other arrangements by mail or telephone. I decided therefore that the fall quarter of 1996 would be my last term of teaching and coordinating. By doing so, I gave up a two-quarter sabbatical to travel to Poland as a visiting professor. I didn't want to leave Helen behind, and I was not sure what my status might become by being away that long without family. Helen decided she would teach her students to the end of the school year in the summer of 1997 when she would also retire. We would both have completed thirty-four years of teaching.

Even though I had made the decision to retire from academic life, I actually resisted it on one day and was all for it on the next. I enjoyed teaching and studying American culture, as well as my coordinating responsibilities, but I realized that I had accomplished as much as I could in both areas. Some of my colleagues suggested that I go into administrative work since our division had a director's position open. I thought about this since I was doing some of that type of supervision already, but I would have to oversee disciplines outside of my academic training, and I thought this undesirable. Had I taken that route I would never have written some of the works that became a part of my future. The direction I was taking in my roots study and creative writing would have ceased.

I was indeed ready to launch into a new life, and I finally recognized that writing and travel provided the change in my world that I so needed. I thought at the time that short stories and poems would be my main genres. Little did I know where my need to write would lead and how ancestry research would link into those writing endeavors.

– Chapter 28 –

The first two years of retirement 1997-1998 were devoted to carrying out plans for our future and travel. Helen and I thought at the time that we were on our way to becoming snowbirds. In addition to our family home of thirty years in Bremerton, we had a condo in Seattle's Belltown neighborhood and a two bedroom rental home in Tucson, Arizona, that we had purchased three years earlier, thinking that we would sell our home in Bremerton and then spend six months of each following year in Seattle and Tucson. A major happening altered this plan. Our daughter and son-in-law provided us with Coleman, our first grandchild, in February 1996. That meant we would spend most of our time in the Pacific Northwest except for periods of travel. Since we needed to accomplish transition between these changing goals, we decided to take our RV south for the winter of 1997-1998. We would arrange for the sale of our house in Tucson and fulfill a wish that we'd had for some time, to live in the sunshine for one winter instead of the drizzling rain in the Pacific Northwest. We both also looked forward to more intensive investigation of the Native American cultures of the Southwest; she for their arts and I for their overall cultural patterns. I had in fact included significant aspects of American Indian cultures of the Southwest in my American West course. These features of the class were gained by extensive research and travel to the States of Arizona and New Mexico.

On one of our earlier trips to the Southwest in 1981 to visit with relatives during the Christmas holidays, Helen and I and family had traveled to the territory of the Navaho Nation north of Flagstaff, Arizona. We drove through the Hopi Indian Reservation and visited at Second Mesa. We stopped at art galleries in that sparely populated high plateau country and marveled at their turquoise jewelry, pottery, and woven wool blankets. Helen especially enjoyed this visit and bought bracelets, earrings, and wool rugs as gifts for others and herself. The Navaho use of natural dyes and patterns of design typical of their native culture gave me the feeling of a genuine culture, not governed mainly by consumer production. Following these visits at galleries we drove north to Chinle, Arizona, and stopped at Canyon De Chelly National Monument where we were totally captivated by the stark beauty of the sheer canyon walls. Afterwards we stopped alongside the road and saw hogans in the twilight where lanterns shined from windows. That high plateau country held many of these dwellings that spread out sparsely over a large area. Viewed from the light of the setting sun, the scene looked like an enormous painter's canvass, beautiful and to be remembered forever.

Later during that holiday visit Helen and I drove to New Mexico. On one early morning drive west from Albuquerque to the ruins of the ancient Anasazi Indian culture at Chaco Canyon National Historic Park, we saw smoke rising from chimneys on a mesa just to the south of the highway. Deciding that this place had to be Acoma Pueblo, we detoured and stopped for a visit. We parked below the mesa and walked up the slope and found an open art shop, a surprise to us since it was only 7 a.m. We entered the shop and purchased some black and white pottery. As we were escorted out the door by the shopkeeper artisan, we noticed a gathering before what had to be a Spanish mission church. Indians were lining up for a procession. We asked our hostess what the assembly was for, and she answered that it was the annual blessing of the Pueblo. We asked if we could join, and she said it would be OK. We approached the procession as it was beginning to move towards the northwest corner of the Pueblo and joined the group at the end of the line. The column was lead by a middle aged stocky man, and he was followed by others from old to younger and finally to children. Behind them we walked, much to the delight of the children who peeked back at us and giggled.

The cortege proceeded to the first corner of the mesa, past adobe houses where a few of the very old stood in witness by their doorways. The procession soon stopped and a blanket was laid on the ground. Shredded pieces of corn were spread by hand on the blanket. Then the natives chanted in their native tongue. Helen and I glanced at each other in amazement. We were the only outsiders present for this ceremony. Our expressions changed quickly to startled looks when we heard high-powered rifle shots thundering from all around the periphery of the mesa. Men stood on all sides of the mesa and were firing at the desert below. I surmised that they were re-enacting the driving out of the Spanish in 1680. Before we could adjust to the sounds, the procession started moving again, towards the second corner.

We continued in our position at the back of the line. We weaved through some narrow streets separating adobe houses. As we rounded a corner, another burst of shots rang out. The procession came to a halt, but the shots continued. I looked up at the roof of a three-story structure, and there stood a young warrior. He was firing bullets from a pistol pointed directly skyward, but he was looking down at Helen and me. I whispered to Helen to stay put and keep looking at the man. We waited, but not for long. The broad-shouldered, squat headman came walking to the end of the procession. He glanced at the two of us, but didn't hesitate when he saw what we were looking at. He raised his arm and shook his glove-covered hand at the man on the roof, shouting in his native tongue. There was no doubt about what he was yelling. The young man lowered his revolver, climbed off the house and disappeared. The leader of the procession glanced again at us, but he didn't say anything as he walked by to the head of the line and started the procession once again.

I was struck by the significance of the encounter. We two white people had received a rebuke by a solitary young Indian man. He was probably re-enacting for himself a version of the driving out of the Spanish from Indian Territory and culture. I couldn't help but think about race and ethnic rivalries that had lead to many confrontations and battles over the years of the settling of the American West. There were still tensions, of course, as young Indians left their villages or reservations and moved to cities about the country. Past federal government treaties and reservations still caused rankling and legal suits. I knew all too well about alcoholism and unemployment on these reservations, but I also had witnessed their arts and treasures. Helen and I felt privileged to have been present at this ceremony. Fortunately the procession leader had nipped the disruption to the blessing of the village. He had also refrained from castigating us for our presence. I thanked him in my heart for his forbearance and solemnly swore to do my best to return the favor in my community and in my travels. At the end of the walk to the four corners of the mesa with pauses and chanting at each stop, the procession members filed into the mission church past the shaman who had stood over a smoldering fire, looking stoically to the west as formal witness, I'm sure, for the blessing.

A mesa hovers hundreds of feet above
the saguaro cacti on the desert floor.
On top dreamy Acoma Pueblo smokes
lore from mesquite fires in adobe stoves.
A shaman, smoldering embers like blood
at this feet, witnesses an ancient rite again,
the blessing of the town. Lines of the people pour
powdery corn on cloth and chant and chant.

To keep alive the sense of pueblo self—
of a place the ground the rock the winds of the range
and of those that came and lived and died before—
a procession of souls circles the holy soil
and men of age recall the Pueblo Revolt
by firing rifle bullets at ghosts below.

Helen and I walked back to our rental car and continued our drive to the Chaco Canyon ruins. After an hour we arrived there and marveled at the formation of the village in structures made of adobe and stone. We noticed round holes in the stone ceilings of the subterranean spaces below where ladders once protruded to allow men and boys of each clan to enter these sacred chambers. The remains of buildings faced the path of the sun to allow the warmth of that sacred planet to best heat the buildings. I recalled reading about these ruins and the complicated rituals of the Anasazi and wondered why stereotypes of savages clouded their history. In fact they had an integrated, meaningful culture.

Our next stop was Taos, New Mexico. We wanted to see the pueblos that were still occupied by natives, but also to see what had attracted Georgia O'Keeffe as well as D.H. Lawrence to this region. Helen told me it was the special light from the sun in the clear air of New Mexico that brought the painter. I knew that the writer came to be near an authentic culture. We arrived in the evening at Taos, and it was cold but there was no threat of snow or blizzard. In the bright renowned light that Ansel Adams had praised, we saw Taos Pueblo, occupied by native tribal families. I had seen photos of it and imagined seeing natives sitting on the rooftops of the east and west ends of the structures, aiding the sun god in moving across the sky from rising to setting. I also thought about Carl Jung's visit to Taos in about 1920. He came to the United States to deliver lectures at Clark University and had requested that the coordinator of the conference arrange for him to travel to Taos, specifically to meet a head shaman of the pueblo. At the time Jung conversed with the shaman via interpreters about the rituals of the native peoples, thus enlarging his philologist knowledge. He asked the shaman what he thought about the white Americans he had encountered. The shaman replied that Americans walked with their heads and chests thrust forward. He added that he thought that Americans thought with their heads rather than with their hearts as was true of the Pueblo people.

Helen and I also visited the house that Mabel Dodge had occupied. It was large enough to accommodate the many visitors she had over the years, Spanish in architecture, and situated on a spacious plot of land. I thought of her many artist guests, of her affair and marriage to Luhan, a Taos Indian man, and of the art she produced here. Yes, I thought, this place was truly inspirational. We left Taos the next day and drove towards Santa Fe and stopped nearby at San Ildefonson Pueblo to see the black pottery of Maria Martinez. Her son Popidai still lived in the pueblo, and we visited his gallery/studio where we were fortunate to be able to buy a piece of his work, a small round piece of black pottery similar to what his famous mother had produced. Again I was thankful for this opportunity to visit and acquire a small but precious part of this culture. We stayed the night at Santa Fe, enjoying this contemporary artist community, visiting its galleries and enjoying the southwest cuisine. Having used up our available time, we drove back to Tucson the next day, and after another day of visiting we said our goodbyes and left for home.

– Chapter 29 –

That earlier visit to Arizona and New Mexico had given us good reason to consider the Southwest as a potential second home for our senior years. Now in the fall of 1997 we were back in Arizona on our first year of retirement, but the arrival of our grandson made our future as snowbirds no longer possible. We did enjoy driving our RV from Washington to Arizona, stopping along the way at many of our national parks, including Zion, Bryce Canyon, Arches, Canyonlands, and the Grand Canyon. We also visited Monument Valley. We spent a full month at these places and enjoyed their beauty and remarked continuously on how fortunate we were to have these stark natural wonders in our country. We were particularly attracted to the stop at Monument Valley where we took a tour and visited a Native American village that included a stop at a hogan where the woman of the house gave us a demonstration of weaving wool from their sheep. She also showed us how to cart the wool and prepare it for natural dyes.

I used my free time in the evening to continue my reading in literature, favoring at this time Thomas Hardy and D. H. Lawrence. *Tess of the D'Urbervilles*, *The Return of the Native* and *Jude the Obscure* provided me with much needed instruction in how to organize materials and character into thematic line. D. H. Lawrence's *Sons and Lovers*, *Lady Chatterley's Lover*, and *The Plumed Serpent* were books that I read also for their skillful development of character and plot line. I also wanted to read *The Plumed Serpent* because it had been inspired by his visit to the Southwest and Mabel Dodge at Taos. We did enjoy our time in Arizona, first at Tucson in the fall of 1997 and later in the winter of 1998 in the Phoenix area. Seeing the sun almost daily was welcomed by both of us. We enjoyed hiking the desert trails, for they were a new experience to us who were used to alpine trails in the mountain ranges of Washington. Walking among tall cactus and seeing wild donkeys and roadrunners were all new visual images for us. We encountered only one rattlesnake in our many hikes and that was from a distance. We didn't even get to hear the rattle of its tail in warning to us intruders. We also didn't like the sandy trails and the inevitable dumping of small stones from our boots.

An incident during this time gave support to our decision to not live in Tucson on any permanent basis. We had our bicycles stolen from the back bumper of our motor home. The robbery also brought the ethnic rivalry issue that arose in my family history in Russia to life in contemporary America. We carried our bikes on this trip because we both enjoyed riding them for exercise and because one could see more from them than from our RV or car. Stopping and poking into parks, biking trails, side roads and small business districts was also easier on bikes. On our way down to Arizona we had enjoyed riding them in our national parks, especially at the Grand Canyon on our twelve-day stay there.

We had booked a three-month stay at a fashionable RV park in South Tucson. This place had all the features of an upscale facility with swimming pool, exercise room, hot tubs, and meeting rooms. It was secured by a corrugated wire fence around the periphery of the paved parking spots that included electric power and other utilities for the RV's. We liked the location because it had many paved roads that allowed for riding and visiting nearby shopping malls and parks. One day we encountered a foreshadowing of what was to come. We had peddled about two miles when we stopped at a hardware store. I was looking for a wrench to use on the bikes. I noticed as we parked and secured our bikes that the shop had iron grates on all exterior windows as well as the entrance door. After we entered, we saw, much to our surprise, that all merchandise was enclosed in glass counters that were locked. One had to get a clerk to open a counter if you wanted to look at an item. I couldn't find anything I wanted, so we left and rode back to our RV Park. On the way Helen remarked that all of the stores customers but us were Hispanic. I judged that we had ridden into the proverbial other side of town that I knew from my youth.

That evening we were in our pajamas, watching the late evening news and weather reports on television when I thought I heard a bump on the rear of the RV where we stored our bicycles on a rake with chain and lock. It was such a weak sound that I thought a bird had accidentally struck or landed on one of the bikes. I turned the sound on the TV down and listened, but I didn't hear anything. Since we were about to go to bed, I decided to put on slippers and check out our vehicle, car, and bicycles. To my amazement our bikes were gone. The sound that I heard must have been the cutting of the chain. I looked around the area and down the roads separating the RV's, but saw nothing. There were no sounds or sights of any movement. Since it was late and there were no night guards on duty, I decided to wait until the morning to report the theft.

The first thing the next day I went to the security station of the facility and reported the robbery. A guard accompanied me to our RV, and he invited me to walk the fence with him around the perimeter of the park. Quite a distance away and near the far end of the area, we saw that the fence had been cut from the ground up to about six feet. This was the exit for the thief. The guard said to me, "I'm glad you didn't go after the robber when you found your bikes missing. Sometimes they carry guns." He then gave me the address of the police station to report the robbery. He told me that a neighboring mobile home park was on the other side of the fence. He added that the culprit was likely an illegal immigrant from Mexico who was working for a Coyote, a person who escorts illegal aliens into the country. The bicycles were probably part of his payment for his passage into the United States.

Helen and I drove our car through the mobile home park next door and saw no trace of our bikes. We then went to the police station and filled out forms. The police told us essentially the same story that we had heard from the RV park security guard that an illegal alien had probably stolen the bikes. There were frequent reports of such thefts of bikes, golf clubs, and other valuable items from neighborhoods in the area. The policeman who took our information also said that it was unlikely that any investigation would be made since there were other more serious crimes such as assault and battery, major theft and even murder that occupied their limited investigative personnel. He added that contacting our insurance company and giving them the theft report and report number was our best bet.

I found out through conversation with other visitors to Tucson and from relatives that Tucson was a gathering point for illegal aliens from Mexico. Their status didn't stop Tucson business people and homeowners from hiring them to do menial jobs, especially outdoor work in the summer heat, such as gardening and yard maintenance. Many other white people told me also that Hispanics were the problem. I thought that Coyotes were the real problem, and I couldn't understand how one could leap to such a generalization about Hispanics in the Tucson area. Most of them were legal residents with jobs and families. I didn't condone the theft, but I was aware of the problem of unemployment in Mexico. I actually felt sorry for the thief and his apparent poverty. I certainly wasn't going to jump to any conclusions about an ethnic group in general.

John Steinbeck's *Grapes of Wrath* and the Joad family came into my thoughts. They were fourth and fifth generation white Americans who were forced to move out of Oklahoma because of drought and subsequent loss of their farm. When they sought work in California, they were employed at cheap wages and encouraged to move on once the local harvest of fruit or vegetables was completed. If they didn't move on to the next harvest area farther north, police gave them a bad time with unwarranted searches, vagrancy charges, auto and driver license problems, and even false charges of theft. They weren't illegal aliens, but they were treated in the same fashion.

During our stay in Tucson we upgraded and sold our two-bedroom home and then moved our RV to the Phoenix area where we had friends living in a complex that had double wides, Arizona rooms and RV parking. The place had swimming pools, hot tub shelters, golf course, exercise facilities and gathering places for residents. Helen and I joined groups that did hiking in the surrounding mountains.

We did day hikes normally and again enjoyed the sunshine and desert flora and fauna. We occasionally saw roadrunners and other smaller wild animals. On one hike up a mountainside, we reached a viewpoint where we could see Phoenix. I thought about the Hohokam, an ancient Indian tribe that had preceded the American Westward Movement. I also pondered over the modern urban sprawl that lay before us in the distance. I remembered how the Hohokams had built water aqueducts to their villages from mountain streams and how they had established trading routes to other parts of the Far West. In some ways it was a minor Silk Road. I also recalled how they had abandoned their villages because of drought. They moved east as far as the Mississippi River Valley. While looking at the vast numbers of homes and shopping malls that spread out from Phoenix to other cities in the vicinity, I wondered about the aquifer water levels and the capacity of local rivers to feed this modern snowbird paradise.

— DESERT —

A solitary tarantula
scurries off the trail to security
behind a large stone.
Saguaro cacti guard the arroyo,
balance precariously on steep slopes.
Coyote cubs scramble from a den,
yelp at mother's return.
A burro brays, protecting two companions,
asserts his claim against intruders.

Reaching the summit, I look across
at a city of two million people
that arose on the ruins of the Hohokam.
Many of the newcomers are retirees,
waiting for rivers to dry and aquifers to empty.

Later driving north over a mountain pass
I descend a winding road to the Colorado River.
On the opposite bank an oasis
of casinos lines the river.
Crossing a bridge, I park
in acres of autos and buses.

Entering the nearest casino,
I join the congregation,
walking among altars of the temple.
Worshippers address themselves to the
rush of tumblers and silver.

I feel the sting of these services
like mistletoe on a paloverde tree.

— Chapter 30 —

We worked hard on getting as much as possible out of the Phoenix area, for it was not likely that we would be back except for visits with friends and relatives. We purchased new bicycles with insurance money proceeds. Thanks to an insurance provision of comparable current value, we were able to get lighter, better bikes with more features. We took long rides and breathed in the air and views of the desert. We saw many Hispanics working in cotton fields and other agricultural capacities. We hadn't encountered any of them as residents, nor did we see them at other retirement communities that we visited. However, they did landscaping and gardening work at these places. We were warned about potential theft at night and the need to keep vehicles locked and nothing of value stored outside. When we drove into Phoenix, through the Los Angeles like sprawl of the metropolitan area, we saw enclaves of tiny homes and old cars and pickups where these workers and families lived. We didn't witness any confrontations between ethnic groups, but a boundary was evident although Hispanics shopped in most of the local grocery stores and shopping malls. They brought to my mind my own ancestors who traveled to Odessa by train to get medical care and do some shopping. It was likely that they stood out since they spoke German and dressed in heavy clothing of their own making. The same was true when they went into neighboring Russian towns by horse and wagon to sell goods or get supplies. They were then recognized as a separate group, and as the world wars neared, they were regarded with suspicion since the local Russians thought they might be spies for the Kaiser or Chancellor of Germany.

Our next adventure in the Southwest was to travel with our motor home in a caravan of RVs into Mexico. My sister and brother-in-law and their friends did an annual trip down to Puerto Penasco in the Gulf of California. This small town and resort area was across the water from the northern part of Baja California. Its attractions were good parking for vehicles, excellent prices, good food and saltwater fishing. Since the rest of the group drove from Tucson west towards Phoenix, we met them at a casino near Chandler, Arizona. From there we drove about a hundred miles to the location of our visit. RV spots had been reserved, and we were near the water and close to an excellent restaurant. Days were spent on the beach absorbing the sun and flying kites. Afternoons and evenings were spent at happy hour and evening meals at the restaurant. American tourists were the primary diners, and we didn't see much of the locals except for waiters and bartenders. We did take in a Sunday mass at my sister's insistence although I hadn't been in a Catholic church for many years. There we did meet the locals, for the church was filled with Mexican families. We were the curiosity, and we were accepted without reservation. I didn't engage in any discussion about Hispanics on this stay in Mexico, but I sensed that there were concerns about security among our group. Some of them did talk about their excursions into Mexico for dental work and to buy prescription drugs that were far more reasonable than in Arizona. Overall it was a good visit, and it was near the culmination of our stay in the Southwest, so I let politics rest for the time being, especially on our return drive into the United States.

When the end of March 2008 approached and our RV rental space contract was nearing its end, we packed our belongings, said our good-byes, and traveled west into Southern California, stopping near Palm Springs, California. We wanted to scout out the area for future month long visits when we needed to get out of the rain in the Puget Sound. After several days we moved our RV to a park on the north side of Los Angeles near to where our relative lived. We spent the next several days visiting with her and around the area. She had a particular interest in movie stars, especially dead ones of considerable fame, so we went to cemeteries to see the gravesites of Marilyn Monroe and Dean Martin. She filled a bedroom in her home with memorabilia of Shirley Temple, one of her favorite stars. We visited the new Getty Art Museum on the hillside above Santa Monica, the new Symphony Hall in downtown L.A., and the Norton Simon Art Museum in Pasadena. Our relative had graduated from UCLA and had lived in the area for most of her adult life. Although we shared many interests with her, especially European travels and art museums, I was troubled by her attitudes towards minorities, especially Hispanics and Black Americans. I didn't quarrel with her about it for she was elderly, and I had to admit to myself that I didn't hear or read daily about the crimes that were committed by some members of these ethnic groups. I was sure, however, that the majority of them were just as law abiding and upstanding as most white Americans. Once again stereotyping was the villain.

We left the Los Angeles Metropolitan area and moved our RV and attached car up I.5. towards Seattle. We made several stops on the way north at Napa Valley and in northern California to visit other relatives, but we arrived back home in Bremerton safely after a week of freeway travel among the eighteen-wheelers and heavy automobile traffic. We had no mishaps on our seven month and five thousand miles of driving in both the western part of the United States and in Mexico. We hadn't received any tickets, suffered any accidents, or the need for repairs of any of our vehicles. The only exception was the theft of our bicycles in Tucson. Although the incidents and observations of near segregation of minorities was a negative, we did experience a great beginning for our retirement lives and now looked forward to the rest of it.

Chapter 31

The truth was that traveling had now asserted itself well into our futures. We were well traveled in the United States, Canada, and to some extent in Mexico, and we had made two trips to Europe prior to this time. Both were lengthy sojourns of two months in the first instance and six weeks in the second, covering France, Italy, Austria, and Germany in the first case and Germany, Iceland, the Netherlands, Belgium, and France in the second instance. After the summer in Bremerton and Seattle at our two homes and a lot of visiting with our children and grandchild, Helen and I left for Spain in late September of 1998. Although I had always enjoyed the people of these countries and tried to stay in B&B's, local hotels and away from American establishments so that we would come more in contact with the languages and people of these countries, I was now even more conscious of the importance of making contact with as many of them as possible. I wanted to make my own judgments about them and to witness in particular their treatment of us. Quite frankly I wanted to become more of a citizen of the world since both Helen and I had ancestors who had lived in several countries. I also wanted to behave in a respectful way to people of other ethnic backgrounds, hoping that I would be treated likewise by them. There was too much turmoil and destruction in the past that was caused by misunderstandings, and I wanted to become an advocate of better relationships.

In preparation for this month long journey in Spain and Portugal, I read a history of the Iberian Peninsula and some of the writings of two writers, Federico Garcia Lorca and Jose Saramago. I read Lorca's selected poems and pondered his violent death at the hands of Francisco Franco's military. I was determined to reserve some time for homage to him at Granada. I also read Saramago's *The Death of Ricardo Reis* and *Blindness* and intended to spend some time in the Algarve region of Portugal. The reading of the history and selected literature told me that I was going into a section of Europe that had a history of ethnic and religious conflict equal to that of my ancestors in Russia and the Soviet Union. The Moors had conquered Spain and controlled it for several centuries, but eventually the Moors were driven out of the Iberian Peninsula and both events had their impact on Spain and its varied peoples. Religion was at the basis of the conflict, and Jewish people as well as Muslims were either driven out of the country or were forced to convert to Christianity. Much violence accompanied these overturns. It seemed that I wasn't able to travel at all without running into upheaval somewhat similar to what I had learned caused immense suffering for my own ancestry.

We arrived in Madrid and enjoyed nearly a week there with side visits to Toledo and Segovia. We visited the major art museums and the presidential palace of Madrid and spent time at tapa cafes and enjoyed just walking the streets of this capitol city. On one late evening, as we were walking on a crowded street in a construction area where the walking quarters were tight, I felt someone bump into me, but thought nothing of it because of the crowded conditions. Helen, who was walking several paces behind me, said later that she saw a man reach towards my back pocket when another man bumped into me. Since I didn't carry a wallet in my back pocket on excursions in foreign cities especially at night, Helen, who knew my habits, didn't respond until they were gone. I hadn't felt the touch, so I congratulated myself on my good judgment of carrying most of my valuables in a concealed waist wallet. I did carry small bills and one credit card in a front pocket wallet. Our side trip to Toledo was by train. On that rail journey we met an English woman who was traveling alone.

She told us that on the previous day, she had been sunning herself in a Madrid Park when she was attacked and robbed. She was in anguish yet because it was in the middle of the day, and she screamed, but no one of many people who were at the park came to her assistance. We commiserated with her, and she stayed with us throughout the Toledo visit with no adverse happenings. The side trip to Segovia was by bus, and we had a fine time walking the streets and visiting a castle. We discovered a restaurant that had a specialty of suckling pig, so we decided to return on another day to enjoy dinner and a stay at a hotel.

After we picked up a rental car in Madrid, we drove to Segovia and found a hotel and did the dinner we had promised ourselves. It was well worth the second visit and time. We then drove south for a weekend of rest on the beaches at Salema, Portugal. We found the beach and hotel at Salema just what was needed at this point in our journey. The local restaurants served fresh seafood that we saw brought onto the shore by local fishermen daily. Locally grown vegetables were also delivered and sold daily at stands near the beach. These foods along with wine from local vintners made our stay restful and full of Portuguese character. Strangely enough Spanish servers at several restaurant stops on our journey south had told us that it was dangerous to go into Portugal. I surmised later, after the experience we had at Salema, that these advisories were just a way to keep tourist money in Spain and not in Portugal.

Back in Spain we stopped at a hotel in Seville. Our stay included visits to a bull fighting ring, walks in parks and visits to castles and cathedrals, but the primary pleasure was an evening at Los Gios, a nightclub in the old Jewish quarter that featured a flamenco show of huge attraction. In fact the two-hour show went by so quickly that I felt cheated. The guitar music, dancers, clapping of castanets and the singing were so unusual and absorbing that it has led to a lifetime enthusiasm for me. When Paco de Luca, a musician from Andalusia came to Tacoma, Washington, several years later, I booked tickets for Helen and me months in advance. It was worth it. I also became a follower of John Williams, an Australian guitar player, who has specialized in recording Spanish guitar music.

Our two week car rental was due to end by the time we would reach Granada, so we went on our way and stopped for overnights at Tarifa, Gibraltar, and Nerja. All of these stops were pleasurable, and we were delighted with our reception by all Spanish people that we met on the streets, in the restaurants, at museums, and at local hotels. We dropped our car when we arrived in Granada because of the heavy traffic and took a cab to our hotel. We were located just at the base of the hill that was topped by the Alhambra. We were close to a major shopping market and cathedral and just a short walk to the museum home of Lorca, the poet. Our four days here were filled with wondrous happenings. One of the best was a visit to the Alhambra. The former mosque was magnificent, and we were grateful that the Spanish had left it standing. It was not only attractive to us, but the renowned American poet Washington Irving had written a classic poem about it.

On our way back to our hotel in the late afternoon, we stopped at several luthier shops on the street leading down to our hotel. I was delighted to see such craftsmanship in the guitars that hung on the walls. I was invited to take any of them down for a look, but I didn't want to embarrass myself with some feeble attempt at strumming on such an instrument. I did promise myself that I would take lessons in the future and buy a hand made guitar from Spain. Another visitor at the second shop we entered did take a guitar down and played a long tune with precision, finger picking instead of strumming. I loved the tone of the instrument and the skillful playing of the chords and riffs of the tune. A woman walked into the store and started singing, and the proprietor of the shop started clapping. It was a remarkable ending to our day.

We visited the cathedral the next day and had an encounter with some women who were giving out free single flowers. They were using the flowers to conceal their groping hands. We also watched three men crossing through the market: one had a mastiff on lease, another did an erratic, odd dance as he walked by, and the third rushed intently with a bag full of bottles of wine. Our visit to Lorca's former home, now a public museum, was next. The house was surrounded by flower gardens of considerable size, and the collection of Lorca memorabilia inside made the stop unforgettable. At least now he was appreciated.

While in Andalusia, stop at Granada and visit the Alhambra—
its gardens and pools triggered Washington Irving's imagination.
Stroll through Lorca's Memorial Garden, a tribute to dance, deep song and
bullfighting.
Row upon row of flowering shrubs circle his home,
remind you to lay bouquets in the Granada hills where Franco's Army buried him.
Climb to the Albaicin quarter, near some gypsy caves, and lunch on *media barca*.
Enter a luthier's shop below on a hillside street and view acoustic guitars.
Be patient and stay, even if you must decline the offer
to try out one of these rosewood and spruce sculptures,
for at any moment a guitarist will walk in and pull one off the wall.
He will likely begin by running through scales, chords, and arpeggios,
listening intently for just the right tone and maybe a false string vibration.
When he begins to play, say a tune by Albeniz, maybe "Zambra Granadina,"
a woman, whom you hadn't seen, raises her arms and claps a set of castanets.
Slowly, as if rehearsed, she swivels her body and clicks her heels
in rhythmic counterpoint to the visceral bass notes of the guitar
and the luthier's staccato clapping and high-pitched singing.
Before long the three will take you to that place
Of mystery and spirit, a place called *duende*.

We flew to Barcelona the next day and for several days enjoyed the art galleries of Miro and Picasso and saw other works by artists such as Dali at other local art museums. We delighted in the Gaudi designed cathedral that was being built and would not be finished even during our life times. Walking *La Rambla* and other streets and squares of the city occupied much of our time. We were delighted to find out that many of the Spanish people on the streets were on holiday. It was October, apparently a national time for vacations. Again tapas were our favorite foods. We took bus tours to get a full view of the overall city. On Sunday morning we were out looking for a place for brunch when we happened into a side street that lead down to a square. We walked towards it to see if the square had a nice restaurant. As we approached the square, several people were standing in the middle of the narrow passageway. It was obvious that they were intoxicated, so we moved slowly by them and could see that there was nothing open in the square ahead, so we turned and started back out the way we had come. Two men seemed intent on blocking our way, but a Spanish woman started berating them for their bad behavior. She was making such a fuss that both men began arguing with her. We walked on by them before the men realized that we were gone. It was obvious that the women had prevented an altercation.

We left for London and the United States the next afternoon, and we had experienced a fulfilling month of travel, but it did not totally relieve my mind of the conflicts that result from differences in nationality, ethnicity, and religion. Why, I thought, do these troubles continue when Helen and I always felt welcomed and received thoughtful consideration by all but a few people that we had met in our travels? We have always rejoiced in the arts, crafts and common lives of the people of the countries we've visited. Is it ethnicity, religion, and nationality that continue to hamper peace or is it the perceptions that people have of these concepts or the demonizing of outsiders by cunning rulers?

– Chapter 32 –

After returning home, we settled into family life again. We cared for our grandson on two days of each week with a one night's stay over. We continued to entertain our family at birthdays and holidays, taking all of them out for occasional dinners. Upgrading our Bremerton home also kept us busy, for we weren't sure at all that it was going to be our last permanent residence. We took advantage of Seattle's varied cultural life and attended classical guitar and symphony performances at Benaroya Hall and art exhibits at SAM and Frye Art Museum. Meany Hall at the University of Washington offered dance, chamber music, and solo performances by musicians on various instruments. The Seattle Public Library, Town Hall, The Elliott Book Company and various other literary venues provided us with readings by local and national writers. I wrote poems during this time and read them at Seattle bookstores and once at Seattle's Frye Art Museum. I published a few poems, but mostly I received rejection notices.

We entered this active period of our lives in 1999 when a circumstance interfered with this pleasant situation. I was carefully following newspaper and television reports on the actions of the Immigration Naturalization Service in Seattle. The central headquarters of the INS was on the south side of the International District. As I read the accounts of the crowded conditions at the facility, and the difficulties immigrants were having in getting registered for naturalization, in getting appointments with INS officials, and in combating notices of deportation, I would occasionally stroll to the INS building to witness the lines of immigrants in queues from the front door of the facility to the sidewalks and down the street for several blocks. I had read in some accounts that these people didn't have appointments but were waiting in line to obtain appointments. Sometimes the lines moved at a reasonable pace, but at other times they were horribly slow. If you didn't reach the appointment office by closing time, you would have to reappear the next day and get back in line. It was a first come first serve arrangement, so an immigrant might repeat this process for days without getting an appointment. Since many of these people had jobs, this process almost guaranteed that some couldn't fulfill their responsibility to register. Failure to do so meant deportation. For some of them returning to their home countries meant prison terms or worse. As I watched this procedure, sometimes in the rain and sometimes in bitter cold, I couldn't help but think of what Magdalena and family had experienced in the Soviet Union. I realized that I was witnessing injustices to immigrants, especially those with minority racial and ethnic backgrounds.

As I continued to follow the reports in the newspapers and sometimes in television news programs, I learned that the INS had detention centers for immigrants who were out of compliance with their visas, who were waiting for trials about their possible deportation, or were being held as illegal entrants into the country. These detention centers were full and had serious problems in housing and food service. Some of the incarcerated were in limbo. The INS courts had ruled to deport these individuals, but their home countries refused to accept them, and so they were held indefinitely. Some of these inmates were from Vietnam, Laos, and Cambodia while others were from Nicaragua or Columbia, but many were from Mexico. A few others were from the Middle East.

Some of these inmates had established families and had wives and children living in the area. A few owned small businesses. Others had worked in restaurants, auto shops, retail businesses, or in the fruit orchards of Yakima and Wenatchee. Without the breadwinners to pay the rent and buy groceries, these families were in jeopardy and faced eviction notices from their landlords. There was sympathy for these wives and children, especially since they were allowed only a two-hour visitation to see their husbands and fathers. If they happened to live in Port Angeles or the Tri-Cities on the east side of the Cascade Mountain Range, they had to drive for a couple of hours and maybe take a ferry to get to a 1 to 3 P.M. visiting period. They would then have to make the return home later in the day, incurring expenses they couldn't afford.

As I dug deeper into the problems of these immigrants, I felt strongly that there were violations of human rights against the inmates at the detention centers. I decided to attend INS hearings in their courtrooms. Some of these hearings were held in a building on Third Avenue in downtown Seattle, so I went to see for myself what kind of justice was being done. I entered the building, checked in at a registry, and took the elevator up to the twelfth floor. INS hearing courts were open to the public, but trials on deportation or other offenses to the code were not. I entered the office labeled INS Hearing Courts. An armed guard flashed a metal detector over my arms and legs and then nodded his head allowing me to enter the courtroom. I glanced behind him and noticed that the place was well prepared for any aggressive behavior since tiny offices on a back wall had bulletproof glass and very small openings for speaking to secretaries. I entered the courtroom and saw twenty or so people in the front rows of chairs. I sat down in the last row and took out a notebook I had in my jacket pocket. I listened carefully to what was being said by these people although much of it was in Asian and Spanish languages. In one case a person seated in the second row asked a lawyer if he had time to represent another client. The lawyer who was seated in the first row said yes and mentioned a fee.

The judge entered the courtroom and sat down behind a large desk that set on a platform, giving him full view of the occupants of the room. He switched on various electronic devices that included a microphone. After opening a folder and spreading out papers, he announced the first hearing of the day. He read the name of the petitioner and asked the person to identify himself and to take a chair at the table in the front of the room. He then asked if counsel was present and if a translator was needed. Two other people, the translator and lawyer, moved forward and took chairs on either side of the petitioner. Satisfied that all were identified properly, the judge explained the case before the bench. In this case the petitioner was a Mexican fisherman who captained a fishing vessel that operated out of various west coast American cities. This man was up for deportation because he had failed to report periodically to INS officials concerning his whereabouts and the location of his family members, a wife and three children. He possessed a green card for working legally in the United States. The judge asked the petitioner why he hadn't met his reporting obligations. The fisherman answered the question in Spanish, and the translator reported that the captain had fishing routes that were specified by the owners of the vessel that sometimes kept him at sea longer than he had anticipated. The owners of the boat didn't allow captains to make long journeys to port until they had caught their quota of fish; thus he couldn't meet his INS appointments without jeopardizing his job. The judge asked the clerk of the court if there were any other infractions by the petitioner. She said no. The judge than ordered a deportation hearing in three weeks time in his courtroom. The attorney for the captain asked if his client couldn't just be given a warning to appear on time for future INS reports, for he lived in California when in port, and it was difficult for him to make trips to Seattle. The judge said no and adjourned the case to the hearing as scheduled.

The petitioner looked worried as the translator informed him of the judge's decision. Several people who sat behind the petitioner shook their heads and uttered "no's". But before any further remarks the judge read out the number of the next case and asked the petitioner and counsel to identify themselves. The judge then proceeded to read the charge against this petitioner. The person was a student who had attended the University of Washington on a student visa. He was from Jordan and was now out of compliance with the conditions of his visa. He was working and no longer attended classes at the university. The judge asked counsel if the charges were accurate. The counsel answered in the affirmative, but said there were reasons why the student was employed rather than in college. The judge told the counsel to gather supporting evidence for his client and then announced a deportation hearing in one month's time. The judge asked if the date for the hearing was acceptable. No objections were offered, so he adjourned the hearing until the deportation trial.

I sat through several other hearings that were not quite as abrupt as the first two were. Another student was in violation of his student visa and became alarmed at the announcement of a deportation trial, claiming that he would be jailed if was returned to his home country of Nicaragua. He further argued that his life would be in jeopardy. The judge asked the petitioner and counsel if they could verify these claims. The petitioner offered to bring his brother, also in the United States on a student visa, to the deportation hearing to give testimony on his behalf. The judge replied that the witness would be admissible, but to bring documentation regarding the danger to his life. Another student in violation was given a stern warning by the judge and was allowed to leave without any further hearings. I wrote in my notebook that the judge was very matter-of-fact in his judgments and didn't appear to show any sympathy or even clear interest in the petitioners before his bench. I thought that maybe the judge's docket was crammed with cases and might justify his cold demeanor.

The next day I returned to the courtroom and after about fifteen minutes of the first hearing, I was approached by a guard and asked to accompany him out of the courtroom. After we arrived in the outer room, he asked me to follow him to the INS Hearing Administrator's office. I asked him if there was a problem. He only replied that the administrator wanted to talk to me about my note taking. I followed the guard into the hallway where we approached a very sturdy metal door. The guard flashed his badge over a sensor, and a voice came from a speaker. I looked up and saw the speaker as well as a camera that were pointed at us. The voice asked about the purpose of the request for admission. The guard answered that he was escorting a visitor from courtroom number 3 to the administrator's office at the request of the administrator. The door's lock clicked, and the guard opened the door telling me to knock on the second door on the right side of the hallway.

After I was admitted inside the office, a Mr. Smith introduced himself and asked for my identity and purpose in taking notes in courtroom number 3. I told him I was a retired professor and that I was interested in the immigration issue that was getting so much coverage in the local newspapers. He asked me if I was working for any newspaper or political group. I said no, but that I had lectured on American history and culture for the last twenty-five years of my career. He seemed very relieved and went to a nearby bookshelf and pulled out an INS hearing manual that he gave to me. He said the work would explain the procedures and purposes of the courts under his jurisdiction. He said also that the judges in these courtrooms were hard pressed to deal with the number of cases on their dockets. He supplied more answers about the courts in response to my questions. I didn't mention the detention centers since they were not under his supervision. At the end of our meeting he welcomed me back for future hearings.

I did just that. In the next weeks I attended more hearings in the same courtroom although there were three others on the same floor of the building. I continued being concerned about the judge's attitude. He had a sort of Clark Gable look to him with dark hair, dapper shirt and tie, and mustache. He did occasionally grant warnings rather than further hearings, but generally he was short in his comments and moved quickly to deportation hearing date decisions. I continued to follow the newspaper coverage of the INS actions in arrests, deportations, or problems at detention centers. I also joined the Northwest Immigrant Rights Project, an organization located in Seattle that offered legal aid to immigrants, support for families of the detained, and developed support for changes in federal legislation affecting immigrants. Finally I joined the ACLU, for they also had a few attorneys assigned to assist immigrants with their legal problems.

Later in the year I researched more on Seattle's INS. I found out that they were responsible for processing thousands of applications per year for naturalization and that generally they approved the majority of them. They also had to rule on government benefit applications from immigrants and found again that most were eligible. The INS was also responsible for inspecting passengers, vehicles, and aircraft entering the State of Washington at two airports, six seaports, and fourteen land border crossings. They had substantial duties and the evidence at the time was that they were doing these jobs fairly well. Of course they were watched carefully by immigration rights groups and the ACLU.

The detention centers, on the other hand, were overcrowded and kept more and more detainees in jail indefinitely. A Seattle federal prosecutor helped many of them file habeas corpus petitions. Because of this action many were released back into society. Federal courts also released detainees who had petitioned them for freedom. The 9th US Circuit Court of Appeals affirmed the decisions of lower courts. The ACLU increased their commitment by forming an Immigrants Rights Project, putting their resources into various actions in favor of immigrants and INS detainees. At the time resolving injustices to immigrants looked promising, so I left the issue as it was, but in the back of my mind I still had suppressed feelings about my own extended family members who had suffered forced migration, broken promises, and imprisonment in mining and forest camps in the Gulag, largely because of their ethnic and religious backgrounds. I felt an obligation to do what I could to stop such injustices from happening again in my time and country.

At the same time I was actually somewhat disturbed with myself for these continuing preoccupations with immigrant and human rights issues. Why couldn't I just forget them and settle into retirement and smell the roses. Why did I always need a goal or a mission? Why had my life been filled with obligations and accomplishments? I even wondered if a quote in The New Yorker magazine article ("True North" Feb. 18-Feb. 25, 2002) might apply to me. In it a North Dakota businessman said in reference to himself and other North Dakotans, "We have this deep-seated Scandinavian, Teutonic outlook—a combination of dark Lutheranism and German Catholicism, which adds to a primal sense that somehow we're not worthy." Or was this feeling just another detour on the road that I was meant to travel?

During the middle of the year when I was still investigating the INS I was drawn back to family, but in this case it wasn't back to my lineage study. My mother had a stroke and was admitted to intensive care at a hospital in Minot. She was eighty-four years old and pretty much homebound because of two hip replacements. Upon request I gave permission to her doctor and hospital staff to do interior studies of her condition, and just a day later, she had a heart attack and another stroke. Her condition was very serious, so all five of us children—now middle-aged adults—went to Minot to be with her. After she was about a week in a coma, our family decided to instruct the hospital staff to pull all life preserving methods from our mother since her brain was completely black. She died after about a day. Since most arrangements for her funeral services and burial had been made, I only had to prepare an obituary that I sent immediately to the local and several state newspapers where relatives lived. I also wrote a eulogy for her funeral services. My sisters made telephone calls to relatives, especially those in state, announcing the day of her services at the funeral home.

One thing that I hadn't done was to arrange for a Lutheran or Catholic service; I did call a local priest to be present at the funeral home ceremony. Surprisingly none of my siblings said anything about what services we should have. Apparently they assumed that I had arranged a religious program. I had not deliberately eliminated this consideration, but I wasn't able to get my mother to tell me what she wanted at her death when we discussed all of the other issues of death and burial years earlier. I would have arranged for whatever she wanted, but when left on my own I guess I thought to do what I would want for myself. To make matters worse mother's stroke and heart attack came unexpectedly. I was in for a lot of grief. Many of my mother's Lutheran relatives arrived at the funeral home chapel, for most of them lived about ninety miles away. My dad was wheeled into the chapel and placed near the front in the middle aisle by his nursing home attendant. He had dementia, so he didn't seem alert to the situation, and he remained silent.

I gave the eulogy, extolling my mothers many virtues, especially her role as parent. I alluded to my hope that she was witnessing this ceremony. I think some of my siblings were aware of my agnostic stance towards religion, but many of the relatives didn't, but they were soon to find out at least some of the truth. The priest spoke and apparently said that I had not requested a religious ceremony. I say apparently since I was in no condition after my heart felt eulogy to hear anything clearly. The lack of attention to me by relatives at the end of the ceremony, the burial at the cemetery, and later at a reception we had arranged at the social room of my mother's former apartment complex made it clear that I had stepped over a line. In some cases relatives from my mother's side did not even show up at the reception, but their icy stares as they left the funeral chapel told me that in their minds I had made an unforgivable error. Yes, I had broken a family tradition, one that Heckers and Petersons had followed for hundreds of years. In my view any creator who would not receive my mother on her own saintly merits was unworthy of any devotion.

PART III

WRITINGS ABOUT THE JOURNEY

2000-2011

_____

— Chapter 33 —

Life went on for Helen and me in our normal routines. Helen was the primary caregiver for our two grandchildren on two days of the week after Michelle, our daughter, birthed Katelin in September of 2000. When Helen wasn't actively involved with family or luncheons with former teacher friends, she worked on her artistic palette, our yard. She had our handyman, a hedge trimmer primarily, do bonsai on our many tams around our circular drive. Once she learned the technique, she trimmed them thereafter. We had eliminated grass from our front yard and replaced it with rhododendrons and azaleas. Helen cared for and trimmed these plants also. The result of her efforts was so picturesque that people would stop and praise the beautiful landscape she had created. In our backyard we had a garden, primarily of lettuce, tomatoes, cucumbers, string beans, zucchini and spinach. We also planted strawberries and raspberries. Two rows of grapes, one red and one white, stood beside the garden next to our plum tree and across from our apple trees. Flowers—dahlias, geraniums, tulips, and daffodils—were scattered in groups throughout the garden area and in among the scrubs. All of these plants kept us busy, especially in the fall, but Helen was the chief gardener.

I was the repairman and builder. I had built a wraparound deck on the south and west sides of the house in the early 1970's, but the structure, designed by our son Jeff, was now weather beaten and needed repairs in many places. We decided to replace it. Our handy man and I tore down the old deck, and Shannon, our son-in-law, built a new one with treated lumber. During one-summer years earlier, I had roofed the house with medium butt cedar shakes. These were still good but required cleaning and stain every four years. This kind of work, along with cleaning roof gutters and wood chopping, kept me busy, and for both of us these yard, garden and house improvement activities were still satisfying. These tasks seemed to mirror what our ancestors had done in South Russia and North Dakota. Had we added a few chickens and goats we would have come close to self-sufficiency as they had been.

I also continued with my literary work, writing and reading my poems in venues in both Seattle and the Kitsap Peninsula, especially in Bremerton and Poulsbo. I continued to study the classics that I had collected but hadn't had time to read. One of them that I had read only in parts was the Old Testament. Since I recognized that religion was one of the universals of mankind, and a cause of contention among races and ethnic groups in my journey, I decided to give it a solid go. I bought a literary guide to the bible and also a new copy of the King James edition. I spent a couple of hours each evening reading the two texts side by side. I suspected that most people, regardless of how religious they claimed to be, hadn't read the entire Bible, and my experience reading it revealed why.

I launched into this reading with my own bias. I believed the bible was literature, and I wanted to know how it came into being and by what processes and writers. In my mind it was the creation of prophets, monks, rabbis, and other men of letters. To be sure Ibsen, Hardy, Schopenhauer, and Joseph Campbell influenced me in this attitude. Ibsen and Hardy were literary mentors during my student years in college and university. Later I taught plays and novels from both of them in my literature classes. The reading project was worthwhile, revealing many insights into religion in general and Christianity in particular. I recalled how land divisions made by Russia's government under Catherine the Great and Alexander I included a requirement that there not be any mixing of religious affiliations in any of the land grants. Lutherans, Catholics, Mennonites and Orthodox Russian Christians were kept apart to lessen problems.

These potential disturbances also mirrored in my mind the similar rivalries and territorial conflicts in the animal world.

My conclusions about the Bible and the human condition I found in my journal notes from the summer of 1999. From June to September I had read 1,216 pages and had written 16 pages of notes. The story of creation and then Noah and his Ark establish "the create and then destroy" patterns of the early Bible. There is much killing and violence, not only in the early bible, but there's even more in later sections and chapters of this book. Next, we have God give Moses the Ten Commandments, listing the infractions against a moral life. In Deuteronomy we get the punishments for these failures. Isaac and Rebecca, Samson and Delilah, Boaz and Ruth, and David and Bathsheba show relationships filled with violations of the Ten Commandments that mirror the human condition to the present. To compensate for giving up the pleasures of life and for shouldering the duties of life, there is the promise of a paradise in the afterlife beyond judgment day. These few comments are an oversimplification of the issues involved, especially for someone like myself who believes in spiritual life and ethical behavior. Having made that caveat, I will summarize the rest of my notes.

"The Old Testament is the story of the Hebrew people, attempting to survive in a chaotic world. It's about their search for ways to control human appetites and natural instincts that threaten human survival. The Ten Commandments are a list of the difficulties—parental control, sibling rivalries, theft, sex, etc.—that have to be overpowered. Religious rivalries fit into the same general category—whose father is better, whose king is better, whose race is better, whose moral code is better—and all developed from the first family of Eden that expanded to group and to nations until nationalism dominated and caused most of the calamities of the Twentieth Century. Can globalism fare better?"

I could add to this assessment my findings in Schopenhauer's *The World as Will and Representation*. His will is the universal law of the thing, the savage struggle for primacy and for procreation that leads to unrest. One might also see the will as a creative force to be used in the arts. His notion of representation complicates the problem even further, for the thing that each of us see individually is not equally there for all of us. We each see the reflection of the thing in our eyes that is then interpreted by our experience, memories, and ability to use words to name things; thus each of us has an individual conception of the thing. In other words we live in a world of appearances.

Perhaps what we need now is a further use of the human imagination to create another outside force to deal with these assaults on human harmony. If we desire to follow the old pattern and use fear and punishment, then we could create outer space creatures from another galaxy. This construction would be no different, however, than the creation from heaven as it is now. The Hebrews were the first mythmakers, but now we need something new to transcend their creation. It must be centered on unity of all mankind in this world not in another. We must celebrate this life, as does the voice in Wallace Stevens's poem, "Sunday Morning." Walter Pater advocates the same notion in his work *The Renaissance.* Beyond the witnessing of greatness in the arts, we should be participants, learning to play an instrument, drawing and painting our conceptions, writing out our thoughts in poems, stories, and plays, dancing whatever steps are within our reach, and reciting lines from our favorite, most captivating writers. These acquired skills and arts should then be carried into our work. Any design, whether it be for a house, condominium, or commercial building or bridge, or boat, or dress, or suit, or vehicle, or bullet train, or solar panel, or class in spelling, arithmetic, or physical therapy regimen, or film production, or vegetable garden and corn field, should carry the fruits of our ecstasy. Actual engagements such as these will help us transcend the bonds of excessive consumption and greed, giving nature and its resources a chance to survive our global condition.

To accomplish this alteration in wants, we must eliminate the inequalities we burden each other with in family, group, ethnic rivalries, and race. Nature provides humans with examples of variation in reproduction. Fathers and mothers come from different stocks, and each offspring carries genes from both, but dominant traits from one or the other give us different heights, body frames, eye and hair colors, weights, personalities, intellects and even feelings. Some of these characteristics come from earlier generations. Look at any family portrait from two or three generations ago or at your own generation, and this variation is striking. So why complain about or fear those from other backgrounds who are also different. It may be that we should exalt marriages from different ethnic backgrounds and races so that future families will possess all of these differences: colors of skin, eyes, hair; shape of heads and bodies; and variations in intellect and personality. We could then hopefully accept all of humanity as products of our own common heritage.

Until these fundamental changes are made, I must content myself with a few modest writings to help dispel these problems. Others of greater capacity and literary accomplishment have tried as well to get the general public to revise their conceptions of others. Mark Twain said in his travel book *Innocents Abroad* that "Travel is fatal to prejudice, bigotry, and narrow-mindedness. Broad, wholesome charitable views of men and women cannot be acquired by vegetating in one little corner of the earth all one's lifetime." John Steinbeck wrote *The Russian Journal* to deflect the cold war from emerging by showing the people of different parts of Russia as considerate, helpful, and honest. In our time Rick Steves, a travel guru from Edmonds, Washington advocates travel as a political act. He too experienced what Twain and Steinbeck felt. People are not vile and dangerous but fun loving and sympathetic. Political leaders who crave power use propaganda to drive people into xenophobia, fear and defensive violence.

– Chapter 34 –

For my part I decided to write a historical novel about a Seattle Immigration Naturalization Service hearing judge. In that work he evolved from being a "fences-up" judge to one who had sympathy for the immigrants who stood before his court. I had prepared myself earlier for this writing when I attended INS Hearings in Seattle. I had also read the local newspaper accounts of the many challenges facing these courts. I abandoned that earlier pursuit when personal interests intervened. More importantly the 9/11/2001 bombings in New York and Washington, D.C., changed the national climate back to hysteria and xenophobia.

But now I determined that I couldn't let what I had learned in my lineage studies and reading just fade away. My life's work in education demanded that I act. I had to do something, however little that might be, so I started my novel in early 2001 and continued until I had a rough draft of it in late 2001. There was a three quarter sequence course in fiction writing at the University of Washington in the evening extension program, so I registered, hoping to get some professional advice on my rather ambitious undertaking. I hoped eventually to publish a finished manuscript and thus make my contribution to alter the attitudes towards and treatment of immigrants in the United States by both citizens and government agencies. After submitting my rough draft in the 3-quarter course sequence and making revisions to it, it took me until early 2003 to get a finished manuscript entitled "Expiation."

At the beginning of the writing of "Expiation" I didn't have a full outline of the work. I did have a few specific guidelines. I gave my INS judge a German name—George Schwartz—and provided him with my family background. He would then have a mixed ethnic background of German and Scandinavian. By the time of the action of the novel he became involved with a woman of Scandinavian-American heritage, thus providing potential tension in the relationship. Just as I had been, George Schwartz was confronted in middle age with knowledge that his family had secrets. In other words he would find out what I discovered about my roots through my Uncle Adam of Salem, Oregon and Magdalena (Hecker) Reiswich of Hamburg, Germany. George would be confronted with the fact that the immigrants that came before his court were suffering the same problems and injustices that his own relatives had faced in South Russia and later in the Soviet Union. George would travel to Germany to meet distant relations in Munich and Hamburg and learn first hand about the immense injustices these families experienced and that only a few of them survived.

I chose to present George as a single man who had grown up in Mandan, North Dakota, attended college and law school at the University of North Dakota in Grand Forks, North Dakota, and joined the INS at Seattle after completion of his education. To fill in his history prior to the action of the novel, I provided him with relationships with women, including one INS prosecutor who appeared before his bench. Janice, a journalist and reporter for the *Seattle Post Intelligencer*, is his intended at the time of the major conflict in the novel. She had the INS courts in Seattle as her jurisdiction and brought her knowledge of these courts and their actions into her relationship with George. Her basic view was that the immigrants were not getting fair treatment and reasonable justice as a rule. Janice appreciated George's responsibilities, but nevertheless she argued for a more sympathetic viewpoint from him.

As a matter of strategy she took George to lunch in the International District where ethnic backgrounds of people were similar to the majority of those who appeared before his bench. The exception, as she pointed out to him repeatedly, were Japanese Americans who had been removed from the district after Pearl Harbor by the F.B.I. and other government officials. She also took George on visits to sections of Seattle where mosques, temples and synagogues existed. Since she herself had been raised in the mid-west and had experienced some ethnic and racial discord, she thought it important to have George mix with these individuals under normal social circumstances outside of the established rules and decorum of the courts. When George told her that he was aware that he had long lost relatives in Germany who had experienced severe treatment and suffering because of their ethnic backgrounds, she encouraged him to travel and meet them, hoping that these encounters would alter his "fences-up" judicial bearing and attitudes. George eventually heeded her advice and took vacation time to make the journey alone. What he encountered when he met with relatives in both Munich and Hamburg were their stories of loss and death in Stalin's collectives and work camps with no refuge in courts or other legal alternatives. After a week of intense discussions with these relatives, he returned to Seattle determined to take a closer look at what kind of justice he was handing out to immigrants in his courtroom. He didn't change his stance easily on his professional work, but his visit with relatives in Germany and a thorough analysis of his rulings eventually caused him to experience a change of heart. Once that hurdle was surmounted he quickly became an advocate of justice for immigrants in his courtroom.

As had often happened during my journey, an episode occurred during this time of writing that gave me hope not only for my historical novel but also for the improvement of ethnic and racial relationships that I sought. A relatively new mosque that had been built in Seattle near Northgate Mall had been vandalized. The story was covered extensively by the local news media. The damage wasn't extensive, but it was clear from graffiti at the site that the villains planned to return and do even greater violence if the mosque was not closed. Seattle police investigated and wrote up a crime report, but they weren't successful at identifying the troublemakers. They speculated that rednecks from small towns northeast of Seattle were involved.

The clergy of other religions in the metropolitan area decided to act. Ministers, priests, and rabbis and their parishioners circled the mosque at its next scheduled services and defended it against attack. Again the news media covered the gathering with photos of hundreds of citizens carrying signs and banners warning against any further vandalism. The protest worked, for there were no additional actions against this mosque.

Janice's own background and family came into the picture as her relationship with George deepened. Her mother and sister were prejudiced against ethnic Germans. George had to confront these challenges. Janice's mother lived in an assisted-living facility north of Everett, Washington, and George and Janice visited her there. It wasn't just ethnic backgrounds that had to be faced, but it was religion also. George had been raised Catholic, but now he was agnostic. He was considerate of those who had religious affiliation because he believed everyone should follow their consciences on this matter. Janice's brother also lived near Everett and was a Boeing engineer. Janice's sister from Wisconsin came to visit, and her presence further aroused conflict in George's life. He didn't have to work too hard with these potential relatives on ethnic and religious differences because Janice worked with them on those issues. One incident at Pike's Place Market helped Janice in this endeavor. A Mong flower arranger and salesperson came to Janice's mother's aid when she stumbled and fell on the floor in front of the Mong woman's flower table. The Mong woman quickly brought a chair for Janice's mother to sit on after the accident. The Mong woman's actions and warmth had overcome the ethnic and language barrier.

As time passed George wasn't satisfied with his own change of heart and courtroom sympathies. He decided to confront other justices in the Seattle INS Hearing courts as well as the court administrator. Beyond these efforts he also moved to rally other INS justices in other jurisdictions of West Coast states. George also worked to correct errors he had made in past court decisions in Seattle and Alaska, another part of the Seattle INS jurisdiction. Eventually George Schwartz became so well known and admired by advocate groups for immigrants that he was appointed by the Justice Department to give the annual oath at Seattle Center to qualified immigrants who were being naturalized as citizens of the United States.

Judge George Schwartz didn't go without his detractors during this process. He had confrontations with another "fences-up" judge in weekly meetings called by the INS court administrator. George had an ally among his counterparts, a Japanese-American judge who agreed with George's new viewpoint. George also suffered vandalism to his car in his condo's garage, and a close call when an automobile nearly ran him down on a street near his condominium. Upon police investigation the red neck owner of the vehicle was apprehended and admitted that he had committed the action because he believed that George Schwartz's legal decisions were a threat to American society.

Running parallel to George's professional life in "Expiation" was Janice's life as reporter. She attended Washington State court sessions, both civil and criminal, as well as INS hearings. She visited INS detention centers, meetings of advocates for immigrants, and the homes of some court impacted immigrant families. She also scheduled meetings with prosecutors of the US Customs Department. These contacts and gatherings provided her with important information and opinion for her weekly news articles in the *Seattle P.I.* As a consequence of her actions and reporting news articles, the readers of "Expiation" were able to follow not only the particulars of George Schwartz's professional life, but they were also able to get a different perspective from a professional reporter's point-of-view.

– Chapter 35 –

During the same time period as the writing of "Expiation," I worked on another project that had the aim also of correcting wrongs in the treatment of immigrants. In this instance I was not a writer but a literary agent. Maria Kreiser sent me a letter that bore good news in early January 2001. She related that she had written the story of Magdalena's life from 1928-1974, the dates from her birth in Munchen, South Russia, to her family's eventual immigration from the Soviet Union to Germany. She completed the research and writing so that she could give the manuscript to Magdalena on her seventieth birthday. I rejoiced when I read that my suggestion that this story be written was finally fulfilled. Since Maria only knew the portion of her mother's journey from her own birth in 1961 in the Ural Mountains to 1974, she spent an afternoon of each week for about a year with her mother in discussions about Magdalena's years in South Russia, about the years of W W II, about her family's exodus to Poland and Brandenburg, Germany in late 1944, and finally about Magdalena's and her father's years as refugees in the Gulag.

Maria was well equipped to do the research and writing because she had studied at the University of Hamburg and earned a B.A. degree in Slavic Studies. She was fluent in English, German and Russian, so she could handle the historical background of her mother's years prior to her immigration with family to Germany. Maria took notes at each session with her mother and asked pertinent questions about specific historical events in each phase of Magdalena's life. Maria was diligent in getting the details associated with Stalin's first five-year collectivization program, the infamous starvation period of 1931-33 when Magdalena was only four years old and millions died including her twin sisters, and the problems for Magdalena's parents who were trying to survive while belonging to a collective. As the afternoon interviews progressed into life in the forest camps of the Ural Mountains, Maria was more familiar with the story since she had spent her youth there until she was thirteen years old.

In her letter to me Maria included a four-page English language summary of her manuscript. She must have labored hard at this job since it was highly detailed and carefully written. The reason for the summary was that the one hundred and sixty page manuscript was written in High German, a language that I had only a weak association with, except for a month long, two evenings a week course in conversational German Helen and I had taken when we made our first trip to meet our German relatives in 1990. The memoir was named "My Life in God's Hands," and Maria asked me if I couldn't get it translated and published in the United States.

I was delighted to receive the one hundred and sixty page manuscript and the photographs that accompanied it, and I was eager to take on the jobs of finding translator and publisher since the work reinforced my current writing objectives. One photograph in particular caught my attention. It showed Maria and her fifth grade classmates, some ethnic German and Polish but mostly Russian, in a school portrait taken at their school in the Ural Mountains. All of the students were in uniform and many wore scarves. These scarves indicated that the students were members of Lenin's Communist Youth, sworn to carry out the program of the Soviet regime. In the background of the photo was a statue of Lenin, sitting in a chair with book in hand draped between his legs. He had a revolutionary look to him by the thrust of his chest and head forward into the future. Maria stood in the last row in the photo and had a pensive look on her face. In her descriptive letter Maria, now a mature woman, college graduate and mother of two daughters, wrote that she was young and had felt pressure at this school in the Soviet Union because the educational system was communist, atheist, and totalitarian.

— Photograph of Maria and Classmates in the Ural Mountains —

As I viewed her apprehensive look in the photo, I thought about the duplicity she had experienced in her Soviet school. At home she spoke Low German, the dialect of her parents, and took instruction from her mother in Catholicism and German culture. She prayed and learned about the sacraments of the church. Magdalena taught her how to cook German recipes, about names days (the celebration of a saint born on the same day as the birthday celebrant) and other German rituals. She practiced the German language and songs when visiting other German refugees in their homes. These practices were forbidden and were punishable by the Gulag camp administration. Maria's older sister Irma had the same experiences.

On the other hand, at school she became fluent in Russian, listened to the propaganda on the tenets of communism and the supremacy of the State and heard condemnatory remarks against religion. As I thought about her situation as a pupil in a Soviet school, I recalled George Orwell's mockery of the Soviet way when he wrote that in this type of State "some pigs were more equal than others." Of course at her age she wouldn't have known about this assessment of a totalitarian government. She had to practice duplicity and had to feign agreement to what she was taught. She had to think in two different languages and express conflicting ideas according to where she was at any particular time.

Once I had the German language manuscript in hand I had several problems to overcome, but one in particular needed immediate attention. I knew the general content of the manuscript from Maria's summary, but I didn't know how well it was written, what the style was like, and how it measured up against history. Fortunately I had a colleague at my former college who was still teaching. He was ethnically German, a former citizen of Potsdam, Germany, and possessed a Ph.D. in American literature and history from the University of Potsdam. He now taught German and American Culture at Olympic College. I contacted Professor Bernd Richter and asked him if he would read the manuscript and give me his assessment.

I was lucky in overcoming this first problem associated with "My Life in God's Hands." Bernd Richter was not only a German trained scholar, but he was well versed in the literature that came out of the Soviet Gulag. He had read some history on the topic, especially Solzhenitsyn's works, but he had also read many memoirs by survivors of the gulag. A few of these writers were Jewish, one or two were Polish, and others were German or Russian. So he looked at the writing from a well-grounded critical perspective. The manuscript must have caught his attention, for he was a busy faculty member with family, but nevertheless he finished the manuscript in about two weeks and gave me a telephone call. He said we should meet for lunch where he would present his findings and return the manuscript.

We met at a favorite faculty restaurant, and Bernd related that he was impressed with the manuscript and it deserved my attention and efforts in its behalf. He gave two additional reasons. One was that the work was from a woman's perspective that was unique in his experience with the form. Secondly, it was about German nationalists who survived Stalin's collectivization program, WWII and the Gulag. To have these three together in one book was exemplary. Finally Bernd said the book was well written and in a suitable style. I was delighted and asked him if he wouldn't translate the work into English. He said he would be honored to undertake the job, but he didn't think he had a good enough command of the American idiom and colloquial expressions to meet the needs of an American audience.

— Chapter 36 —

The next difficulties in this project were twofold. I had to find both translator and publisher. Getting either would be a Herculean task, for Maria Kreiser was unknown, didn't have any publication record, and the subject of the memoir, Magdalena (Hecker) Reiswich, was also unknown. Magdalena now lived in Hamburg with her husband Christian and both were retired, he from a machinist's job and she as nurses aide in a Hamburg hospital. Since I had failed myself to get my historical novel published, I knew I would have to get creative. Deciding to build a platform from which to operate, I established the Sojourner Literary Agency, a business to give prospective translators and publishers a sense that I was credible. I registered and licensed the agency with the State of Washington and set out to accomplish my tasks. I fortunately had done the proper legwork in the local library, researching the work of literary agents and copying examples of both author/agent and author/publisher contract forms.

Directing my first efforts at universities with German departments and publishing arms, I sent out inquiry letters to ten university presses that had comparable publications on their lists, outlining the memoir's subject, the historical context of the work, and potential audiences. I also requested the names of German language professors who might be interested in a translation job. I received responses from most of the editors, and they wished me well but declined to request a manuscript of the work for review. I repeated this process with a few other university press editors, but again I received encouragement but no takers. I decided that it was unlikely that I would find any university press for the "My Life in God's Hands" manuscript. I also reasoned that a translation of this work for little pay and maybe just English translation copyright was not going to look that important on a professor's curriculum vitae. I then contacted the Germans from Russia Heritage Society in Bismarck, North Dakota. Since the subject of the memoir was a German from Russia, I reasoned that this society would be interested in bringing this work to light. I had purchased books from the society in the past and knew that they in fact published or sold a number of texts on South Russia and the German colonists. They were interested in the manuscript for possible publication, and they also provided the name and address of a potential translator who lived in Minneapolis, Minnesota.

The translator's name was James Gesselle, and he came from the same background as I did. He had a major difference and advantage; he was raised near his German from Russia family and had been taught their German dialect as well as some Russian. In addition he had lived within a German-American culture that clearly resembled Magdalena's early life in Munchen, Russia. James's family had immigrated in the late Nineteenth Century from a village in South Russia that was near Munchen. Beyond that James held an M.A. degree in the teaching of German from Stanford University, so he would have no difficulty with Maria's High German manuscript.

Even with these positive conditions for a translator, I still had a major problem. How would I know if his translation was true to the manuscript? I had an answer in my colleague Bernd Richter who agreed to assist me in evaluating the translation. I contacted James Gesselle and explained the contents and context of the manuscript and subject. He was so intrigued and willing that he offered to translate without pay except for copyright on the English translation if, that is, he found the work credible. I sent him the manuscript and asked him to translate the first fifteen pages. He did and within a week I had the pages in hand and his assurance that the memoir was fully worthy of translation and publication. I turned the pages over to Bernd, and he said he would re-read the pages in Maria's German and make checkmarks wherever there was a critical decision on English word choice. Using that selection process Bernd read the translated pages. He called me three days later and said I should immediately agree to have Mr. Gesselle translate the work, for he hadn't missed a beat in his choice of English words at the critical junctures he had checked.

James Gesselle agreed to translate the manuscript so long as I agreed to handle the work of getting a contract with GRHS to publish it. In addition he would work with his associates to set up the cover, lay out the text, select and place photographs and do editing and illustrations. He agreed that I should be involved, if I wanted, as well on the technical side of the publication of the text. The next year and a half involved a lot of correspondence and negotiations to get the manuscript finished and agreed to by all parties. There were, of course, other critical considerations. One major bump in the road was contract negotiation with the Board of Directors of GRHS. We agreed on a flat 8% royalty to the author per volume sold with an initial printing of one thousand books. The BOD wanted the right to publish a paperback edition as well as a CD version with appropriate royalties to the author. They also wanted 8% royalties for the GRHS if I found a producer for a film of the memoir. These considerations were in dispute for some time, but I compromised on most of them in exchange for their agreement to publish the first edition as a hardback. They argued on purely economic grounds for a paperback first edition. It was a deal breaking problem, but I thought I had given way enough times to get this one consideration. I so wanted this condition in the contract to give Magdalena's journey the best presentation possible. James Gesselle was willing to help on the issue. He succeeded in getting himself elected to the Board of Directors of GRHS, and subsequently the board agreed to do the first edition in hardbound.

Meanwhile James Gesselle and colleagues put together for my review suggestions for the cover and illustrations of the book. Magdalena's photograph, taken by the German SS in western Poland in late 1944 when she was sixteen and being processed for entry into Germany, was selected for the cover. Illustrations included a map of South Russia, a death certificate of Magdalena's mother and two young daughters who were killed in the Allied bombing at Brandenburg in early 1945, and various photographs including the one of Maria with classmates in a Soviet school in the Ural Mountains. These attachments to the text met my agreement, but we had trouble selecting a title. We all agreed that "My Life in God's Hands" overemphasized the religious element in the narrative. We consented finally to the title, *Though My Soul More Bent*, a quote from Milton's poem "On blindness." It preserved the note of faith the book contained and added a literary aspect to the work. (In hindsight I wish we had selected *Magdalena* or *Magdalena's Journey* as title.)

Just at the time when the publishing arrangements for Magdalena's memoir where nearly completed, I was struck by another blow from within my family. My dad died in the nursing home that he had been in for six years. The head of the nursing staff contacted me by telephone just days before his passing, telling me about my dad's serious condition and requested my instructions. There was a caveat in the request. I was informed that if my dad could speak for himself he would prefer to stay in bed rather than to be taken to intensive care at a local hospital in Minot. I knew the situation well, for I had authorized several other hospitalizations for him in the past three years. I had traveled to see him twice during this period after my mother's death, and he had said quite bluntly that there was no future for him. Although he suffered from dementia, I felt confident that he knew what he was saying. I had the legal right to decide his fate at the moment although he was not likely to live very long under any condition. I told the staff not to call an ambulance, and I made arrangements to travel to Minot. I called my brothers and sisters, and he passed at age 88 when we were in route to be at his side.

Once again I was faced as I had been for my mother's funeral some years earlier, or so I thought at the time, with deciding what to do about a service for him in the nursing home's chapel. Much to my surprise when I discussed the services with the nursing home's administration, I was told that my dad had been attending both Catholic and Lutheran services on Sundays for about a year. I called the priest who served the nursing home Catholic residents, and he agreed, not only to provide a mass for my father, but he also said he would arrange to have the Lutheran minister present in whatever capacity he wanted to serve. The Lutheran minister did share in the services. When I delivered my dad's eulogy at the service, I included my mother in my comments and acknowledged the mistake I had made at her service. Fortunately there were a few of my Lutheran Peterson relatives present. Since I delayed his funeral a few days, he was buried next to mom under their joint headstone on his eighty-ninth birthday. That evening at a reception we toasted him with his favorite drink, boilermakers.

Upon returning to Bainbridge Island later in 2003, I immediately concluded all contracts for the publication of Magdalena's memoir. The GRHS made arrangement for a local publishing company in Bismarck to print the work in about one thousand copies. Advanced advertising was done for early discounts on purchase before publication, and the book was scheduled to be in hand by the fall of 2003. I was delighted with the prospect of finally getting the printed text to Magdalena and Maria. I was proud of Maria for her writing and for her background knowledge of the subject that she had skillfully woven into a book. I couldn't be more grateful to Bernd Richter for the aid he had generously supplied, not just for the reading of the original German text and advice about translation, but also for the blurb he provided for the book's paper cover. James Gesselle had my highest regards for expertly translating the original manuscript and for handling many aspects of the book's format. One drawback was the book's price. It was offered at $25.00 with a discount of $3.00 for early purchase. I should have argued for a lower price, for my major concern was always to get the story to as many people as possible.

Magdalena and Maria echoed my elation with the publication of *Though My Soul More Bent.* Maria had received a few advance copies of the work, and it wasn't long before I received photographs of Maria and Magdalena holding the book together while exhibiting radiant smiles. Finally Solzhenitsyn's recommendation to print narratives by refugees from the Gulag had come true. Now I hoped the reader's of the book would feel the injustices that were done to Magdalena's family and work to prevent such things from happening again to others. Helen and I traveled to Hamburg to further celebrate the publication of the work in the fall of 2004. We spent several days with our relatives, rejoicing also in the good fortune they had experienced in Germany since their emigration in 1974.

Although I had read most of the memoir in sections as it was translated, now I was able to sit down and read the memoir in full, feeling various negative emotions from deep sorrow to anger as my surviving Hecker relatives struggled through each phase of their long, tortured journey. At the end of reading the book I cheered at the triumph of 1974 when Magdalena and family left the Soviet Union to begin a free and prosperous life in Hamburg, Germany.

Since Maria was not able to do the writer's work of readings and various other aspects of selling the memoir, I did what I could from my distant vantage point to promote the book. I bought and gave copies of the work to some of my immediate family at the advance discount rate. I photocopied the advance purchase forms of the GRHS discount rate offer and mailed it to many relatives including those I had met or heard about in my early research work. A distribution company was not hired by GRHS to circulate the book due to cost, so the only place of purchase was the bookstore of the GRHS in Bismarck. I researched and located the chapter affiliates of the AHSGR in the Puget Sound. This National Historical Society of Germans from Russia was affiliated with the GRHS, so I contacted program chairs of several of these Puget Sound chapters and presented the memoir at their gatherings. An unexpected benefit came to me as a result of these meetings. I met people who knew Heckers from North Dakota, especially ones from the Dickinson/Belfield region. I didn't know how some of these fit into the Hecker family tree, but I contacted those I could reach and received more information about my lineage.

In concurrence with my efforts, GRHS sold the book at their annual membership conference, and overall the memoir had six months or so of good sales. A professor at the North Dakota State University at Fargo used the memoir as textbook in his course on immigration. I suggested that GRHS circulate copies of the book to library associations and major reviewers of this kind of work to encourage sales. Had the book sold out in the first year or so GRHS would have, as agreed, offered a paperback edition and maybe even a digital version. None of these options was forthcoming since the GRHS hadn't recouped their investment yet, thus an opportunity of reaching a wider audience was lost.

I was disappointed since I had hoped for more distribution and a resulting increase in awareness by the general public to the misfortunes and tragedies of immigrants relocating in foreign lands. I had also hoped that a broader spectrum of people would become aware of the Soviet Gulag from a common person's vantage point and a woman's point-of-view. Hopefully reader's, with their enhanced perspectives, would keep an eye out for any new examples of this form of slavery and work to stop it. At least they might support organizations, such as local Immigration Rights Groups or the ACLU, that were devoting a lot of effort, time and money on behalf of these victims. I returned to my own efforts to stop injustices such as these through my writing and hopefully publication. I also continued to support the local Immigrant's Rights Group and the ACLU.

– Chapter 37 –

The bumpy road I traveled offered new creative avenues during this period. Helen and I moved fulltime to our condo in the Belltown neighborhood of Seattle after selling our home of thirty-five years in Bremerton in the fall of 2003, just as *Though My Soul More Bent* was published and I finished writing "Expiation." I continued to seek a publisher for my historical novel and read from the manuscript at some literary venues. In addition we took the opportunity to take up letterpress and bookmaking since Seattle had schools that taught such skills. We registered in classes and did projects through 2004 and 2005, learning the craft while featuring our grandchildren Coleman and Katelin in our works. Since the wars in Afghanistan and Iraq were underway, I decided next to produce a work that opposed these conflicts with a letterpress chapbook titled "War." It was clear to me that my work on immigration was leading me to other forms of activism. In "War" I used words such as revenge, Manichean, illusion, arrogance, control and intransigence to illustrate the mindset of the Bush Administration that led us into the Iraqi war. I included woodblock prints in the chapbook showing the dollar sign and oil production as the real motivations for this military engagement. To show my abhorrence to these conflicts, I included woodblock prints of the bombings of Hiroshima and Nagasaki. To counter these negative motivations for these wars, I ended the chapbook with a section on peace, using the words negotiation, impartiality, objectivity, humility, empathy and wisdom to show how we could keep out of such senseless destruction. I printed "War" under my newly created imprint Crab Walk Press in 2006. The chapbook didn't sell well, and some of the poems I read at venues against the wars found some support but eventually that dried up and criticism for my position followed.

My efforts placed me in a position to see how difficult it is to go against the established emotional climate of a period of time. Following 9/11, patriotism was exalted as defense for mounting wars. It was our patriotic duty to support our troops. The Bush Administration sought support in this fashion even though the logic and justification were slim in merit to warrant such costly and violent incursions into two countries. In my thinking I supported the attack on the al-Queda in Afghanistan, but continuing the war as a nation-building venture was counterproductive and sure to lead the United States into failure and huge costs in human life and money. Motivations for the invasion of Iraq included control of oil production for American oil companies and revenge against Sadam Hussein. The assault on Iraq was a gross mistake that cost us heavily financially and in human destruction and has led us down the road of imperialism. I clearly saw that emotion trumps reason when propaganda celebrates words such as freedom, liberty and patriotism as justification for military aggression. My venture into activism brought me to recognize what had happened to my relatives in Russia when they became victims of the same tactics used by the Russian government. I didn't retreat from my position, but I did attempt to soften the title of the chapbook by changing the title to "War or Peace". But even this change didn't alter the reception of the work.

I found time also during this three-year period to revise my historical novel. Since I had no luck in attracting a publisher, I decided it needed an overhaul. The title was changed from "Expiation" to "Strangers Before the Bench." I hired a professional editor to review the work and to make suggestions for editing and revisions. I spent a year of so doing these alterations. I gave the female lead character a greater role in the book, and I found ways to make George more personable. I added materials on immigrants, making them more suitable for sympathy as well. I was intent on making my voice heard on the importance of treating immigrants with their best interests in mind.

There were other ways of getting my viewpoint out on racial and social issues. I published a series of four travel articles on a trip Helen and I took to China during this period. My motive was to show how the people we encountered on this journey were normal and sympathetic to foreigners. Again I was emulating Twain, Steinbeck and Steves to convince readers that they needed to overcome stereotypes and demonizing techniques that are often used by governments to justify their aggression. Besides these articles I also printed illustrated letterpress broadsides. My first effort was a fourteen-line poem titled "Sun Catcher" that had woodblock cuts featuring a spider and a sun catcher mobile. The second broadside was a sonnet about our experience in visiting Acoma Pueblo in New Mexico. I included a wood block cut of the mesa and pueblo dwellings in the print. I named the work simply "Acoma Pueblo."

— Chapter 38 —

As much as Helen and I enjoyed this creative work in Seattle, other changes entered our lives. As we had planned, we sold our condo in Seattle and moved to a larger unit in a newly built condominium complex on Bainbridge Island in November of 2006. It was a strategic move for us since we had both our children and grandchildren on the Kitsap Peninsula at Bremerton and Kingston. Twelve years was enough of constant ferryboat transportation back and forth across Elliott Bay. On Bainbridge Island we could keep our closeness to Seattle without need of a car and easier and cheaper visitations with our children and grandchildren. Just as Seattle had influenced us to more creative lives, so did our new home. Art, music and literary events were fostered on this island. I joined a writing group and worked to add poems to a collection of poems I had written. Some of the poems were about my ancestors on both sides of my family. I couldn't get the pursuit of my roots very far from my thinking. And just as these notions impacted my thoughts, other events drew me away from and back to my ancestry studies and goals for that pursuit.

I was diagnosed with prostate cancer in April of 2007, and for the rest of that year I had hormone therapy with two months of radiation treatments in October and November. After that time period my PSA dropped, and my cancer went into remission. The threat that I faced had a surreal quality to it. I felt healthy and vigorous, and the only thing that slowed me down was the effect of the drugs and the radiation treatments; consequently, during the summer of 2007 Helen and I took a ten-day cruise of some of the Baltic countries and cities, starting and ending in Copenhagen.

Visiting Oslo, Stockholm, Helsinki, St. Petersburg, Tallinn, and Gdansk gave us a favorable opinion of the peoples of these cities. We encountered no difficulties and were normally met with smiles, helpful suggestions and directions. In particular we were impressed with what our guide told us in Oslo. Norway admitted immigrants from various countries in the Middle East and Africa. Since it was national policy that employment in the country required language fluency in both Norwegian and English, the government provided support and education for these newcomers until they had the necessary skills for jobs. I assumed that the number of immigrants was not large, but nevertheless this kind of thoughtful planning must have resulted in productive citizens. We thoroughly enjoyed standing in the room where Noble Prizes were presented, visiting the Hermitage Art Museum, and walking the streets of each city, especially those of Tallinn and Gdansk. After the cruise we then took a side trip of ten days to Iceland, where we visited and toured with my Icelandic relatives.

But after our return home and I started the radiation treatments that ended in early December, I was left with a serious rash and a feeling of lethargy that I had never experienced during my physically active life up to this time. The energy drain that I felt forced me to give up my position as President of the Home Owner's Association of our new condominium complex that I had been elected to in March of 2007. In that one year I had taken the lead in getting our complex through its first year, the transitional year of ownership from developer to association. In some ways it was a relief to give up the position since I was still working on my ancestry studies, and I didn't have the energy for both.

Maria e-mailed me during this time. She informed me that she had sent two pages of her German manuscript of "My Life in God's Hands" to a Hamburg newspaper in answer to their request from readers for stories about refugees from the former Soviet Union. The excerpt from her work was printed along with several others, and she subsequently received a telephone call from a Hamburg literary agent. After the agent learned that the pages were from a German language manuscript that had been published in English translation in the United States, she requested a copy of the manuscript. Maria asked me what she should do about the request since I was her exclusive literary agent. I told her to provide a copy of the German language manuscript, explain that I was her agent, and give my e-mail address to the agent if she was interested in promoting the work in Germany. Within a week I received an e-mail from Dorothee Engle of Hamburg. She explained that she was convinced that the manuscript could be published in Germany. I replied that if she wanted to sell the memoir to a German publisher, I would agree to a co-agent arrangement.

In a short time I received another e-mail from Dorothee accepting my offer. I contacted a literary properties attorney in Seattle and had a contract drawn up. After receiving the contract I faxed it to Ms. Engle for signature. I received her signed copy by mail after a week's time. I had no idea what the publishing prospects were for the memoir, but it was certainly worth trying. In about two weeks I received another e-mail from Ms. Engle, acknowledging that Herder Verlag of Freiburg, Germany, a two hundred year old publishing house, had made an offer to print the German language manuscript. She forwarded a lengthy contract that she had negotiated that included rights to foreign publication, film and other mediums of publication. I had Ms Engle negotiate an amendment to the contract, excluding any English translation of the manuscript or sale of it in this form to English language countries such as England, Australia, and the United States.

Herder Verlag agreed to the terms, signed the contract and assigned an editor to the project. Maria didn't have to make any major changes to the manuscript, except for a few editing alterations. She received her advanced royalty with the agreement by Herder to print an initial edition in paperback of 3,500 copies. The title of the memoir was changed to *Herbstfrucht* (Autumn Fruit) and the cover photograph was of an older woman leading heavily clad children on a march down a snow-covered road. Magdalena Reiswich was listed as author, Maria was given credit as ghostwriter, and Dorothee Engle was listed as literary agent. I accepted these alterations since I believed Herder was a reputable publisher with considerable knowledge of how to reach German readers of memoirs.

Once again I saw this publishing opportunity as another means of getting Magdalena's story to an expanded audience. I didn't care about literary agency credits on the title page of the book since I was receiving my equal share of the commission. I was mostly concerned about getting the story told in as many forms as possible, alerting the reading audience to this narrative of broken promises, starvation, and death. Maybe, I hoped, these future generations wouldn't allow this travesty of justice to happen again. Herder released the memoir at the 2008 Frankfurt Book Fair. Helen and I arranged to meet Maria and Kai-Uwe in Frankfurt to celebrate this second publication of Magdalena's journey. We were all excited at the appearance of the book and hoped it would do well in distribution numbers. We also met the current fifth generation Herder family member who managed the publishing house and encouraged him to promote the book for filming, thus dramatically extending its audience reach. For our part Helen and I found that our presence at the release of the memoir was a fitting conclusion to our journey that fall of 2008 when we had visited Athens, cruised the Greek Isles, stayed in Alexandria, Egypt, and finished our voyage with five days on our own in Istanbul, Turkey. Sympathetic and wholesome people greeted us at all of these ports of varied ethnic groups and religious affiliations.

— Chapter 39 —

After we returned to Bainbridge Island, I was ready to return to writing, but now to a new genre. An editor-in-chief of a prominent historical society press in the Middle West suggested it to me. I had written a letter of inquiry to her upon returning home asking her to consider publishing the second version of my historical novel, now titled "Strangers Before the Bench." After reading my description of the work as a discovery of a buried family history that was in fact true to my family lineage, she suggested that I write a memoir on the topic, for she thought it would attract an audience better than a historical novel could at the present time. It was late December 2008, so I began work on my memoir after the holidays in early 2009.

At the time I was sixty-nine years old, and I was aware that my age and potential return of cancer put this new venture in writing on a high priority level if I was ever going to finish it. I decided to take a leave of absence from my poetry-writing group, and I gave up temporarily writing any poems, literary reviews, and travel articles. I also put aside any plans I had for chapbooks and broadsides. Doing so gave me some anguish since I had several ideas that I was eager to do in letterpress form. In fact I did let my imagination work a bit on some of these genres, but only in outline form. There was an exception, however. I had been writing a poem for each grandchild's birthday, so I had to continue that writing commitment, and it had my fullest attention. With that exception I started my work on the memoir, utilizing whatever faculties of imagination and the subconscious I possessed.

Although I was familiar with the memoir genre and had read a few recent publications, such as Frank McCourt's *Angela's Ashes* and Tobias Wolff's *This Boy's Life*, I had a lot of reading to do. I found Jill Ker Conway's *The Road to Coorain* and *True North* much to my liking. She also had academic training, and a life that began in the outback of Australia that was not too much different from my rural upbringing in the Siberia of the United States. Another memoirist came to my attention who also came from modest beginnings and traveled along the academic route. Mary Karr's *Liar's Club* and *Lit* found space on my reading shelf. But W. S. Merwin's *Summer Doorways* had a style, tone and voice that brought me back to it repeatedly. As the years wore on, I read other memoirs by Joan Didion, Gunter Grass, Fethiye Cetin, Tom Grimes, and Frank Conroy, among others. I had decided to keep my reading of this genre spaced throughout the writing period of my memoir that came to be titled Full Circle.

I also looked for craft articles on this form and found several excellent ones in journals I subscribed to like *Poets and Writers*, *The Poetry Review*, and *The Writer's Chronicle*. Jill Ker Conway and William Zinsser provided broader analyses of the memoir form in several of their books on memoir and autobiography. Finally I was fortunate to read Daniel Mendelsohn's *The Lost: A Search for Six of Six Million*, a memoir that had similarities to my own memoir endeavor. I also attended readings by memoirists such as Glenn Rockowitz who presented his *Rodeo in Joliet*. Our Field's End Writer's Roundtables at Bainbridge Island's Public Library featured some informative talks by other published memoirists such as Warren Read. So I was on my way to grasping structure and voice in memoir.

After a few months of this preparation that had always suited me well, that is spending a lot of time reading and taking notes on a subject—the eternal scholar—I realized that I had to start doing some writing. Since the memoir is based on fact, I put together a rudimentary outline that would guide my writing. Fortunately I had been a journal keeper for the past twenty-five years and could turn to my many notebooks, both larger lined ones and other smaller pocket sized ones, the latter that I carried with me at most times. The smaller notebooks contained factual information about daily doings—what I thought and notes on events I attended. The larger notebooks were ones devoted to travel and my speculative thoughts on readings in literature, philosophy and philology. I also had four journal volumes handcrafted by a local bookmaker and kept record in these of our family's activities over the years. These notes were often extracted from my smaller notebooks and remain the best overview of our family. Other sources of facts were Helen's photo albums that contained family ancestry materials, our many journeys, and other public events like birthdays, marriages, and vacations to visit grandparents and the like. These were vital to my memoir since she had included airline tickets, hotel account summaries and samples of paper money from various countries prior to the Euro.

These materials were extensive and required my attention before I could put them to use. I leafed through them and used post-it labels with key words to identify useable contents. I marveled at how right I had been to distrust the human memory, and in this case my own, because as I worked on an outline I was wrong about dates and sometimes places and corrected my writing by reference to these notebooks and albums. These errors in memory also held true for some of my relatives, and I had to correct them later in the last section of my manuscript. I was still spinning my wheels, getting memoirs read and taking notes rather than writing. I decided to forge ahead with sections of the memoir that best attracted my attention regardless of the chronology. I started with the seminal meeting I had with Uncle Adam in Oregon. I learned exceedingly more on that weekend in Salem with him than I knew altogether about my paternal ancestry. Unfortunately, some of what I had learned then was speculative and untrue.

My academic training caused me to dig deeper to find more information. I contacted the genealogical arm of the Seattle Public Library about my great-grandmother's grave location at Plantersville, Texas. They referred me to several web sites in Texas and to some critical essays written by scholars on cemeteries in Grimes County, Texas. I ordered copies of several essays and looked at the Texas State Historical

Association's web site, The Handbook of Texas Online. These sources gave me the context of immigration to southeastern Texas. After the Civil War southerners from Mississippi and Alabama moved west to get land and to set up cotton plantations. There were freed slaves available for sharecropping and thus cotton raising flourished in the area. Because of political considerations some other estate holders in Grimes County wanted sharecroppers from Germany and South Russia. These property owners sent recruiters to these countries, offering information about farming and about reduced passenger fees on both ships and railroads to get to Texas. Two important recruiters were Casimer Keifel, a former teacher in the German villages north of Odessa, and Father Klein who eventually established a Catholic Church at Plantersville, Texas. Recruiters like these could easily have convinced Martin Hecker to take his family to Texas. Kiefel spoke Martin's language and knew his culture. He was from the village of Selz near to Martin's village of Munchen. Father Klein was of Martin's faith and that was extremely important to the Hecker's of South Russia. The fact that they could immigrate without much passage money and start-up capital also fit their circumstances.

Another factor that appealed to Martin Hecker was rail transportation. The Heckers and other colonists in South Russia had adapted to and felt comfortable with this form of transportation. They had sent their grain for export by train to Odessa. They rode the train to Odessa for medical and shopping purposes. In the United States transcontinental railroads were laid prior to their immigration in 1891, giving them a way to get from New York City to Kansas City, Missouri. From there splinter lines were available to take them south to Texas. But again this was logical but speculative. Fortunately I had made contact with two academics in Texas, Dona B. Reeves-Marquardt and Lewis R. Marquardt. Their essays, e-mails and telephone conversations on Germans from Russia who had immigrated to Grimes County, Texas provided me with the context of the Hecker passage and settlement in Plantersville. The two scholars provided me with their notes from interviews with elderly Texans and genealogists who knew directly the Plantersville farm situation. In these notes the names of Keifel and Klein occur as recruiters of Germans from South Russia. Also in these notes the interviewees had stated that the common route for immigrants was from Odessa to Hamburg by rail, to New York by ship, and to Texas by rail. Finally and most importantly to me were the notes about the Plantersville cemetery. Again interviewees had referred to a woman who died in childbirth and was buried in this cemetery but in an unmarked grave. Since Martin Hecker had little money, it was possible and Dona Marquardt thought it was very likely that Christine Hecker who died in childbirth was buried there.

Since I had drawn a blank on the Martin Heckers on passenger lists in 1891 at Hamburg and New York, Donna Reeves-Marquardt suggested that I use the German spelling of Hecker (Hacker, umlaut over the a) to find them on passenger lists. It worked. Martin and Christine Hecker and their nine children left Hamburg on the <u>Augusta Victoria</u> on May 15, 1891 and landed in New York later in May 1891. So finally I had evidence of their passage and arrival in America. Since the aforementioned interviewee notes confirmed the common route for farmers from South Russia was by rail to Texas, it was clear that the Heckers had used rail and not ship to arrive in Texas. In the process of checking these passenger lists I found other names such as Jacob Brucker and Martin Herzog, both heads of family from South Russia who were listed later on the 1900 census sheets for Plantersville, Texas. These families had traveled to Texas in 1891 and 1892 and had farmed alongside the Martin Hecker's there.

Since three of Jacob Brucker's children married children of Martin Hecker in Texas, another condition of their cultural patterns became clear. They encouraged and arranged marriages within their cultural groups. Martin Herzog's daughter Anna Mary Herzog married John Hecker, son of Martin and Christine Hecker in 1903 at Plantersville just before the Herzog and now Hecker families moved to Kansas. Father Klein was the priest who married them in the Plantersville Catholic Church. I received a copy of their marriage certificate from Beth Hecker, wife of Lucus Hecker, son of John and Anna Mary (Herzog) Hecker, and Beth said that the elder Herzogs and Heckers had arranged for the marriage. Later in a telephone conversation with Selma (Hecker) Schmidt of Dickinson, North Dakota, I related this information about arranged marriages among the Hecker, Brucker, and Herzog clans. Selma said it was true for her father Mike as well. His dad, Frank Hecker, one of the original Hecker immigrants, arranged his son's marriage. So the practice of arranged marriages continued in North Dakota.

Beth Hecker was another relative I had been fortunate to come into contact with during the writing of this memoir. Beth was also a dedicated researcher into the Hecker clan, and she had conversations with her mother-in-law, when Anna Mary was in her later years of life. Anna Mary confirmed that she and John Hecker were married at the behest of their elders even though she wanted to enter a convent and become a nun. She also told Beth Hecker that their farming life at Plantersville, Texas was difficult. As a youngster she had to take her place in the cotton fields with her parents and siblings, pulling a heavy sack of cotton between the rows of cotton in stifling heat. She told Beth that their lives were like that of indentured servants. In other words the prospects in Texas were not good and subsequently all of the Heckers, Bruckers, and some of the Herzogs moved out of Texas in the early years of the Twentieth Century.

Another reason for their out-migration from Texas was the political conflicts at the time. The Germans from Russia couldn't rid themselves of political, ethnic and racial turmoil. In early 1900 a White Man's Union Association was formed in Grimes County. This organization was formed to select candidates to run on the Democratic Party ticket against the Populist Republican Coalition who came to Grimes County after the Civil War and became elected officials of the county. The Republicans used Black American voters to keep their control of the county offices and policies. The Democratic Party coalition that limited its membership to whites won elections from 1900 to 1958, thus racial prejudice and political chicanery were rampant in Plantersville just as it had been under the later Alexanders and Bolsheviks in South Russia.

Another error in my earlier research on the Heckers was their method of getting to North Dakota. They didn't follow the harvest north with horse and wagon as Adam Hecker of Salem and I had surmised. They took the train, the transportation they had always used.

When I was growing up in North Dakota, it was common for combining crews to follow the harvest from Texas to the Upper Plains. Farmers along that route who had smaller land holdings and crops couldn't afford the expensive combines and labor to take down their crops, so they hired combining crews who had self-propelled combines and trucks that could carry the combines and haul heavy loads of grain to elevators. I remembered those times from my youth and naturally thought that this was possible earlier, only much slower. As it turned out, John Hecker and wife took the train to Kansas because the Herzog's had family there, and it was possible to get homestead land. The Bruckers of Texas were the first to take the train to North Dakota, and they found work in the railroads of Mandan. Next my grandfather Frank Hecker and his brother Mathias took their families to Mandan by train and secured jobs on the railroad. That left Martin and his large family who took the train further west to Belfield, North Dakota to join his brothers and their families on still available homestead land.

So I learned more about the social mores of the Germans from Russia who had settled in Texas. People in Plantersville and even later in North Dakota must have easily recognized them since they spoke a dialect of German, some Russian, but very little English. Adam Hecker of Salem told me that his father, my Great-Grandfather Martin, never spoke any English. He and family wore heavy clothing, mostly homemade, and their cuisine was decidedly German. Did they celebrate their names-days? Did they keep strict observance of the Catholic Church calendar and ritual? Surely they did. But how long would these social and religious obligations hold their attentions, especially when confronted by the American Way of Life that encourages individuality and self-interest?

Following those discoveries of crucial social mores and writing about the critical time I spent with Adam, I studied and wrote about the meetings with other paternal relatives at meetings and through travel. I also thoroughly reviewed the United States census and immigration records as well as State and County information about naturalization, obituaries, and other official documents. Since I had knowledge of the GRHS of Bismarck, North Dakota, I ordered valuable reference works from their bookstore and later used these as well as their resourceful web site data in my writing. These activities added dimension to my earlier findings, but they didn't change the facts about the Hecker's journey after settlement outside of Texas.

After writing the first sections of the memoir in long hand with ballpoint and side notes in pencil, I took to the computer to get typed copy of what I had written so far. It had been some time since I had finished "Strangers Before the Bench." I trudged along with the typing, but I failed to attain the joy of writing by getting immersed with the creative activity as I had with my historical novel, poems and travel articles. I remembered the importance in the past year of being involved with a writing group where I had combined old poems with new until I had a collection that I titled "Beneath the Surface." I was on the lookout for such a group that focused on memoir. I put out feelers and attended discussions and presentations at the Field's End Writing Roundtables and found a few writers who were considering writing memoirs, but nothing developed.

As sometimes happened on this highway that I traveled, the curves and hills would smooth out to a straight, flat surface, and I would pick up speed. Just such an opportunity to gain momentum came when Maria Kreiser sent me an e-mail stating that she was arranging to take her mother to her birthplace in what was now the Ukraine. Maria's older sister Irma had agreed to travel there as well. The route would start with a flight from Hamburg to Kiev via Munich, Germany. From Kiev travel would continue on a German Cruise ship down the Dnipro River to the last stop at Odessa, stopping along the way at various places including Yalta. From Odessa we could arrange a trip north to Munchen, Magdalena's birthplace and my own great-grandfather's birthplace as well. I didn't respond right away and had questions about the journey, sights along the way, and expenses. I knew that Helen's ancestral village was also near Odessa, so she would benefit in her own ancestral investigations. I picked up a travel book on the Ukraine and read it quickly, noting the names of writers like Gogol, Babel, Pushkin and Chekhov. Magdalena's husband Christian had been a Volga German, and his youth had been spent near Kiev. He had hoped to visit there in his retirement, but he died in 2007, and it was clear that she wanted to see her husband's former homeland as well as her own.

The historical significance of the Ukraine, the romance of the Cossack country, the attraction of getting to Yalta, the meeting place of the big three—Roosevelt, Churchill and Stalin—quickly took hold of my imagination and before long I was booking our passage with Maria's assistance. I liked the idea that this voyage would also connect the last two cruises that Helen and I had taken, one to the Baltic capitals of Norway, Denmark, Finland and Russia in 2007 and the Greek Isles, Egypt, and Turkey in 2008. This journey would link the mouth of the Black Sea at the Bosporus to the north end of the Black Sea at Odessa. We would experience the route the Swedes and Poles sought to own to get to the wealth of the Silk Road and the Mediterranean Sea. I was giddy with anticipation and began reading Chekhov, Gogol, Babel and Mikhail Sholokov. This trip I hoped would energize my quest to write my memoir.

– Chapter 40 –

We took the trip to the Ukraine in May of 2010. Helen and I flew direct from Seattle to Frankfurt on Lufthansa and then on another flight to Hamburg. We were picked up at the airport by Maria and her older daughter Ann-Sophie and driven to Maria's home in a suburb. After lunch with Maria and Magdalena, we walked to a nearby cemetery to see Christian's grave. It displayed a granite headstone with the family name Reiswich towards the bottom. He deserved a rest like this in a peaceful, well-manicured cemetery after his life in the Gulag. Christian's surname was on the right side of the monument with his years of life below, 1926-2007. Above his first name was a white cross. Room for Magdalena was on the left side of the stone. In between the two surnames and crosses was a white statue of an angel. There were plants blooming in front of the gravestone and down both sides of the gravesite. Magdalena talked to us through our interpreter Maria and said that Christian had wanted to fly to the Ukraine and then cruise down the Dnipro River to the Black Sea because we would start at Kiev in the area where he lived in his youth. Magdalena cried briefly but noted that she would keep his memory in mind when we got to Kiev, thus fulfilling his dream visit for him.

— *Photo of Christian and Magdalena on the Sofa of their Home* —

The journey into my ancestry and its outcomes was never very far from my thoughts, and so the next day we visited the Hamburg Immigration Museum to seek passenger lists for my great-grandparents, Martin and Christine Hecker. We didn't find anything in the records. Nearly six months later in this lineage search I would discover that had I used the German spelling of Hecker, that is Hacker, umlaut over the letter a, I would have located the record. We were successful, however, in another matter. We had coffee with Dorothee Engel, my co-literary agent, at the museum's café. We discussed the publishing record for *Herbstfrucht,* Magdalena's memoir in German. The memoir had reached more readers than the English version, but after nine months sales stagnated, so my hopes of a broad audience educated about fear and xenophobia was diminished. Germany was suffering some setbacks in its economy, and there was considerable unemployment in the country that didn't encourage the reading of a refugee's account from a repatriated German now living in the country.

Helen and I flew from Hamburg the next day, a Saturday, with Magdalena, her two daughters, Maria and Irma, and a friend of Irma's, a retired Lufthansa commercial jet pilot. After a brief stop at Munich, we went on to Kiev where we were transported to the <u>MS Dnepr Star</u>, a German cruise ship, and got settled in and had dinner before retiring. The next day, Sunday May 9, we remained at our dockage and were able to participate in the Ukrainian celebration of their independence from the German Army at the end of World War II. It was their Fourth of July! Interestingly Helen and I found out that she, a small group of Scandinavians and I were the only non-Germans passengers aboard this German vessel in a harbor extolling the Ukrainian victory over the Germans of the Third Reich. I told Helen I would get an American flag and hang it out of our cabin window. She laughed at my jest. Fortunately as we found out that day and later as the voyage continued, Ukrainians didn't hold any grudges against present-day Germans and in fact celebrated the German colonists who had started many of the villages in the Odessa region two hundred years earlier.

Kiev surprised us by its efficient mass transit system, its many well-designed and built commercial buildings and its many restaurants, including a McDonald's across the highway from our dock. All of us rode a cable car to the upper city where we saw St. Sophia's Cathedral and across the large square from it stood St. Michael's Cathedral. In between these structures was the National Ministry building. Just across the way from the government building was a monument to the millions who died in the starvation era of 1932-33 under Stalin's regime in what was then the Soviet Union. Magdalena's twin sisters were victims of this government-orchestrated travesty, and she stood quietly, bowing her head to the memory of those two toddlers. We all took turns comforting her, and she wiped her eyes with a handkerchief, telling us that she was glad to see this recognition by the Ukrainians of that turbulent era. Fortunately for Helen and I the monument had both Ukrainian and English language citations. They read, "For the Millions of Ukrainian-Victims of the Famine-Genocide of 1932-1933." Below the words was the sentence, "Erected in 1993." That was just shortly after the collapse of the Soviet Union. This admission stood even though now in 2010 the newly elected President of the Ukraine had signed an agreement with the Russians that would keep the country out of NATO and the European Union. As we walked about the upper city, the number of large new hotels, restaurants and other commercial buildings lining the streets impressed us. The

Ukrainians were moving ahead in their capitol city with aggressive building and renovation. It was also encouraging to see the number of rebuilt churches in what had been a churchless Soviet era.

— Photo of Monument to Victims of the Famine-Genocide of 1932-1933 —

The lower city was a Times Square like area with many large hotels, office buildings and even a chic McDonald's of an imposing size not ordinarily seen in the United States. In the middle of these structures was a large open square with a few statues of prominent political figures. This is where public festivals like their Independence Day were celebrated. Thousands of people stood in this center area and along the sidewalks surrounding the square. A parade was scheduled to begin after the President of the Ukraine gave a speech from a temporary podium structure. Bleachers, also temporary, across the street held a symphony orchestra that had been playing for a considerable time. Magdalena engaged in conversations with older people standing near our group and was accepted by them, especially since she was speaking Russian. Some older men wore military uniforms of the era that had seen the driving out of the German Army. The street life was lively and crowded with some drinking on side streets, but there was no rowdiness. This was obviously a joyful national event that could have been mistaken for a national holiday in the United States except for the languages being spoken around us. None of the spectators paid much attention to the English that Helen and I spoke with our relatives.

After the recently elected President finished his address from across the Square, cheering erupted throughout the crowd, and a parade started its movement down the central boulevard with multiple bands, people on floats, soldiers marching in formation, and military equipment, including tanks and trucks. There was one group Maria identified for us as a left-wing organization that displayed posters and cheered to their own music, but we were never clear on what they stood for or against. The police and military guards that were about the area in small numbers didn't engage them or even seem concerned. This was a good sign of acceptance of opposition. The parade moved towards the waterfront, but before it got there, it arrived at another large square where the tanks were parked and the parade started unwinding. People climbed onto the military trucks and tanks, getting their pictures taken. It was clear that many of these well-attired people were from other cities in the country and had come here on holiday. Again Magdalena engaged in conversations with older gentlemen dressed in uniform of an earlier era.

It was easy to see by her cheerful attitude that she was happy to see her late husband's former homeland in such high spirits.

Later in the day we toured a reconstructed 19th century village. I wondered if they were similar to those of our ancestral villages near Odessa. Again there were a lot of Ukrainians, and it was so crowded that our bus was parked many blocks away from the village, but it was a pleasant occasion and Magdalena was clearly at home among these houses and outbuildings that must have reminded her of her youth. There were many vendors at this site, selling crafts and food, and sales looked very promising. I found the clothing and wood sculptures especially attractive, but the size of the ones that I admired were too large to haul along for the rest of our journey. Next our tour bus took us to a National Museum that celebrated a former monastery, its churches, and other buildings including schools for artists. Magdalena was clearly joyful that religion was once again appreciated as it had been before the Soviet era. We were guided into a lower section of the monastery grounds where monks now lived and practiced their rituals. We visited their gardens and some caves where we saw mummified bodies in coffins with glass tops. These viewing surfaces were improvements for tourist attraction. The caves, however, were not altered except for air conditioning in the narrow passageways. Our bus drove us back to the Star, and it left the dock at 6 PM to begin the voyage to the Black Sea and Odessa, our most anticipated and cherished destination. These two days at Kiev were a fine beginning of our cruise since spirits were high among the people, and the condition of the city that we saw was decidedly upscale.

The MS Dnepr Star was a long and narrow vessel that now carried its capacity of four hundred passengers plus crew. The shape of the boat allowed it to navigate the locks that connected the three lakes that we had to traverse on our way south. It took us two full days to reach our first stop in what had been Cossack country. Along the passage we had lectures, meals, and we witnessed the ship's movement through the locks. At the Captain's Cocktail Hour on our first evening Helen and I met a couple from Germany. He had worked as an engineer for Raytheon in the United States for about twenty years where he and his wife birthed, raised and educated a daughter. After I explained our mission of visiting ancestral villages near Odessa, and my hope that the literary output of two books from the lineage study would end in a movie production to reach an even larger audience, they told me that their daughter was a scriptwriter living in Berlin. Once again an unexpected meeting pointed towards my quest of getting the story of the Hecker family's tragic fate out to a wider audience. After our cruise ended, and we had returned to the United States, I engaged in a correspondence with the scriptwriter that resulted in an excellent and imaginative idea for a movie script on Magdalena's life in the Soviet Union.

— *Photo of Captain's Cocktail Hour on Cruise Ship* —

By the time we reached Zaporizhya we were ready to see some sights on land. We were transported by bus to Khartytsya Island where we visited a Cossack Museum that exhibited the weapons, boats, swords, costumes, gems, photographs of Hetmen (the political and military leaders of the Cossacks), and a model of the old fort where the military arm of this group of people had met and planned their campaigns. We then drove down Lenin Strasse, a long paved road down the heart of Zaporizhya. We saw a hydroelectric dam, built in the 1930's with American engineering design that later powered much of the heavy industry developed by the Soviets. Our Ukrainian guide admitted that the industrial output was now outmoded and that high unemployment was the result. Many professionally trained residents were now commercial vendors, selling clothes, electronic machines and foods they bought in Moscow, Kiev and Odessa and transported back to Zaporizhya. This city was a letdown after Kiev, for we saw very few new buildings, and side streets were narrow with old, small structures on them. Some of the streets were not paved and the ones that were looked shabby. Our guide related that the Ukrainian government was working to modernize the buildings, roads, bridges and industry of the city. At the other end of Lenin Strasse was a huge statue of Lenin that looked as weather beaten and dismal as the city we had just passed through. Our last visit was at a model of an old Cossack fort where we were entertained by acting Cossacks in traditional garb who gave demonstrations of horsemanship and military prowess. Waiters and waitresses, wearing Cossack era costumes, served us a meal typical of an earlier time, including homemade vodka. I couldn't help but think of Gogol's *Taras Bulba* and Skolokov's *The Don Flows Home to the Sea*, each of which had presented a more realistic view of the old Cossack life. We would, for instance, have dipped our vodka out of buckets with metal cups rather than having it served to us in wine glasses.

Back in our cruise ship we continued our journey to the Black Sea, stopping at Kerson, a major shipbuilding and vessel repair port near the entrance to the Black Sea. Our Captain and crew had to get permission to enter into the Black Sea as well as pass security checks while we passengers toured in smaller boats to a village along the channel not far from Kerson. Like at Zaporizhya, Ukrainians entertained us in traditional costume both aboard the vessels and in the village. We heard the traditional music of these people and saw many vendor displays of handcrafted clothing and crafts. We also toured a typical house of the village. Along the channel on the way back to our ship, we saw also many small vacation dachas of Russians and Ukrainians. They were often painted in bright colors, especially blue.

Our next destination was Sevastopol, a port located on the Crimean Peninsula. This was our stop for two days. On the first day we were transported to Yalta and visited the Livadia Palace, the conference location of the Big Three—Roosevelt, Churchill, and Stalin—and the broad walk of the city of Yalta that displayed fancy shops, hotels and restaurants as well as the summer villas of wealthy Russians, Ukrainians and a few Europeans. I was delighted to see finally the summer Palace of Nicholas II and the meeting place where our leaders of that time determined the division of Europe at the ending of World War II. We stood at the entry doors to the conference room where these important agreements were hammered out by these leaders and their many advisors. Photographs of those sessions were hung around the large room and displayed the looks of these men and the apparel of that period. One of our guides told us the story of how Churchill had tried to buy one of the marble lions on a huge terrace facing the Black Sea, but Stalin had replied that he didn't own the lions, the people of the Soviet Union did. We also visited another nearby palace, much smaller and less dramatic where Churchill had headquartered during his stay in Yalta. Later on that first day we were bused to the broad walk of Yalta, and Helen and I strolled down to where larger-than-life statues of Anton Chekhov's main characters in his story "The Lady With the Pet Dog" were displayed. I had my picture taken as I stood between the woman and her dog and her suitor, a gentleman banker from Moscow. Chekhov had maintained a white dacha in the city at one period of his life. The literary aspects of the cruise were often foremost in my mind.

On our second day at Sevastopol we bussed to Bakhchisarai, the old capitol of the Crimean Khanate. We visited a summer palace of the Khan of the era, and it held a marble fountain that the Khan had erected to commemorate the death of a young and beautiful Polish woman in his harem. She had refused to return his love and died after one year. He apparently had felt the emotion of his attraction to her and grieved for her. Alexander Pushkin celebrated this unrequited love by writing a poem about it. Thanks to Catherine the Great this palace and religious center were spared when she drove the Turkish Muslims out of the Crimea. On our way back to our cruise ship we passed the place where the Battle of Balaclava was fought in the Crimean War of 1854 that pitched the forces of the British cavalry led by Lord Cardigan against Russian military forces. In this instance Alfred Lord Tennyson wrote the poem "The Charge of the Light Brigade" to memorialize the tragic conflict. Again I was reminded of the seemingly unstoppable ethnic and national conflicts in the history of this region. The one consolation was the literary response to these events.

– Chapter 41 –

The next night we made our passage across the Black Sea towards Odessa with just one interim stop before reaching our final port destination. During the crossing we encountered such a violent storm that our Russian captain changed course, so we would avoid the worst of the turbulence. Once again I was experiencing the tumult of my journey, but this time it wasn't on roads with cracked surfaces, washouts, and dead ends. Now the highway was an angry sea, rolling our ship from side to side and up an down deep swells and causing waves to smash over railings and against our cabin windows. We docked at the Port of Odessa one day early, much to our satisfaction, giving us an extra day to explore Odessa where our ancestors had shipped their grain crops and visited by train for shopping and medical purposes. Our group walked the streets of the city, admiring the statues of Richelieu, Catherine the Great, and Pushkin as well as the Potemkin Stairs, the Opera House and the many fine buildings exhibiting French architectural influence. We also walked Deribasovskya Street to people watch and sit in the well-manicured park at its far end. After lunch of stuffed white fish, as recommended in a book by Ilya Kaminsky, a former resident of Odessa, we visited the Odessa Literary Museum where Pushkin, Gogol, Chekhov and Babel were featured along with many Ukrainian writers. Next to the museum was a cheerful outdoor park exhibition of humorous statues of many artists and writers of the region. This city of a half million residents was not what our relatives had seen, but it was a favorable, multi-ethnic population even in 1867 when Mark Twain visited it and wrote admiringly about its wide streets, low buildings and many tree bordered sidewalks, leaving him with enough feeling of comfort and familiarity to proclaim it was like America.

— *Photo of Me with Pushkin* —

Our next venture into the environs of Odessa was on the next day by bus. We drove through many sections of the city, some sumptuous and expensive with modern homes, apartments, and condominium structures. Other districts that we passed through had modest apartment buildings of the working class with some graffiti and run down buildings. Even here restoration was underway. We stopped to view churches, civic buildings, such as the City Hall where Odessa's Mayor conducted official business, and several hotels, but the featured visit was to the Fine Arts Museum. This multi-storied building was packed with sculpture and paintings, both old and modern. We spent nearly two hours wandering from floor to floor and room to room. I was struck by the darkness of the colors, especially on the older paintings that might have been a commentary on the Russian and Soviet eras. On our return trip to our ship, Magdalena pointed out the railroad station that she had used some seventy years earlier when she and her dad Johannes Hecker had brought one of the younger children of the family to Odessa for medical attention.

That evening I telephoned Serge Yazilerov, the guide I had hired to take us to our ancestral villages the next day. He was a Professor of Engineering at the Polytechnic University of Odessa who had a sideline guide service. Individual members of the GRHS who had traveled many times to this area to visit their ancestral villages had recommended him to me. Serge spoke excellent English, welcomed us to the Ukraine and agreed to pick us up at 7:00 a.m. the next morning. I informed our group at dinner that we were all set for the real goal of our tour, exploring our ancestral villages of Munchen, Elsass, and Josephstal. The first village was in the Beresan District that was north of Odessa and the other two were to the west of the city. We had agreed to go north first to Munchen since it was farther away and more difficult to get to and would occupy the morning and early afternoon of the day. To say the least we were all excited about the forthcoming journey, but there was also some anxiety, for we weren't exactly sure what we would encounter. Magdalena had the most at stake since she was born in Munchen and had experienced life there.

Early the next day our guide and his driver and van picked us up at our ship's dock. We five—Magdalena, Irma, Maria, and Helen and I—climbed into the van, introduced ourselves to Serge and the driver and then took our seats for the three hour drive north to Munchen. We all checked our luggage to make sure we had our cameras, water, food, extra clothes, and umbrellas. Along the way we looked at maps and village plats Serge had with him. Most of these materials were in Ukrainian or Russian, so Serge had placed tags on the villages we were traveling to and red markers on the routes we would travel. He also had some historical material in German that Magdalena and daughters reviewed as we drove along. After several hours and about

David A. Hecker, Ph.D.

seventy-five miles of driving, we encountered a road made of melon-sized rocks that rattled our van's suspension, bringing we passengers back to the Prologue of this narrative. The telling of the journey was over, not just for this tour in the Ukraine, but for my twenty-four year search for roots as well.

Epilogue

2011

The writing of the memoir was not finished, however, when we returned to Bainbridge Island in late May 2010. I had not only to finish the writing and editing of my memoir, but I had two obstacles to overcome. I was rear-ended and suffered whiplash on June 15, 2010, so I had to undergo physical therapy for a year. In September 2010 I experienced a significant increase in my PSA ratings, so I had to return to a hormone therapy regimen. After nine months of treatment, once again the cancer went into remission in June of 2011. During this time period between June 15, 2010 and June of 2011, I forged ahead with my memoir, writing and editing. I decided I had to complete it. I worried that I might not finish it, and occasionally when I woke up in the middle of the night, I would direct a prayer to whatever, if anything besides my own grit were in charge, to give me the energy, focus and time to complete my book. In some ways the pursuit of my memoir was a relief, for it kept my mind from lingering over and fretting about both the whiplash and the cancer.

Fortunately another very important and happy event in August 2010 also kept my mind off the whiplash and cancer. Helen and I celebrated our Fiftieth Wedding Anniversary by taking our entire nuclear family of nine on a cruise to Alaska. We sailed on the Norwegian Pearl that featured every type of restaurant, cuisine, and activity. The one-week roundtrip journey out of Seattle sailed to Juneau and Glacier Bay with additional stops at Skagway,

Ketchikan, and Victoria, Vancouver Island, and each stop met every-one's expectations. Each location also provided side trips; for instance at Skagway the rest of our entourage took the train to White Pass on the Yukon Route Railroad. In addition the grandkids were kept busy in the swimming pools, bowling alleys, game rooms, and cafes while the older set enjoyed the hot tubs, massage parlors, music and dance floors in the evenings. Another feature of the cruise was that there were passengers from all over the globe, and we all heard for-eign languages and saw individuals from various races and many countries.

But for Helen and I the enjoyment came from watching our fam-ily members enjoy the voyage. In addition we recognized that we had kept up some of our ancestral heritage traits. We enjoyed fam-ily and our nuclear family in particular, and kept in contact with our extended families. We did not move as they had from vil-lage to village or country to country with extended family mem-bers in one ethnic group and religious affiliation. Our fourth generation family in the United States moved individually and mixed with various ethnic groups, races, and religious affiliations. On the other hand, and unknown to Helen and I when we met, married, had children and moved to Minnesota and later Washington, we were from German lineages that had lived in villages of Germany, South Russia, and North Dakota that were within seventy-five miles of each other. The time frame extended for three centuries. A fascinating point that we both commented on, as we reflected on our Fiftieth Anniversary, was that our marriage had not been arranged. We found each other while attending college where we both pursued careers in education.

— Photo of Helen and David on 50th Anniversary —

What is there left to say about the ups and downs of this road I've followed for these past many years? The journey was much longer than I had expected it to be. I thought I had reached Full Circle several times before I actually got there. At one point when I completed the family tree portion of the project, I thought the work about family and relatives was finished. But then came the idea to share the story of my wandering family with other Germans from Russia, immigrants rights advocates, teachers of history and literature, and interested citizens who might help others avoid these catastrophes. That goal led me to get Magdalena's memoir published, not once but twice. Again I concluded that I had arrived at Full Circle. My life in education with its commitment to aid others in reaching their full potential intervened, and I wrote "Expiation" and its revision "Strangers Before the Bench." Then I concluded I had truly reached my goal, but no it wasn't over yet. I began to focus on travel and travel writing as a means of helping other people and myself to overcome fear, stereotypes and xenophobia. I wrote travel pieces and journeyed to Europe, Central Europe, Asia and South America, intending to visit relatives and to gain more understanding of other peoples and their cultures. Again something was missing. What was absent was a recounting of my own journey between 1987 and 2011 in memoir form under the title Full Circle.

Some of the writing of Full Circle occurred between our return from the May 2010 travel to the Ukraine and now in the late fall of 2011. Visiting the villages of old South Russia with relatives provided me with the stimulus to move ahead with the writing of the many drafts and edits of the text. During and before the process of completion of my memoir, I encountered sour notes. Uncle Adam of Salem died within a year of our momentous meeting at his home in 1987. I had to drive ahead without his further guidance. Bernd Richter, who provided his expertise during the early phases of the publication process of Magdalena's memoir, ended his life before seeing the work published in Germany. My desire to influence the general public about immigrants has been weak. Magdalena's memoir has reached modest numbers of readers in both the United States and Germany. My historical novel rests in a box on a shelf in my study. I published some travel articles but again the numbers aren't significant. What will happen with my memoir is yet to be seen, as are my efforts to get a film version of Magdalena's memoir produced.

A more favorable result of writing the memoir is that I met with and reached out to many relatives, academic researchers, librarians, web sites, government agencies, and historical societies that all proved necessary to get me to the end of this journey. As a result of these contacts, I have gained considerable information about my Hecker clan. One of my most important findings was about their social and religious alignments. From Germany to Russia to other countries, the Heckers and other German families moved together, arranged marriages within their families, practiced the Catholic faith and followed the same social patterns. In addition I have extended my knowledge about the problems of ethnic, religious and racial rivalries, and have tried to fulfill my quest to help resolve these troubles. Along the way I also changed my writing efforts from academic position papers and reviews of books to more creative forms such as poems, travel pieces, a historical novel and finally a memoir. I'm grateful for these opportunities that have enriched my life. Hopefully I've helped others in their quests to tell their family stories and hopefully readers of all of them have benefited as well.

I feel that I've become a better person because of this journey, a more acceptant person towards others of different ethnic, religious, and racial backgrounds. I believe I'm a better and truer American because of this quest. I've exposed the negative forces that are against the American Dream and our exceptionalist destiny, and I've advocated that others open their minds to the great variety of peoples and creeds in the world. I believe if they do so, our global societies will be richer and more creative. This acceptance can lead these multi-lingual groups to create visions of higher civilizations. It is true that I've become discouraged recently by the negative reception of the latest ethnic addition to our population, Muslims who practice Islam. The Koran was burned in public by an American Caucasian preacher, but he represented a small congregation and didn't attract much support for his position. In fact it looked as if he was using the episode to increase his church attendance. Some objections were made to establishing a mosque in New York City within blocks of the site of the 9/11 bombings, but again the resistance lost traction as the economic support and size of the mosque were revealed. One other objection occurred in a southern state to a proposed development that included retail businesses and a mosque. When it was revealed that the financing and support came from American-Muslims, the resistance lessened. In each of these cases the problem seems to be that the clamor comes from misunderstanding. Objectors mistake the common adherents to Islam as people belonging to the militant terrorist minority, the jihad.

Hopefully as John Steinbeck believed the process of assimilation in America works, that as a newly arrived minority attains economic value, it is accepted into the American fold. In this vein I witnessed the changes in my own family. Traveling as they did in highly defined singular groups of one ethnic background, language, religion, and cultural mores, they gave way in time to more variety and not necessarily less family cohesion. I believe it all depends on allowing individual conscience and choice to prevail. Arranging marriages along ethnic, religious and cultural lines has given way to individual selection based on friendship, love, shared passions, and common goals.

I've also discovered the ironies of my family's travail. Yes, Napoleon did cause our first forced migration, but later he sold the Louisiana Territory to the United States, thus providing homestead land for later Heckers. The Russians did renege on their promises to German colonists in South Russia, but the result was another forced immigration to the United States where constitutional guarantees and economic opportunities prevail for most citizens. My great-grandfather's first experience of farming in Texas mirrored the employment of Russian and Polish laborers in South Russia by German villagers. Not the least irony on the broader front is that as we have involved our military in wars around the globe, we accept into our borders more racial and ethnic minorities. Many more Koreans, Vietnamese, Mong, Cambodian and other Asians are now Americans because of the Korean and Vietnamese Wars. Our forays into Afghanistan and Iraq and now Libya are adding more of these ethnic minorities into the United States as refugees and perhaps citizens. Hopefully we will accept, learn and prosper with all of these additions to our culture.

Not everything I'd hoped for was attained on this journey. There are shortcomings that could still be overcome through technology and advances in resources. For instance I don't have copies of any passports of relatives in their many national boundary crossings. I've never seen a photograph of my Great-Grandmother Christine (Schmidt) Hecker, and I still don't have any verifying evidence of her death or precise burial place in Grimes County, Texas. Maybe these will surface as more documents are copied and made available to genealogists.

Finally as I finish writing this epilogue, I think of why I attempted this memoir, and although I've stated the main reasons repeatedly— to find out about my family and to spread the word about the dangers of xenophobia—I now add legacy. It's my retirement's legacy to my family and the world, but even more importantly it's a legacy to my grandchildren, especially the youngest who probably won't remember much about me if I perish at the age when my grandfathers' died. Aiden and Katelin are three and eleven years old. When my grandfathers' passed, I was two when the first went and ten when the second left. I didn't get to know either of them in life, but I know them now because of this lineage search. If my grandchildren find the time and want to know about their family heritage and me, they'll be able to read Full Circle. If they do so, they'll add another dimension to the title of this work.

ACKNOWLEDGMENTS

Memoirs demand collaboration from a multitude of sources. Family members, distant relatives, libraries, historical associations and societies, academic researchers, genealogical groups, web sites, and government bureaus all contributed to this memoir. Since many are listed in the pages of this work, I will not repeat them although my gratitude to all is deeply felt. If I overlooked anyone or any group, each has my sincere apology. I thank Olympic College, colleagues and students for the platform and opportunity to compare American immigrant experience to my findings about my family who crossed national and continental boundaries, living in several nations where they confronted problems of race, ethnic background and religion. The American Studies Association, of which I was a member throughout my teaching of American Cultural History and program development at Olympic College, provided me with vital information and many national conference sessions on race, ethnicity and immigration topics. Many memoirists provided me with models and reading them during my writing for nearly three years inspired me to continue and complete this writing. Again I mentioned some of them in the pages of this memoir, but for those I've forgotten to identify, I offer my heartfelt regrets. Libraries have been sanctuaries for me since my youth, and I'm grateful to all of them for engendering my love for history, literature and writing, but I especially give thanks to Bainbridge Island's Public Library and librarians for without their assistance, facilities, books, web sites, and Writer's Roundtables I wouldn't have finished this book. One of the presenters on the memoir at the library was Warren Read, the author of *The Lyncher In Me: A Search for Redemption in the Face of History.* He reviewed my outline and the initial draft of my memoir and provided valuable insights into the work and gave me encouragement when I needed it.

Although I have referred to many organizations, both public and private, that gave me help in completing my memoir, I want especially to express my appreciation to the Germans from Russia Heritage Society of Bismarck, North Dakota. I was able to purchase many resources from its bookstore that provided the historical background of immigration opportunities and routes that my German ancestors claimed and used to establish new homes in South Russia and the United States. This society with its many committees also identified my ancestors and created family trees by surname and village both in Germany and in South Russia. They as well provided me with other family trees of German colonists who lived near, traveled with and intermarried into the Hecker family in Germany, South Russia and the United States. I especially want to identify Dennis Roth and David Kilwien for their contributions in these matters. This society also contributed to the circulation of the history of my ancestors by publishing *Though My Soul More Bent*, a memoir about Magdalena (Hecker) Reiswick without which it is unlikely that Herder Verlog of Freiburg would have published the German language version of the work under the title *Herbstfruct*. The Hecker family is indebted to Maria Kreiser, the author of the German manuscript of Magdalena's memoir, and to James Gesselle for translating and handling the details for publishing the English version of the work.

To my wife Helen and our children (Jeffrey and Michelle), grandchildren (Coleman, Katelin, and Aiden), and son and daughter-in-law (Shannon and Michelle), I thank all of you for your forbearance when I was physically present but mentally absent while my mind floated down avenues of thought about lineage. Also to Helen I extend my appreciation for reading the manuscript and suggesting improvements as well as serving as memory source on names and places of our nearly forgotten past. To other extended family members who I have identified in the text of this memoir, I want now to repeat their names. At the beginning of the journey Adam Hecker of Salem was pivotal in this book. Other relatives of great value were Selma (Hecker) Schmidt, Leonard Hecker, Jr., Sister Reinhardt Hecker, and Emma Frank. Later on in this voyage and at critically important moments came the contributions of Therese and Larry Uri and Beth and Luke Hecker, all of the Kansas branch of the Hecker clan. Another source of vital information about the Hecker family in Texas came from Dona Reeves-Marquardt. Finally, but not the least of my appreciation, goes to my Germans from Russia relatives Magdalena and Christian Reiswick, Maria and Kai-Uwe Kreiser and daughters and Irma Aschert and family.